The Appeal of Tochigi

なぜ人は栃木に魅せられるのか

栃木の自然と文化再発見

英語で発信

Delphiの会 [編著]

随想舎

はじめに

　私たちデルファイの会は、活動を始めて8年になります。結成は、『英語で発信　栃木の歴史（2012年5月刊　下野新聞社）』の編集作業に取り掛かったときでした。私たちのこの著作物は「英語で発信」というユニークさが認められ、「全国新聞社出版協議会ふるさと自費出版大賞・優秀賞」という栄誉に輝きました（2013年5月）。

　もともと栃木大好き人間の5人が集まって、まずは自分の足元・栃木の歴史を知ることから始めよう、そしてもっと掘り下げてみようと挑戦したのが最初でした。

　会の名称は、「汝自身を知れ」というデルファイの神殿に刻まれた古代ギリシアの格言に基づきます。私たちの思いにぴったりだったからです。栃木県には自然、史跡、建造物、伝説、人物など私たちに興味を与え、私たちを魅了する事柄がたくさんあります。『英語で発信　栃木の歴史』をまとめていく中で、私たちはふるさと栃木が持つ「惹きつける力」を再確認いたしました。栃木の自然や文化の「魅力度」は実はもっと高いぞというのが実感です。

　本書は、有名、無名を問わず、栃木が持つさまざまな魅力を日本語と英語で発信することによって、より多くの方々、ひいては、外国の人々にも、栃木が持つ魅力を十分堪能してもらいたい、そんな気持ちで執筆・編集に掛かったものです。私たちは、時間をかけて丁寧に作業を進め、このたび「英語で発信」シリーズ2作目として『栃木の自然・文化編』をまとめ、出版する運びとなりました。なお、3作目『栃木の人物編』は、原稿執筆がほぼ終了し最終チェックの段階に入っております。近いうちに出版する予定です。

　本書の構成は、6章立てにし、各章の冒頭に栃木県の地図を掲載して、取り扱う事項や地名を明記し、併せて掲載ページを記入しました。索引として活用していただきたいと思います。また、本文中の写真や図表はオリジナルにこだわり、随想舎の編集スタッフの意見も取り入れて、よりアピールするものといたしました。少しでも「魅せる栃木」に近づけるよう工夫したところです。

「知れば知るほど、好きになる」(The more you know, the more you love)

　読者の方々が、「栃木を知れば知るほど、栃木が好きになる」ことを願っております。

　これからの日本はますます国際化が進んでいくでしょう。2020年の東京オリンピック・パラリンピックも迫ってまいります。「英語で発信」という私たちの一連の取り組みは、インパクトのある試みになると自負しています。

　もとより私たちは、その道の専門家ではありません。素人の立場で「栃木の魅力」を発信していきたい、その思いから出版に漕ぎ着けたものです。皆さまのご感想、またご叱正をお待ちしております。

　本書の原稿執筆が完了し、印刷の初校の段階になって、「那須疏水」が「世界かんがい施設遺産」に登録されたという嬉しいニュースが入ってきました。

　もう少し早ければ本文に書き加えることができたのにと悔しい思いです。約130年前に疏水の工事に着工した先人たちの苦労を偲び、地元関係者の喜びはいかばかりかと想像しながら、この吉報を「まえがき」に書き加えました。

　なお、本書の執筆・編集に当たり、多くの方々のご協力をいただき、感謝にたえません。特に、元高校長で植物愛好者の山口正夫氏には、「栃木の地名を由来に持つ植物写真と説明」の提供をいただきました。各章末に1ページ分を取り、掲載させていただきました。また、桜井実氏には「コウシンソウ」(34ページ掲載)、柏村祐司氏には「提灯もみ」(207ページ掲載)の写真提供をいただきました。

　心からお礼を申し上げます。

　最後になりますが、随想舎の石川栄介氏や編集スタッフの方々にはいろいろな面でお手を煩わし、多大なお世話をいただきました。心からの感謝を申し上げます。

デルファイの会　一同

なぜ、人は栃木に魅せられるのか
目　次

第1章　世界に誇る遺産

世界遺産：日光の社寺 ……………………………………………… 3

鑁阿寺そして樺崎寺跡 ……………………………………………… 11

奥日光の湿原 ………………………………………………………… 14

渡良瀬遊水地 ………………………………………………………… 16

日本最古の学校・足利学校 ………………………………………… 18

笠石神社と侍塚古墳 ………………………………………………… 22

第2章　山・川・温泉

栃木の名峰　男体山 ………………………………………………… 29

伝説の山　庚申山 …………………………………………………… 33

名瀑　華厳滝 ………………………………………………………… 37

水の動脈　鬼怒川 …………………………………………………… 42

鮎おどる那珂川　やな ……………………………………………… 47

荒野を潤す那須疏水 ………………………………………………… 49

那須七湯 ……………………………………………………………… 53

塩原温泉郷 …………………………………………………………… 57

日光湯元温泉 ………………………………………………………… 65

日本列島のへそ　たぬま …………………………………………… 70

奇岩　御前岩 ………………………………………………………… 72

The Appeal of Tochigi
CONTENTS

Chapter 1 Historically Valuable Heritages

World Heritage: Shrines and Temples of Nikko 3

Ban'na-ji Temple and the Ruins of the Kabasaki-ji Temple 11

Oku-Nikko-shitsugen 14

Watarase Retarding Basin 16

Oldest Academy in Japan: Ashikaga Gakko 18

Kasaishi Shrine and Samuraizuka Tomb Mounds 22

Chapter 2 Mountains, Rivers and Hot Springs

Mt. Nantai: the Most Admired Mountain in Tochigi 29

Mt. Koshin: a Mountain with a Legend 33

Kegon Waterfalls 37

the Kinu River 42

Yana 47

Nasuno-ga-hara Canals 49

Seven Hot Springs in Nasu 53

Shiobara Hot Spring Resort 57

Nikko Yumoto Hot Springs 65

Tanuma, Center of Japan 70

Gozen-iwa 72

第3章 史跡・城跡・街道

古代の道 東山道 …………………………………77

鎌倉街道中道 …………………………………81

なるほど名城・唐沢山 …………………………85

天下を決めた小山評定 …………………………89

日光杉並木街道 …………………………………92

測量基準点：観象台跡 …………………………96

消えた県都の近代化産業遺産 …………………99

「桜並木ここにありき」 ………………………105

清流戻る渡良瀬川 ………………………………109

御用邸と御料牧場 ………………………………115

中世の歴史を語る小山城（祇園城） …………121

歴史に名を残す景勝「太平山」 ………………125

第4章 祈りと救い

栃木の神社のいろいろ …………………………133

宇都宮二荒山神社 ………………………………136

木幡神社 …………………………………………139

羽黒山神社 ………………………………………142

古峰神社 …………………………………………146

時代でつづる栃木の仏教 ………………………149

下野薬師寺跡 ……………………………………155

下野国分寺・国分尼寺 …………………………159

高田山専修寺 ……………………………………163

円通寺大澤文庫 …………………………………167

Chapter 3 Historic Sites, Castle Ruins and Highways

Ancient Highway: Tosando ⸺ 77

Kamakura-kaido Nakatsumichi ⸺ 81

A Renowned Castle on Mt. Karasawa ⸺ 85

War Council at Oyama ⸺ 89

Nikko Cryptomeria Avenues ⸺ 92

Ground Datum Line in Nasu ⸺ 96

Vanished Industrial Modernization Heritage of Utsunomiya 99

There Once was a Cherry-tree Avenue Here ⸺ 105

Watarase River ⸺ 109

Imperial Villas and Imperial Stock Farm ⸺ 115

Oyama-jo Castle (Gion-jo Castle) ⸺ 121

Mt. Ohira ⸺ 125

Chapter 4 Prayers and Salvation

Shrines in Tochigi ⸺ 133

Utsunomiya Futa'arayama Shrine ⸺ 136

Kibata Shrine ⸺ 139

Haguro-san Shrine ⸺ 142

Furumine Shrine ⸺ 146

Buddhism in Tochigi ⸺ 149

the Site of Shimotsuke Yakushi-ji Temple ⸺ 155

Shimotsuke Kokubun-ji and Kokubun-niji ⸺ 159

Takada-san Senju-ji Temple ⸺ 163

Entsuji Temple and Osawa Bunko (Library) ⸺ 167

岩船山高勝寺と地蔵尊‥‥‥‥‥‥‥‥‥‥‥‥‥171

佐貫石仏‥‥‥‥‥‥‥‥‥‥‥‥‥‥‥‥‥‥175

寺山観音寺‥‥‥‥‥‥‥‥‥‥‥‥‥‥‥‥‥177

第5章 伝統の祭り

日光東照宮の「千人武者行列」‥‥‥‥‥‥‥‥183

山あげ祭り‥‥‥‥‥‥‥‥‥‥‥‥‥‥‥‥‥188

発光路の強飯式‥‥‥‥‥‥‥‥‥‥‥‥‥‥‥191

間々田のジャガマイタ‥‥‥‥‥‥‥‥‥‥‥‥193

「悪態まつり」と「瀧流しの式」‥‥‥‥‥‥‥‥196

生子神社の泣き相撲‥‥‥‥‥‥‥‥‥‥‥‥‥198

鹿沼今宮神社の屋台行事‥‥‥‥‥‥‥‥‥‥‥201

野木神社の提灯もみ‥‥‥‥‥‥‥‥‥‥‥‥‥205

第6章 受け継がれる名産品

那須のゆりがね‥‥‥‥‥‥‥‥‥‥‥‥‥‥‥211

大谷石‥‥‥‥‥‥‥‥‥‥‥‥‥‥‥‥‥‥‥214

宇津救命丸‥‥‥‥‥‥‥‥‥‥‥‥‥‥‥‥‥218

足利織物‥‥‥‥‥‥‥‥‥‥‥‥‥‥‥‥‥‥221

結城紬‥‥‥‥‥‥‥‥‥‥‥‥‥‥‥‥‥‥‥224

天明鋳物‥‥‥‥‥‥‥‥‥‥‥‥‥‥‥‥‥‥228

烏山和紙‥‥‥‥‥‥‥‥‥‥‥‥‥‥‥‥‥‥231

武者絵‥‥‥‥‥‥‥‥‥‥‥‥‥‥‥‥‥‥‥233

しもつかれ‥‥‥‥‥‥‥‥‥‥‥‥‥‥‥‥‥235

Iwafune-san Kosho-ji Temple and Jizo Bosatsu ·············· 171

Stone Image of the Buddha at Sanuki ·················· 175

Terayama Kannon-ji Temple ···························· 177

Chapter 5 Festivals and Celebrations

Procession of One Thousand Warriors ················ 183

Yamaage Festival ···································· 188

Gohan-shiki at Hokkoji ······························ 191

Mamada's Jagamaita ································· 193

"Cursing Festival" and "Ceremony of Sake-Pouring" ···· 196

"Nakizumo" at Ikiko Shrine ···························· 198

Imamiya Shrine and its Yataigyoji ···················· 201

Chochin-momi Festival at Nogi Shrine ·················· 205

Chapter 6 Local Products

Nasu no Yurigane ··································· 211

Oya-ishi Stone ····································· 214

Uzukyumeigan ····································· 218

Ashikaga Textile ···································· 221

Yuki Tsumugi ······································ 224

Tenmyo Foundry ···································· 228

Karasuyama Washi (Japanese Paper) ·················· 231

Musha-e, Ukiyo-e Prints of Warriors ················· 233

Shimotsukare ······································ 235

Delphi(デルファイ)とは?

古代ギリシャのパルナソス山麓にあった Apollon(アポロン)を祀る Delphi 神殿の入口には
「汝自身を知れ」(γνωθι σεαυτόν)と書いてあった。

自分自身を知ろう!
栃木を知ろう!

第1章
世界に誇る遺産
Historically Valuable Heritages

日光東照宮　Toshogu Shrine

世界遺産：日光の社寺
World Heritage : Shrines and Temples of Nikko
日光市山内

神橋　Shinkyo

　1999年12月にモロッコのマラケッシで開かれたユネスコ世界遺産委員会の第23回会議において、「日光の社寺」が世界文化遺産として登録された。

　「神橋」近くの東照宮入口には、「日光の社寺」が世界遺産に登録されたことを記念して建てられた石碑があり、その裏面には「日光の社寺」

"Shrines and Temples of Nikko" were inscribed on the World Heritage Cultural List at the Twenty-third session of the World Heritage Committee held in Marrakech, Morocco, in December in 1999.

At the entrance to the Toshogu Shrine, near Shinkyo Bridge, there is a stone monument commemorating the inscription on the World Heritage List. It briefly says why "Shrines and Tem-

がどんな訳で世界遺産に登録され
たかについて簡潔な説明が書かれ
ている。それによると

　8世紀末の日光開山以来、山岳信仰
　の聖地として崇拝され、宗教的霊地
　としての歴史を現在まで継承する「日
　光の社寺」は日本が世界に誇る文化
　遺産です。周囲の文化的景観と一体
　となった二社一寺（二荒山神社、東
　照宮、輪王寺）の103棟の建造物群
　は当時の最高技術によって造られた
　高い水準の芸術的・宗教的作品で、
　世界的にも類例のない貴重な遺産と
　なっています

とある。

日光山

　日光山開山の祖と言われる勝道
上人 (?-817) は下野国南高岡 (現、
栃木県真岡市) の生まれで、幼い時
から遥か遠く北西に聳える日光の
山々に畏敬の念を抱きながら成長
し、二荒山 (男体山) が観世音菩
薩の住む聖地補陀洛であると信じ、
いつの日か、そこに登頂したいと願っ
たのであった。

　上人は、766年 (天平神護2) に
はじめて日光に至り、深沙王の助け
により大谷川の激流を渡り、川の左
岸に四本龍寺を創建した。あたりに
は紫の雲がたなびいていたので、こ

ples of Nikko" were inscribed on the
World Heritage List.

　The Shrines and Temples of Nikko date back to the late 8th century, when the Buddhist priest Shodo
started religious activities in the Nikko mountains. The 103 buildings of
Futarasan-jinja, Toshogu and Rinno-
ji, together with their surrounding
natural settings of equivalent cultural value, are religious buildings that
are characterized by their elaborate
styles of decoration, showing an ex-
ceptionally high quality of workman-
ship.They are considered precious
heritage of a type which cannot be
found anywhere else in the world.

Nikko-san

　The Buddhist priest Shodo (?-817),
founder of Nikko-san, was born in Min-
ami-Takaoka (now, part of Moka City)
in the province of Shimotsuke. He grew
up looking every day at the awe-inspir-
ing mountains in Nikko rising high in
the north-west. He firmly believed that
Mt. Futara (Mt. Nantai) was Mount
Potalaka, the holy residence of the bodhisattva Kannon, and he aspired to
climb to its top one day.

　Shodo first came to Nikko in 766. He
crossed the rapid torrent of the Da'iya-
gawa River with the help of Jinja-oh*
and built a small temple on the left bank
of the river. The temple was first called
Shi'unryu-ji because purple clouds were

勝道上人像　Statue of Priest Shodo

の草庵は「紫雲立寺」と言われたが、後に「四本龍寺」と言われるようになった。それ以来、四本龍寺は満願寺、光明院、そして、輪王寺と名称がたびたび変わっている。

　勝道上人は二荒山登頂を目指して、何年もの間幾多の難行苦行を重ね、782年（延暦元）48歳の時、遂に二荒山の山頂に立つことができたのであった。この様な訳で、勝道上人は日光山開山の祖と言われる。勝道上人は784年（延暦3）には二荒山麓の中禅寺湖畔に中禅寺を建立し立木観音を造っている。

　820年（弘仁11）には、真言宗の開祖弘法大師空海（774-835）が日光にやって来た、と伝えられている。空海は稲荷川の上流、四本龍寺の北西に滝尾神社を建立し、そこに田心姫命を祀った。

　そして、848年（嘉祥元）になると、

rising around the place. It later came to be called Shihonryu-ji. Since then, the name of the the temple was changed several times: from Shihonryu-ji, to Mangan-ji, to Komyo-in, and finally, to Rin'no-ji.

＊Jinja-oh: incamation of Bishamonten, one of the Seven Deities of Good Fortune

　Priest Shodo spent many years experiencing every kind of hardship preparing for the climb to the top of Mt. Futara. In 782, he finally achieved his long-cherished dream and stood on the top of the mountain. He was 48 years old then. This is why Priest Shodo is called founder of Nikko mountains. Later in 784, he built Chuzen-ji Temple by Lake Chuzen-ji at the foot of Mt. Futara and carved a statue of Kan'non out of a standing tree, which is now called Tachiki Kan'non (Standing-tree Kan'non).

　It is said that Kukai (774-835), founder of Shingon Sect of Buddhism, came to Nikko in 820. He built Takino'o Shrine in the north-west of Shihonryu-ji, in the upper reaches of the Inari River, and enshrined Tagori-hime no Mikoto there.

　In 848, Priest En'nin (794-864), a native of the province of Shimotsuke and a high priest of the Tendai Sect, came to visit Nikko and founded Sanbutsu-do, Jogyo-do and Hokke-do.

　The Shihonryu-ji which Priest Shodo built was very close to the Daiya-gawa River and was often inundated

下野国生まれの天台宗の高僧慈覚大師円仁（794-864）が日光を訪れて、三仏堂、常行堂、法華堂などを創建している。

勝道上人が四本龍寺を建てた場所のすぐそばには大谷川が流れ、たびたび洪水を引き起こしたため、四本龍寺は850年（嘉祥3）に安全な恒例山に移された。その際、旧地の四本龍寺は「本宮」と呼んで味耜高彦根命を祀り、恒例山の方は「新宮」と呼んで大己貴命を祀った。これら二つに田心姫命を祀る「滝尾神社」を加えて「日光三社」と言われた。

平安時代に入ると、「本地垂迹」＊の考えが起り、「本宮」は「本宮権現」、「新宮」は「新宮権現」、滝尾神社は「滝尾権現」と呼ばれ、これら三つを合わせて日光三社権現と言われるようになった。日光の三山（男体山、女峰山、太郎山）は、次のように三神、三仏と結びつけられたのである。

＊本地垂迹説：日本の神道の「神」は「仏」が権の姿で現れたもの、即ち、「権現」であるという考え

by floods. So, a new building had to be built at a safer place in Mt. Korei-san in 850. Now the Shihonryu-ji in the former place came to be called Hongu (Former Temple) and the new one came to be called Shingu (New Temple). These two, together with the Takino'o Shrine are called Nikko Sanja (Three Shrines in Nikko).

The Heian Period (794-1192) saw the birth of the Honji Suijaku theory＊. In accordance with this theory, Hongu, Shingu and Takino'o came to be called, respectively, Hongu-gongen, Shingu-gongen, and Takino'o Gongen. And the three mountains in Nikko (Mt. Nantai, Mt. Nyoho, and Mt. Taro) came to be related with the three deities/divinities.

＊Honji Suijaku theory: a theory which emphasized that the Japanese native Shinto deities are 'gongen' (incarnation of Buddhist divinities).

（三山）	（本地三仏）	（垂迹三神）	（権現）
男体山	千手観音	大己貴命	新宮権現
女峰山	阿弥陀如来	田心姫命	滝尾権現
太郎山	馬頭観音	味耜高彦根命	本宮権現

二荒山神社　Futara-san Shrine

日光二荒山神社

　日光二荒山神社は日光二社一寺の一社に当たり、日光山内にある「本社」、中禅寺湖畔にある「中宮祠」、男体山山頂にある「奥宮」の３つの宮から成る。日光山岳信仰の中心として古くから崇拝されてきた神社である。

　ご祭神は大己貴命、田心姫命、味耜高彦根命のご三神である。大己貴命は大国主命の名で知られる神様で、本社及び中宮祠の本殿中央に祀られている。田心姫命は大己貴命のお后で、向かって右側に、そして、大己貴命の御子である味耜高

Nikko Futara-san Shrine

　Nikko Futara-san Shrine is a shrine that comprises "Two Shrines and a Temple of Nikko." This shrine is located in three places: Honja in San'nai, Chugushi near Lake Chuzenji and Okuno-miya on the top of Mt. Nantai. The shrine has been the center of mountain worship in Nikko since ancient days.

　The shrine is dedicated to three gods: Onamuchi no mikoto, Tagori-hime no mikoto, and Ajisuki-takahikone no mikoto. Onamuchi no mikoto is also known by the name of Okuninushi no mikoto and is placed in the center of the main building of Honja and Chugushi. Tagorihime is wife of Onamuchi and is placed to the right of her husband.

彦根命は左側に祀られている。
　二荒山神社の本殿や神橋など23棟が重要文化財に指定されている。

東照宮

　日光東照宮は日光二社一寺のうちの一社に当たる神社で、徳川初代将軍徳川家康（1542－1616）を祀る。家康は1616年（元和2）4月17日に静岡の駿府で75歳の生涯を閉じた。「遺体は久能山におさめ、一周忌が過ぎたなら日光に小さな堂を建てて祀れ」との遺言に従い、駿府の久能山に葬むられ、一年後

Ajisuki-hikone, their son, is placed to the left of his father.
　23 buildings of this shrine, including Honden and Shin-kyo, are designated as Important Cultural Properties.

Toshogu Shrine

　The Toshogu Shrine is a shrine that comprises "Two Shrines and a Temple of Nikko." It is sacred to Tokugawa Ieyasu (1542-1616), the first shogun of the Tokugawa Shogunate. Ieyasu died on April 17 at Sunpu, Shizuoka, at the age of 75. In his last will, he said, "Bury me at Kunozan. And after one year, build a small building in Nikko for me." In accordance with his last will, he was first buried at Kunozan and, after

東照宮参道　the front approach to Toshogu Shrine

に日光に勧請された。

家康の終生の安らぎの地として日光が選ばれるに際し、天台宗の高僧天海僧正の力が大きかった。

当初、第二代将軍徳川秀忠によって日光に建てられた東照社（後の東照宮）は比較的質素な建物であったが、三代将軍家光（1604-1651）の時に社殿の大造替が行われた。1633年（寛永10）のことである。

工事には約4年かかり、1636年（同13）に現在我々が目にする東照社が完成した。

そして、1645年（正保2）には朝廷から東照社に「宮号」が宣下され東照社は東照宮と名前が改められた。

東照宮には、本殿・石の間・拝殿や陽明門など8棟の国宝と34棟の重要文化財がある。

輪王寺・大猷院

輪王寺は日光二社一寺のうちの一寺に当たる寺院で、その歴史は古く、766年（天平神護2）に勝道上人が大谷川の激流を渡って、左岸に現在の輪王寺のはじまりとされる四本龍寺を創建した時まで遡ることができる。

境内には徳川三代将軍徳川家光の霊廟である大猷院があり、その本

one year, his tutelary divided spirit was transferred to Nikko.

Tenkai (1536-1643), a high priest of Tendai Sect of Buddhism, was very influential in deciding on Nikko as the final resting place of Ieyasu.

The Toshosha (later called Toshogu) was built by the second shogun, Hidetada, of the Tokugawa Shogunate. It was a modest building.

In 1633, however, Tokugawa Iemitsu (1604-1651), the third shogun, decided to remodel it. The work took about 4 years and the new Toshosha as we see today was completed in 1636.

In 1645, Toshosha was given permission by the Imperial Court to use 'Gu' in its name and Toshosha was renamed Toshogu.

8 buildings of the Toshogu Shrine including Honden, Ishinoma, and Haiden, are designated as National Treasures and 34 building as Important Cultural Properties.

Rin'no-ji · Taiyu-in Mausoleum

Rin'no-ji Temple is the temple that comprises "Two Shrines and a Temple of Nikko." Its history goes back to the time when Priest Shodo crossed the rapid torrents of the Daiya River in 766 and built Shihonryu-ji Temple (the original name of the Rin'noji) on the left back of the river.

In the precincts of the Taiyu-in Temple are the buildings of Taiyu-in Mausoleum which are dedicated to Tokuga-

雪の大猷院　Taiyu-in Mausoleum in snow

殿・相の間・拝殿が国宝に、そして、その他の37棟が重要文化財に指定されている。

　家光の祖父家康に対する崇敬の念は非常に強いもので、自分が死んだ時には「東照宮のすぐ側に葬るように」と遺言をしている。大猷院の建物の配置は東照宮の方角に向いて建てられている。その装飾、規模、彩色などは東照宮の豪華絢爛さに比べ、全体に控え目で簡素なものとなっている。

wa Iemitsu, the third shogun of the Tokugawa shogunate, who was in office from 1623 to 1651. Its Honden (Main Hall), Ai-no-ma and Haiden (Hall of Worship) have been designated as National Treasures and 37 other buildings are nationally designated Important Cultural Properties.

　Iemitsu had enormous respect for Ieyasu, his grandfather. He expressed his wish to be buried near his grandfather when he died. The Taiyu-in Mausoleum faces the Toshogu Shrine. The arrangement of its buildings is very much like that of the Toshogu Shrine, but its size, decorations, and colors are much simpler and far more reserved.

鑁阿寺そして樺崎寺跡
Ban'na-ji Temple and the Ruins of the Kabasaki-ji Temple
足利市家富町、樺崎町

鑁阿寺

　鑁阿寺は真言宗の寺院で、大日如来をご本尊とし、足利市民から「大日様」とよばれ親しまれている寺院である。2013年8月、鑁阿寺の本堂が中世の建物として県内では始めて国宝に指定された。建築学上はもちろんのこと歴史、文化的にも大変意義深い建物と言われる。

　鑁阿寺のはじまりは、源姓足利氏＊2代目の足利義兼 (?1154-1199) が出家して1196年（建久2）に屋敷内に持仏堂を創建したのがはじまりとされる。

＊藤原秀郷の末裔は藤姓足利氏と呼ばれ , 足利義康の末裔は源姓足利氏と呼ばれる。

　当初の建物は落雷で焼失し、現在の本堂は足利尊氏の父・貞氏が1299年（正安元）に再建したもの

Ban'na-ji Temple

　The Ban'na-ji Temple belongs to the Shingon sect of Buddhism, and is dedicated to Dainichi Nyorai (the Great Sun Buddha). It is popularly called Dainichi-sama (Dear Dainichi) by citizens of Ashikaga. In August, 2013, the hondo (main hall) of the temple was designated as a national treasure. It is the first Medieval building that was designated as a national treasure in Tochigi Prefecture. It is a building of historical, cultural as well as architectural importance.

　Ashikaga Yoshikane (?1154 -1199), the 2nd in the line of the Gensei-Ashikaga family＊, built an austere hall in his premises in 1196 when he renounced the world to be a priest. It was to keep the statue of his personal guardian. This was the beginning of the hondo of the Ban'na-ji Temple.

＊ Descendants of Fujiwara Hidesto are called Tosei-Ashikaga family, while descendants of Ashikaga Yoshiyasu are called Gensei-Ashikaga family.

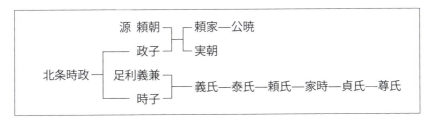

鑁阿寺本堂　Hondō of Ban'na-ji Temple

で、正面、奥行き各17 mの入母屋造り＊、瓦葺きである。

＊入母屋造り：入母屋に造る屋根の様式。

　典型的な密教本堂でありながら、当時の最新の建築様式であった禅宗様式をいち早く取り入れており、その後の宗教建築に大きな影響を与えた。このことが高く評価され、鑁阿寺本堂は国宝に指定された。

The original hondo, however, was struck by lightning and was burned down. The hondo we see today was built in 1299 by Ashikaga Sadauji (1273-1331), father of Ashikaga Takauji.

The hondo is 17m wide by 17m long. It is tile-roofed and is built in the style of irimoya-zukuri＊.

＊ irimoya-zukuri: a building with a gabled, hipped roof

The Main Hall of the Ban'na-ji Temple is a typical building of esoteric Buddhism. It took no time in adopting the Zen style and gave a great influence to religious buildings of later years. This fact was highly valued when it was designated as a national treasure.

樺崎寺跡

　鑁阿寺の北東約4.5kmには、国指定史跡樺崎寺跡がある。樺崎寺は、1189年（文治5）足利義兼が源頼朝に従って奥州藤原泰衡の追討に向かう折、戦勝祈願のために創建したと伝えられる寺院である。自然の山を背景に、かつては、広大な浄土庭園を有したこの寺院は、義兼が平泉で毛越寺や中尊寺を見たことに大きく影響を受けていると考えられる。

　義兼は、晩年出家し、樺崎寺で念仏三昧の日々を送り、1199年（正治元）生入定したと伝えられている。

　なお、義兼は源頼朝の妻政子の妹である時子を妻としているので、頼朝の義兄弟に当たる人である。樺崎寺は明治の神仏分離令により廃寺となった。

Ruins of Kabasaki-ji Temple

About 4.5 km north-east of the Ban'na-ji Temple are the remains of the Kabasaki-ji Temple, a nationally designated historical site. It is said that this temple was founded by Yoshikane in 1189 on his way to Oshu (Northern Japan) when he followed Minamoto no Yoritomo (1147-1199) to subdue Fujiwara no Yasuhira (?-1189). It was to pray for the victory in the coming battle. This temple, with a beautiful background of hills, once had a spacious garden that depicted Jodo (paradise or pure land). It is evident that Yoshikane had the images of the gardens of the Motsuji and the Chusonji Temples in his mind when he built it.

After Yoshikane renounced the world to be a priest, he spent the days of chanting prayers to Amida Buddha. He is said to have died in 1199 in a cave where he was buried alive of his own will.

Incidentally, Yoshikane married Hojo Tokiko, sister of Hojo Masako who was married to Minamoto no Yoritomo. This means that Yoritomo and Yoshikane were brothers-in-law. The Kabasaki-ji Temple was abolished after the ordinance that prohibited the mixture of Shintoism and Buddhism.

樺崎八幡宮　Kabasaki-Hachiman Shrine

奥日光の湿原
Oku-Nikko-shitsugen
奥日光

「奥日光の湿原」は、2005年（平成17）11月8日にラムサール条約のリストに登録された。登録されたのは、湯の湖、湯川、戦場ケ原、小田代原のうち総面積が260.41 haに及ぶ地域である。

湯の湖は面積が35 haの小さな湖で、最大水深14.5mの湖で、三ツ岳の噴火によってできた湖である。湯の湖から流れ出る湯川は戦

Oku-Nikko-shitsugen was added to the Ramsar List of Wetlands of International Importance on Nov. 8, 2005. It covers Lake Yuno-ko, the Yukawa River, Senjo-ga-hara and Odashiro-ga-hara. Its total area covers 260.41 ha.

Lake Yuno-ko (area : 35ha) is a small lake which was formed by the eruption of Mt. Mitsudake. It is 14.5 m deep at its deepest point. The lake drains into the Yukawa River that flows through Senjo-ga-hara Wetland into Lake

湯川　the Yukawa River

場ケ原の中央を流れ、中禅寺湖に流れ込んでいる。

　戦場ケ原は男体山の噴火によって川がせき止められ、その結果できた湖であったが、そこに土砂や水生植物の残骸などが徐々に堆積してできた本州最大級の高層湿原で、現在、ワタスゲ、ホザキシモツケ等100種類以上の湿原性植物の生育が確認されている。

　小田代原は湿原から草原に移行する過程にあり、湿原性植物と草原性植物の両方の生育が確認されている。

Chuzenji.

　Senjo-ga-hara was once a lake formed by a river which was damned up by the eruption of Mt. Nantai. Sands and dead aquatic plants gruadually accumulated over the lake and formed the greatest highland moor in Honshu (Mainland Japan). So far, more than 100 species, such as 'watasuge' and 'hozakishimotsuke', have been identified here.

　Odashiro-ga-hara is now in transition from wetland to grassland, and both wetland plants and grassland plants are identified here.

渡良瀬遊水地
Watarase Retarding Basin

渡良瀬(わたらせ)遊水地は 2012 年（平成24）7 月 3 日にラムサール条約湿地に登録されている。栃木、茨城、群馬、埼玉の 4 県に跨がる総面積 2,861 ha の湿地・貯水池で、思川(おもい)と巴波川(うずま)の二つの川が渡良瀬川に合流する地点にある。

渡良瀬遊水地については、過去において、流域住民にとって苦難に満ちた日々があったことを忘れてはならない。

Watarase Retarding Basin is also on the Ramsar List of Wetlands of International Importance. It was added to the list on July 3, 2012.

Watarase Reservoir is at the place where two rivers, Omoi-gawa and Uzuma-gawa, meet the Watarase River. It extends over Tochigi, Ibaraki, Gunma and Saitama Prefectures, and its total area covers 2,861 ha. of wetland and reservoir.

It must be long remembered that the people who were living around the

渡良瀬遊水地　Watarase Retarding Reservoire

足尾で「銅吹き」と呼ばれる精銅がはじまったのが江戸時代で、以後、銅の生産は徐々に伸び、最盛時には毎年1,300〜1,500tの生産があり一時はオランダに向けて長崎から輸出をしたほどであった。

　しかし、それと共に、銅山から流出する鉱毒によって下流地域の河川や田畑は汚染され、20世紀も近くなるとこれが大きな国家的社会問題となった。鉱毒による被害が大きくなって農民による鉱毒反対運動が激しくなると、政府は下都賀郡谷中村全体を買収してこの地に鉱毒を沈殿させる遊水池を作ることを計画した。1905年のことである。これは谷中村の強制廃村につながり、住民は栃木県那須郡下江川村や北海道に移住を余儀なくされたのである。

　このような悲惨な歴史を秘めた渡良瀬遊水地ではあるが、現在では、葦原が広がり、ヨシキリやセッカなどの高原の鳥など、約260種の鳥類が確認されている。カモ、シギ、チドリなどの水辺の鳥、冬期にはチュウヒ、ハイイロチュウヒ、コチョウゲンボウなどが多数飛来する。

Watarase Reservoir had to go through hard days of sufferings in the past.

It was during the Edo Period that the method of dofuki (a method of refining copper) was introduced, and with it, copper production gradually went up and its annual production reached 1,300〜1,500 tons at its peak and Ashio copper was exported to the Netherlands from Nagasaki.

However, the pollutants flowing out of the copper mine gradually contaminated rivers and fields in the lower reaches. And toward the end of the 19th century, it began to cause a serious social problem. With the expansion of contaminated areas, farmers rose up and the movement against the copper mining grew greater and stronger. In 1905, the Japanese government decided to buy the whole land of Yanaka village and to build a reservoir there for the purpose of depositing pollutants. This meant that Yanaka residents were forced to leave their home. They had to move to Shimo-egawa, Nasu, in the north of Tochigi Prefecture or to Hokkaid.

Watarase Retarding Basin which has an unhappy history in the past is now beautifully covered with reeds. It has been confirmed that about 260 kinds of birds like yoshikiri (reed wablers) and sekka (fan-tailed wablers) inhabit the reservoir. Waterfowls like ducks, snipes, and plovers are also found there. Harriers, gray harriers, and kestrels come flying in winter.

日本最古の学校・足利学校
Oldest Academy in Japan: Ashikaga Gakko

足利市昌平町

　日本最古の学校である足利学校は名刹鑁阿寺に隣接しており、市民の間で「学校様」と親しまれている。

　ん足利学校は、正面に向かって左側が孔子廟エリア、向かって右側が学校エリアに分けられる。この構成は、元の時代に設立された中国北京にある「国子監」や韓国ソウル

Ashikaga Gakko is the oldest academy in Japan. It adjoins the noted temple Ban'na-ji. It is popularly called Gakko-sama ('Dear School') by citizens of Ashikaga City.

Ashikaga Gakko consists of two areas: Area for Confucius' Mausoleum on the left and Area for Gakko on the right. This resembles the constructions

足利学校　Ashikaga Gakko

にある「成均館」と類似している。

　足利学校の創建については、諸説があってはっきりしない。一つは、国学起源説。時期を最も古くとる説で、足利学校は下野国の国学であったとするもの。二つ目は、平安時代の小野篁（802-852）創建説で9世紀前半になるというものだが、信憑性がないとされている。三つ目は、12世紀末の足利義兼創建説。足利義兼（?1154-1199）が鑁阿寺と学校を持っていたところから主張されている説で一番有力である。四つ目は、関東管領上杉憲実創建説。いずれにしても、文献上足利学校の具体像が明らかになるのは、上杉憲実が学校を再興した室町時代中期のころである。

　上杉憲実は、土地を学校に寄付し、初代の庠主（校長）に鎌倉円覚寺から快元という僧を招き、書物類を寄進した。これら書物の中には、宋版「尚書正義」、宋版「礼記正義」など貴重本が多く、国宝に指定されている。また、憲実は「学規三条」という今でいう校則をつくり、学校の基盤をつくった。

　15世紀半ばに来日したキリスト教宣教師フランシスコ・ザビエル（1506-1552）は、本国等に送った通信文の中で足利学校について「坂

of Kokushikan in Beijin, China, which was founded during the Yuan dynasty (1271-1368), and Sungkyunkwan in Seoul, Korea,

We don't know exactly when Ashikaga Gakko was founded. Some people say that its origin can be traced back to the study of classical literature in Shimotsuke Province. Others say that it was founded by Ono no Takamura (802-852) in the first half of the 9th century. Still others say that Ashikaga Yoshikane (?1154-1199), founder of the Ban'na-ji Temple, founded it. And some other people say that it was founded by Uesugi Norizane (1410-1466), shogunal deputy for the Kanto region. Many people believe that the 3rd opinion is most probable. It is not until the Middle of the Muromachi Period when Uesugi Norizane revived the academy that we begin to have some reliable records about it.

Uesugi Norizane invited Buddhist Priest Kaigen as shoshu (principal) of the academy from the Engaku-ji Temple in Kamakura. He donated his estate and books to the academy. Among the books he donated were many valuable books such as *Shosho-Seigi* (Sung edition) and *Raiki-Seigi* (Sung edition). They were designated as national treasure. Norizane also established Gakki Sanjo (Three School Rules), foundation of the academy.

Saint Francis Xavier (1506-1552), who came to Japan in the latter half of

19

東の学院あり。日本国中最も大にして最も有名なり」と記している。また、16世紀に来日した明の鄭舜功も彼の著書「日本一鑑」の中で「下野に大いなる学堂を設け、名付けて学校と題す」と述べている。

16世紀の足利学校は、第7代校長九華の頃で全国から学問を志す人たち（大部分が禅僧）が集まり、その数3,000人にもなったという。儒学を中心に、当時実用的とされた易学、天文学、兵学、医学などが学ばれた。易学や兵学を学んだものは大名に仕え、活躍した。田代三喜、曲阿瀬道三という有名な医者が育ち、医学の発展にも貢献した。

足利学校は、現在、世界遺産登録を目指し官民一体の取組みを進めている。

なお、足利学校は、他の三つの教育遺産群＊とともに、2015年に国が定めた「日本遺産」の第1号に認定された。その正式名称は「近世日本の教育遺産群―学ぶ心・礼節の本源」である。

＊水戸藩校の弘道館（茨城県水戸市）、私塾の咸宜園（大分県日田市）、庶民教育の閑谷学校（岡山県備前市）

the 15th century, noted in his letter to his home country that "Ashikaga Gakko is the largest and most renowned academy in eastern Japan." Cheng Shun-kung, who came to Japan from Ming in the 16th century, wrote in his book *Nihon'ikkan* that 'there is a large learning place in Shimotsuke Province which is named academy.'

In the 16th century when Kyuka was the principal of Ashikaga Gakko, there were about 3,000 people (mostly Zen monks) studying in the academy. They studied Confucianism and such practical subjects as the art of divination, astronomy, military strategy and medicine. Those students who studied the art of divination and military strategy were employed by feudal lords and worked for them. Among the students who studied medicine were Tashiro Sanki and Manase Dosan. They contributed to the development of medicine.

Today, there is a movement by both officials and citizens to have Ashikaga Gakko enlisted on World Heritage List.

Ashikaga Gakko, together with three other Educational Heritages*, was designated by a law enacted in 2015 as the first Japan Heritage. The official name of the law is "Educational Heritage from Early-Modern Japan: the Origins of Academics and Decorum."

* the three Educational Heritages are: Kodokan (the former clan school of Mito), Kangien (the private academy of Hita), and Shizutani Gakko (the former school for common people of Okayama Clan)

釋奠

　足利学校では , 毎年、「釋奠」が行なわれる。かつて、釋奠は冬至の日に行なわれたこともあったが、現在では 11 月 23 日に固定している。釋奠とは孔子とその弟子達にお供えものを捧げて祀る儀式をいう。足利学校では、儒学中心の教育が行なわれており、そのような関係で釋奠が行なわれてきたと考えられる。「釋奠」は上杉憲実の頃に始まったとされる。

字降松

　入徳門から足利学校の敷地に入り、学校門を通ると正面に杏壇門がある。杏壇門の右手前にある松の木が「字降松」と呼ばれる松である。

　かつて、足利学校で学ぶ学徒達は読めない字や意味の分からない表現に出会うと、それを紙に書いてこの松の枝に結びつけておいた。すると、翌朝には、必ず、その紙に振り仮名や注釈がつけられていた。九華和尚が答えを書いたのであった。このことからこの松はやがて字降松と呼ばれるようになった。

Sekiten

Sekiten is an annual festival held at Ashikaga Gakko in honour of Confucius and his disciples. In former days, it was held on the day of winter solstice, but today it is held on November 23rd. It is believed that this festival is observed because the basis of learning at this academy has long been Confucianism. The beginning of this festival goes back to the time of Uesugi Norizane.

Kanafuri-Matsu

When you go through Nyutoku-mon Gate into the precincts of Ashika-ga Gakko and through the second gate called Gakko-mon, you will find the third gate, Kyodan-mon, just in front of you. There is a pine tree on the right of this gate. The pine tree is called Kana-furi-matsu. ('Kanafuri' means 'writing Japanese syllabary next to Chinese characters to show their pronunciations' and 'matsu' means 'a pine tree.')

When students studying at Ashikaga Gakko encountered Chinese characters they could not read or expressions they could not understand, they would write them on a piece of paper and tie it to a branch of this pine tree. The next mornng they were sure to find answers to their questions written on the paper. It was Priest Kyuka who wrote the answers. The pine tree gradually came to be called Kanafuri-matsu.

笠石神社と侍塚古墳
Kasaishi Shrine and Samuraizuka Tomb Mounds
大田原市湯津上

笠石神社 Kasaishi Shrine

　大田原市湯津上には笠石神社という神社があり、そこには那須国造碑（700年）がある。那須国造碑は群馬県高崎市の多胡碑（711年）、宮城県多賀城市の多賀城碑（762年）と共に日本三古碑の一つと言われ、1952年（昭和27）に国宝に指定されている。この碑の上には笠のように大きな石が載せてあるので、通例、笠石といわれる。

There is a stone monument named 'Nasu-no-Kuninomiyatsuko-no-Hi' (Monument Dedicated to the Memory of the Chieftain of Nasu Province) in the Kasaishi Shrine at Yuzukami, Otawara City. It is one of the three oldest monuments in Japan. The other two are the Tago Monument at Takasaki City, Gunma Prefecture, and the Tagajo Monument at Tagajo City, Miyagi Prefecture. The Nasu Monument was designated as a national treasure in

永昌元年己丑四月飛鳥浄御原大宮那須国造
追大壹那須直韋提評督被賜歳次庚子年正月
二壬子日辰節殄故意斯麻呂等立碑銘偲云尓
仰惟殞公廣氏尊胤国家棟梁一世之中重被貳照
一命之期連見再甦尾甲之家骨挑無髄豈報前恩是以
曽子之家无嬬尭仲尼孠之門无有罵者孝之
子不改其語銘夏尭心澄神照軋六月童子意香
助坤作从之大合言顭字故無翼長飛无根更固

那須国造碑
Nasu-no-Kuninomiyatsuko-no-Hi

　那須国造碑は、1,000年近く草むらの中に埋没していたものを1676年（延宝4）に磐城（現、福島県いわき地方）の僧円順が見つけ、このことを武茂郷小口村（現、那珂川町）の里正*であった大金重貞に話した。重貞は早速この碑を調べて自著「那須記」に書き記し、その書を1683年（天和3）にこの地を訪れた徳川光圀（1628-1700）に献上した。

*里正：村長とか庄屋の意。

1952. It is popularly called 'Kasaishi' (a hat stone) because it is capped with a flat stone just like a hat.

The stone monument had been buried under thick grass for more than 1,000 years when it was found in 1676 by Enjun, a priest from the province of Iwaki (now, part of Fukushima Prefecture). Enjun told Ogane Shigesada, village chief, about it, who studied it at once and wrote about it in his book Nasuki. Shigesada presented the book to Tokugawa Mitsukuni (1628-1700) who happened to visit the village in 1683.

The monument had been buried with its front surface underneath, which saved its inscribed characters from wearing out. It is about 148 cm in height and about 48 cm in width and is made of black granite. There are 152 characters inscribed on its surface which roughly tell us:

"Atai'ide, chieftain of the province of Nasu, was appointed 'ko'ori-no-kami' (local governor) by the Imperial Court at Asuka-kiyomihara in April in the 1st year of Eisho. When he died on the 2nd day of January in the year of 'kanoe-ne', his son, Oshimaro, and others built a monument in memory of his great achievements."

The Chinese era name 'Eisho' used in the monument corresponds to the year AD 689 and the year of 'kanoe-ne' corresponds to the year AD 700.

In the 30th Book of Nihon Shoki (oldest official history of Japan), there is

碑は表面を下にして埋もれていたためか、碑文がうまく保存されていた。碑は、高さ約148cm、幅約48cmの黒御影石(くろみかげ)でできていて、全部で152の文字が刻まれている。その文意はほぼ次のようである。

「永昌元年己丑(つちのとうし)の四月、那須国造の直韋提(あたいいで)は、飛鳥浄御原(あすかきよみはら)の大宮から評督(こおりのかみ)の官職を授かった。彼は庚子(かのえね)の歳の正月二日に亡くなった。そこで、彼の遺徳を偲んで息子の意斯麻呂(おしまろ)等が碑銘を立てて祀った。」

碑文の中で「永昌元年」という中国の元号が用いられているが、これは西暦689年にあたり、また、「庚子の歳」は西暦700年にあたる。

「日本書記」巻第三十には、当時、新羅(しらぎ)(古代朝鮮の国名)からやって来た人を那須国に居住させたという記事があり、那須国造碑は渡来人と密接な関係があるのではないかと考えられる。

侍塚古墳

那須国造碑の近く、国道294号線沿いには上侍塚古墳(かみさむらいづか)、下侍塚古墳と呼ばれる二つの美しい前方後方墳がある。上侍塚古墳は那須地方に分布する6基の前方後方墳のなかでは最大規模を誇り、下侍塚古

an article which tells us that people who came from Silla (one of the three kingdoms of ancient Korea) were told to live in the province of Nasu. This leads us to imagine that the Nasu stone monument is closely related with immigrants from ancient Korea.

下侍塚古墳　Lower-samurai-zuka Tomb Mound

Samurai-zuka Tomb Mounds

There are two beautiful zenpo-koho fun (square-front, suare-back ancient tomb mounds) near the Nasu monument along National Route 294: Upper-samurai-zuka tomb mound and Lower-samurai-zuka tomb mound. The Upper mound is the largest in size among the

墳は上侍塚古墳に次ぐ規模である。古墳の築造は、墳形の特徴や出土遺物などから4世紀半ばから後半ごろにかけてと考えられている。

　徳川光圀 (1628-1700) は、この古墳が那須国造碑に記載されている直韋提という人物について何らかの手がかりを与えてくれるのではないかと考え、1692年（元禄5）佐々宗淳に命じて発掘調査をさせた。しかし、被葬者についての手がかりは何も得ることはできなかった。調査後は、埋葬品は元に戻され、古墳は旧に復し、墳丘の崩落を防ぐために松を植え見事に保存され、現在でもその美しい姿を保っている。

square-front, square-back mounds in Nasu area. From the shape of the tomb mound and the articles deposited in it, it is estimated that the upper tomb mound was built from the middle to the latter half of the 4th century.

Tokugawa Mitsukuni (1628-1700), daimyō of the Mito domain, thought that the tomb mound is somehow related to Atai'ide described in the Nasu monument. In 1692, he told Sassa Sojun to excavate it. The excavation, however, gave no clues as to the person buried there. Various articles were returned to the former condition after the excavation and the former shape of the mound was restored. Pine trees were planted to prevent the mound from washouts. This helped to keep the beautiful shape until today.

コウシンソウ(庚申草)

タヌキモ科ムシトリスミレ属

特別天然記念物。日光市足尾の庚申山で発見された。
環境省の絶滅危惧Ⅱ類に指定されている。

第2章
山・川・温泉
Mountains, Rivers and Hot Springs

那須茶臼岳の噴煙　Mt. Nasu-cha'usu and the smoke rising from cha'usu

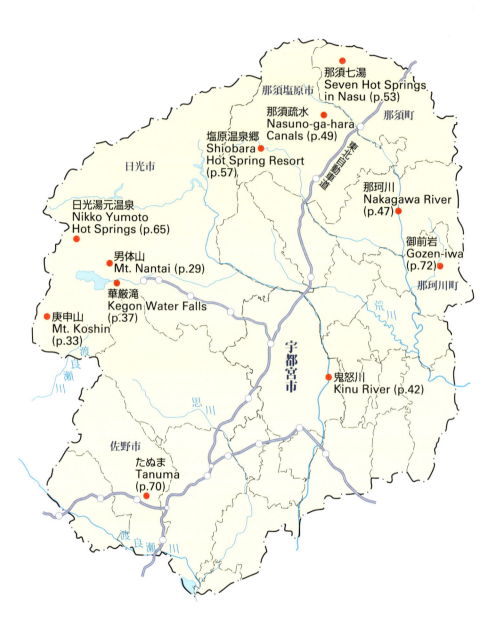

栃木の名峰　男体山
Mt. Nantai: the Most Admired Mountain in Tochigi
日光市

男体山と中禅寺湖　Mt. Nantai and Lake Chuzenji

　男体山（標高2,484m.）は栃木県の北西部に連なる日光連山の主峰の一つで、その美しく雄大な姿は古来人々の心を強く捉えてきた。男体山は、時には、日光山、二荒山とも呼ばれ、古くは、補陀洛山、黒髪山などとも呼ばれた。

　男体山は、古来、山岳修行の中心地で、山頂付近からは、これまでに、

　Mt. Nantai (2,484 m.), one of the highest mountains in Tochigi Prefecture, is located in the north-western part of the prefecture, and its imposing beauty has been admired since the olden times. Mt. Nantai is also known by other names: Nikkosan, Futarasan, and, in ancient times, it was called Fudarakusan and Kurokami-yama.

　Mt. Nantai has been a center of mountain asceticism since ancient

相当数の遺物が出土しており、中には、「二神二獣鏡」や「海獣葡萄鏡」など古墳時代にまで遡るものもあって人々が古くから男体山に惹かれてきたことを物語っている。

なお、男体山は深田久弥氏の「日本百名山」の一つに選ばれている。

勝道上人

かつて、男体山に深く心を惹かれた一人の少年がいた。その少年の名は藤糸といった。藤糸は高岡（現、真岡市）の生まれで、下野薬師寺で受戒して幼名の「藤糸」から「厳朝」と改め、後に、「勝道」と改めている。

勝道(?-817)は男体山登頂を志し、766年（天平神護2）第一回目の登頂を試みたが失敗、その14年後に第二回目の試みをするがこれも失敗に終わった。782年（延暦元）、失敗なら死ぬ覚悟で第三回目の登頂を試みた。上人は出発に当り、神々を祀り、経典を写し、仏像を描き、これを背負って山に登り、「われもし山頂に到らざれば菩提に到らず。」との強い決意で山頂を目指し、遂に、頂上に達することができた。苦渋に

times. So far, various artifacts have been unearthed from its summit. 'Nishin-ni-ju-kyo' (the mirror of two gods and two animals) and 'Kaiju-budo-kyo' (the mirror of sea animals and grapes), to name but a few. Some of them date back to the Kofun period (the late 3rd c.-7th c.), which shows how people have been attracted to the mountain since olden times.

Mt. Nantai is included in the list of 'One Hundred Distinguished Mountains in Japan' selected by Fukada Kyuya.

Shodo Shonin

There once was a boy in Takaoka in the province of Shimotsuke who was profoundly attracted by Mt. Nantai. His name was Fuji'ito. Fuji'ito was born at Takaoka (now, part of Moka City) and was ordained as a Buddhist priest at the Yakushiji Temple, and changed his boyhood name of Fuji'ito to Gencho. He later changed his name again to Shodo.

Shodo (?-817) firmly set his heart on climbing to the top of Mt. Nantai some day. In 766, he tried his first climb, but failed. 14 years later, he tried his second climb and failed again. In 782, he tried his third. Before climbing, he had prayed to gods, copied sacred Buddhist scriptures, and had drawn Buddhist images. He started to climb to the top with these on his back. He was indomitably determined that "he could never at-

満ちた15年の歳月をかけた登頂であった。

　勝道上人の人となりと生涯については弘法大師空海の「沙門勝道歴山水瑩玄珠碑并序（さんすいをへげんじゅをみがくのひならびにじょ）」に詳しい。

伝説：神戦譚

　大昔、日光の男体山と上州（現、群馬県）の赤城山（あかぎやま）が中禅寺湖の所有をめぐって争いをした。男体山の神は大蛇と化し、赤城山の神は百足（むかで）となって激しい戦いを繰り広げたが、戦いは容易に決着がつかなかった。困り果てた男体山の神は鹿島（かしま）の神様に助けを求めた。すると、鹿島の神様は「私が手助けするよりあなたの孫の猿丸に助けてもらうがよい。彼は弓の名人だ。」と教えてくれた。猿丸は相貌が猿に似ていたため猿丸（そうぼう）とよばれていたのであった。

　男体山の神様は早速、猿丸が住んでいるという奥州に出向き、やっとの思いで見つけ出した。男体神は、まず、背中に3つの金の星がある鹿に変身して猿丸の注意を惹いた。猿丸はその鹿を見て、射止めようと後を追いかけて、ついに、男体山まで来てしまった。そこで、鹿はもとの男体神の姿に戻って猿丸に、「私は男

tain enlightenment if he failed to reach the top." At last he succeeded. It was a climb with hardship and of hard will that took 15 years to achieve.

A writing* by Kobo Daishi tells us about the life and the personality of Shodo in detail.

＊Shamon Shodo, Sansui-o-he, Genju-o-migaku no Hi narabini Jo

Legend: A Battle of Gods

Once upon a time, there was a bloody battle between the god of Mt. Nantai in Nikko and the god of Mt. Akagi in Joshu (now, Gunma Prefecture) over the possession of Lake Chuzenji. The god of Nantai transformed himself as a huge serpent and the god of Mt. Akagi as a giant centipede and they fought a long and desparate battle. But it was an indecisive battle. The Nantai god was at a loss what to do and asked the god of Kashima for help. The Kashima god advised him, "Ask Saru-maru, your grandson, for help. He is a master archer." Saru-maru was so called because he looked like a 'saru' (monkey).

The Nantai god at once went to Oshu where Saru-maru was living and managed to find him at last. In order to attract his attention, the Nantai god changed himself as a deer with 3 golden star-spots on the back. Saru-maru saw the deer and, trying to shoot it, followed it and finally came to Mt. Nantai. There the Nantai god showed himself before Saru-maru and said, "I am the god of

体神で、お前の祖父である。今、私は赤城山の神に攻められて難儀している。お前の力を貸してくれぬか。」と頼んだ。

翌朝、赤城山から百足の大軍が男体山に向って押し寄せてきて、男体山の蛇とあちこちで激しい戦いが繰り広げられた。猿丸は、手に弓を持って男体山の頂上から両軍の戦いを眺めていた。折しも、一匹の巨大な百足が大顎で大蛇の頭をかみ砕こうとしているのが目に入った。これを見た猿丸は大百足の右の目を狙って矢を放った。矢は見事百足の目に刺さり、大百足は血を流しながら逃げていった。かくして、男体神は猿丸の加勢を得て赤城神を打ち負かすことができた。

奥日光の「戦場が原」という名前は蛇と百足が戦ったところ、「切込湖」「刈込湖」は百足の足を切って投げ入れたところ、「赤沼」は百足が流した血が溜まったところと言われる。

毎年、1月4日に日光中宮祠で行われる「武射祭」は、赤城山の方向に向けて弓矢を射る行事で、この行事は男体山と赤城山の伝説的な戦いに由来すると言われる。この日、赤城神社では終日社殿を閉ざして、矢除けを願ったという。

Mt. Nantai, your grandfather. I am now in great difficulty fighting against the Akagi god. Will you help me?"

The next morning, a great army of centipedes came rushing toward Mt. Nantai and fierce battles were fought here and there. Saru-maru sat on the top of Mt. Nantai with a bow in his hand and watched both parties fighting desperately. At that moment, he saw a giant centipede about to bite a serpent on the head. Saru-maru aimed his arrow at the right eye of the giant centipede and shot. The arrow hit the eye without fail. The wounded centipete ran away bleeding. In this way, the Nantai god defeated the Akagi god with the help of Saru-maru.

The place name 'Senjo-ga-hara' (battle-field) comes from this battle. The two lakes Kirikomi and Karikomi are where the legs of centipedes were cut off and thrown in. 'Akanuma' (a red pond) came to be so called because the blood shed by centipedes turned its color into red.

During Musha-sai Festival held on January 4 every year at Chugushi, Nikko, people shoot arrows toward Mt. Akagi. This festival is believed to have originated from the legendary battle between the two mountain gods. It is said that the shrine on Mt. Akagi closes all the doors on that day to avoid being shot by the arrows.

伝説の山　庚申山
Mt. Koshin: a Mountain with a Legend

日光市

　庚申山(標高1901m.)は、栃木県の西部に位置する山で、奇岩怪石の山容をなす。山頂近くには猿田彦神社が祀られていて、古来、庚申信仰のメッカとして多くの人々が訪れている。この神社の御祭神は天津祖庚申猿田彦大神、地津主甲子大己貴命、人津霊己巳少彦名命という「天・地・人」の三神である。

庚申山・猿田彦神社　Sarutahiko Shrine at Mt. Kōshin

　庚申信仰は古代中国の道教から生まれたとされ、庚申の日の夜中に人が寝静まった頃、体内に住むと言われる三尸＊という虫が身体から抜け出し、その人の行なった悪事を天帝に報告し、天帝は悪事の軽重に応じて、その人の寿命を決めると考えられた。もし、眠らなければ三尸

　Mt. Koshin(1,901m high) is located in the west of Tochigi Prefecture. There are a lot of strangely-shaped and bizarre-looking rocks here and there on this mountain. Near the summit of this mountain is a shrine named Sarutahiko. It was once the Head Shrine of Koshin Belief. The shrine is dedicated to three gods. Each of the gods is associated with "the heaven," "the earth" and "the human".

　Koshin Belief is said have originated in the Dokyo Belief of ancient China. According to this belief, 'sanshi' ＊ (three worms) creep out of our bodies during the night of a koshin day (a day that comes round once in 60 days in sexagenary cycle) and report to the Heavenly King about every evil-doing we have done so far. After listening to the report, the King decides how long we will live depending on the report by the worms. The three worms, however, cannot creep out of our bodies if we keep awake during that night. So, people used to keep awake all night on a koshin day.

＊Japanese expressions such as 'mushi-ga-shi-raseru' (worms have told me, meaning 'I had a hunch'), and 'mushi-ga-sukanai' (worms do not like it, meaning 'I have a disagreeable feeling') may be related with the three worms.

は身体から抜け出すことが出来ないので、信者は庚申の夜は眠らずに過ごしたという。

＊日本語の「虫の知らせ」、「虫の居所が悪い」、「虫が好かない」などという表現はこの三尸と関係があると言われる。

猿田彦神社の「天・地・人」の三神のご神言に「見まい、聞くまい、話すまい」とあるが、これは、これら三神を三尸になぞらえ、「見まい、聞くまい、話すまい」で天帝に罪を報告させないという意味もあったようである。

庚申山は、江戸時代の中期から後期にかけて多くの参拝者で賑わい、1865年（慶応元）には江戸の庚申講中の参加者が3,000人にもなったという。しかしながら、1946年（昭和21）に猿田彦神社は火災にあい、本殿及びお籠所が焼失してしまった。現在ではその跡地近くに「庚申山荘」が建てられている。

コウシンソウ

庚申山には、コウシンソウと呼ばれるムシトリスミレ属、タヌキ藻科に属する食虫植物が自生している。三好学博士が1889年（明治22）にこの山で発見した植物で、発見された山の名をとってコウシンソウと命名された。6月から7月にかけて咲き、

The divine words of the three gods of the Sarutahiko Shrine go like this: See no evil, Hear no evil, and Speak no evil. This can be interpreted as our wish "Please don't report to the Heavenly King about our evil-doings."

Many people visited Mt. Koshin during the mid- and late-Edo period. It is said that more than 3,000 people took part in the 1865 assembly. But the shrine and its surrouding lodgings were burnt down by a fire in 1946. Today we see the building of Koshin Sanso near its site.

コウシンソウ　koshinso

Koshinso

On Mt.Koshin, we can see 'koshinso' (an insectivorous plant) growing naturally on rocks. It was found by Dr. Miyoshi in 1889 and was named after Mt. Koshin. Koshinso come into flower from June to July. It is designated as nationally protected species.

国の特別天然記念物に指定されている。

南総里見八犬伝

　庚申山は滝沢馬琴 (1767-1848) の伝奇小説「南総里見八犬伝」の舞台にもなっている。小説は、仲間からはぐれて足尾までやって来た八犬士の一人犬飼現八が、茶店の老人から庚申山にまつわる不思議な物語を聞く形で展開する。

　馬琴は庚申山を次のように描写している。「まづあちこちを見かへるに、宝蔵に似たる大石あり。また二重の塀に似たるあり。また屏風に似たるもあり。箪笥の引出してふものに似たるもあり。この余或は舟或は釜、或は鶴亀に似たる自然石の厳々として立てるあり。天造地工の精妙なる、見れども言葉に述べがたく、画くとも筆に写し易からず。」

伝説：サルの花嫁

　昔、庚申山の麓の中才というところに一人の猟師が３人の娘と一緒に住んでいた。ある冬の日、猟師は狩りに出掛けたがあいにく吹雪に襲われ、家に帰る途中、雪で足を滑らせて谷底に落ちて意識を失ってしまった。

　しばらくして、猟師は誰かが自分

Nanso Satomi Hakkenden

Takizawa Bakin (1767-1848) chose Mt. Koshin as a scene for his fantasy romance called *Nanso Satomi Hakkenden* (Eight Dog Samurai of Satomi in Nanso). In the romance, Inukai Genpachi, one of the dog samurai, gets separated from his companion and comes to Ashio. There he is told strange stories about Mt. Koshin by the master of a tea stall.

Bakin describes Mt. Koshin as follows: "When you look around, you see huge rocks formed like a treasure storage, a double fence, and a folding screen. There is also a rock which looks like a chest drawer. There is a boat, a cauldron, a crane-and-tortoise sitting gravely on a natural rock. Their beauty and subtlety cannot be easily described by words nor can they be drawn satisfactorily."

Legend: A Bride of A Monkey

There once lived a hunter and his three daughters in a village called Nakasai at the foot of Mt. Koshin.

One day in winter, the hunter went out for hunting. Unfortunately, however, it soon began to snow heavily. He hurried home in the snowstorm, but on the way, he slipped and fell tumbling down the slope to the bottom of a valley

を揺り動かしているので意識を取り
戻した。猟師は朦朧とした意識の
中で「俺を助けてくれ。助けてくれ
たら俺の娘を嫁にやる。」と言った。
猟師を揺り動かしていたのは人間で
はなく白い猿であった。白猿はこれ
を聞くと小躍りして喜び、早速仲間
を集め、猟師を無事山の麓まで連
れて行った。猟師は別れ際に猿達
に約束した。「三月三日に鏡岩まで
必ず娘を連れて行く。」と。

　家に帰ると、猟師は三人の娘達に
白猿との約束の話をし、誰か猿の嫁
になってくれないか、とためらいなが
ら頼んだ。上の二人の娘は即座に断
わったが、末娘は少し躊躇してから、
「私が行きます。お父っぁんの命の
恩人ですもの。」と言ってくれた。

　約束の日、猟師が末娘を連れて
鏡岩まで行くと白猿が迎えに来てい
た。猟師は娘と別れるのがしのびな
く、3年後の今日この場で再会する
ことを約束して別れた。

　3年後、猟師が鏡岩に行くと、そ
こには仲睦まじい猿の夫婦が待っ
ていた。雌猿の瞳には父親に対する
深い思いやりの眼差しがあった。

and lost his consciousness.

After a while, he came to himself be-
caue someone was shaking him. Half
consciously and half unconsciously, the
hunter said, "Help me. I will give you
one of my daughters as a wife if you help
me." It was a white monkey, not a person, that was shaking him.

When the white monkey heard this,
it jumped with joy and, at once called
his fellow monkeys. They carried him
on their shoulders to Kagami-iwa. The
hunter promised the monkeys that he
would bring his daughter to Kagami-
iwa on March 3, and went back to his
home.

When he reached home, he told his
daughters what had happened and said
to them, "Please, one of you, please
marry the monkey." The two elder
daughters refused at once. The youngest
daughter, after a little hesitation, said,
"Daddy, the monkey saved your life. I
will go and marry the monkey."

On the appointed day, the hunter
took his youngest daughter to Kagami-
iwa, where the white monkey was wait-
ing. The hunter could not bear the sor-
row of parting his daughter and said,
"Let's meet here again 3 years later on
March 3."

Three years later, the hunter went to
Kagami-iwa and found there a couple of
white monkeys who looked very happy.
He saw, in the eyes of the female monkey, the warm deep love for her father.

名瀑 華厳滝
Kegon Waterfalls
日光市中宮祠

華厳滝　Kegon Waterfalls

日光の華厳滝は熊野の「那智の滝」（和歌山県）、奥久慈の「袋田の滝」（茨城県）と共に、日本三名瀑の一つに挙げられる滝である。「華厳」という名称は釈尊の「五時教*」から名付けられたもので、近くには「五時教」を表す「阿含」「方等」「般若」「涅槃」の滝がある。

＊「五時教」：釈尊の一生の間の説法を五期に区分したもの。

昔、華厳滝は「江尻滝」と呼ばれたという。日光を開山した勝道上人の弟子達が818年（弘仁9）に書いた「補陀洛山建立修行日記」には、807年（大同2）の大旱魃の際、上人が「江尻滝」で雨乞いの祈祷をしたという記載がある。

華厳滝は中禅寺湖から流れ出る大尻川が高さ97mの大岩壁を流れ落ちる美しく雄大な滝で、その壮観は古来人々の心をとらえ続けてきた。滝の中間部からは中禅寺湖の伏流水が湧き出て「十二滝」と呼ばれる玉簾のような細い小滝を作って滝に趣を添えている。

日光出身の画家小杉放庵（1881-1964）は次のような歌を詠んでいる。

三千年大華厳経よみつづけ
よみとどろかす滝の音かな

現在では、エレベーターで滝壺近くまで約1分で簡単に下りて行くこ

The Kegon Waterfalls in Nikko is one of the three most renowned falls in Japan. The other two are: the Nachi Waterfalls in Kumano, Wakayama Prefecture, and the Fukuroda Waterfalls in Okukuji, Ibaraki Prefecture. The name Kegon was taken from Goji-kyo*. Near the Kegon Waterfalls are four other falls, Agon, Hoto, Han'nya, and Nehan. These names were also taken from Goji-kyo.

＊Buddha's Teachings Divided into Five Stages

The Kegon Waterfalls was once called Kojiri Falls. In *the Diary of Ascetic Training Days to Establish Mt. Fudaraku* kept by disciples of Priest Shodo in 818, there is a record that Shodo practiced a prayer for rain at the Kojiri Falls when there was a long spell of drought in 807.

The Kegon Waterfalls is a beautiful falls formed by the Ojiri River that tumbles down 97-meter cliffs. People have been fascinated by its majestic view since old times. Underground water from Lake Chuzenji flows out in the middle of the cliffs forming fine water-curtains called 'Juni-taki' (Twelve Cascades).

Kosugi Ho'an (1881-1964), a native of Nikko and a painter, once composed a poem:

Reciting the Great Kegon Sutra
The Falls has been rumbling
For 3,000 long years

Today, we can get to the basin of the Kegon Falls in a minute by an elevator.

とができるが、1930年（昭和5）にエレベーターが出来るまでは、人々は狭い道を徒歩で滝壺近くまで下りていった。この道を拓いた人は星野五郎平という人で独力で10年がかりで道を作ったという。現在、大平から馬返方面に少し下った道路沿い右手に石塔が建っていて、その正面には「左華厳滝壺　白雲滝　涅槃滝」、そして、側面には「明治三十三年十月開鑿竣工　星野五郎平」と刻まれている。今では、この石塔の存在を知る人はほとんどいない。

藤村操：巌頭之感

　1903年（明治36年）5月22日、旧制第一高等学校の学生藤村操は「巌頭之感」を書き残して華厳滝に投身自殺をした。この事件は当時大きく新聞等に報道された。

　藤村操の自殺の原因については、哲学的な悩み説とか失恋説などが挙げられているがいずれの説も真偽のほどは分らない。

　藤村操は旧制一高で夏目漱石の英語の授業を受けていた。藤村操の投身自殺は漱石の心に強い衝撃を与え、彼の作品には次のような表現が見られる。「可哀想に。打ちやって置くと巌頭の吟でも書いて華

But people had to walk down a narrow path to the basin before an elevator was installed in 1930. It was Hoshino Gorobei who cleared the path to the basin. He worked all alone for 10 years to clear the path. A little way down the road leading from Odaira to Umagaeshi, there is a stone monument on the right side. On its front surface is inscribed "Left path will lead to the Basin of the Kegon Falls, the Shirakumo Falls and the Nehan Falls" and on its side is inscribed "Completed in October in the 33rd Year of Meiji by Hoshino Gorobei." Today, few people pay attention to the monument.

Fujimura Misao: At the Top of the Falls

On May 22, 1903, Fujimura Misao, a student of Kyusei Ichiko (the First High School under the Old Education System), jumped down into the Kegon Waterfalls after he wrote his last note "At the Top of the Falls" on the trunk of a tree. The news was reported with big headlines.

Various guesses have been made as to the cause of his suicide. Some said that he had been agonizing over philosophical problems, and others said that he had suffered from a broken heart. The truth lies beyond our guesses.

Fujimura Misao was in a class by Natsume Soseki at Kyusei Ichiko. Fujimura's suicide grealy shocked Soseki. In his novel *Wagahai wa Neko de aru*

嚴頭之感　Gantō-no-kan

("I am a Cat"), we find such expressions as "What a pity. If we leave him alone, he will write 'At the Top of the Falls' note and jump into the falls." or "Help him. It will reward you in return. When we think of his present state of mind, he will probably go to the Kegon Falls." In *Kusamakura* ("Grass Pillow"), Soseki writes "There once was a young man who jumped into the 100 meter-high falls."

The Fujimura's suicide note was soon scraped off by the police, but before it was scraped off, Hoshino Fukujiro, a photographer who lived near Lake Chuzenji, took its picture.

厳滝から飛び込むかも知れない。」（「我輩は猫である」）、「救って御やんなさい。功徳(くどく)になりますよ。あの容子ぢゃ華厳の滝へ出掛けますよ 」（同書）、「昔し巌頭の吟を遺して、五十丈の飛瀑を直下して急湍(きゅうたん)に赴いた青年がある。」「草枕」）

藤村操の「巌頭之感」はすぐに警察によって削りとられたが、その前に中禅寺湖畔で写真館を開いていた星野福次郎という人がカメラにおさめていた。

<table>
<tr>
<td>

巖頭之感

悠々たる哉天壌、
遼々たる哉古今、
五尺の小躯を以て
此大をはからむとす。
ホレーショの哲學竟に何等の
オーソリチィーを價するものぞ。
萬有の眞相は唯だ一言にして悉す、
曰く、「不可解」。
我この恨を懐いて煩悶、
終に死を決するに至る。
既に巖頭に立つに及んで、
胸中何等の不安あるなし。
始めて知る、大なる悲觀は
大なる樂觀に一致するを。（後略）

</td>
<td>

At the Top of the Falls

How spacious Heaven and Earth are!
How eternally Time flies!
I have been trying hard to measure the greatness
with my little five-foot figure!
What authority does Horatio's philosophy have?
The truth of the whole universe can
be expressed in a single word 'inscrutable.'
I have suffered many mental agonies,
And I have finally decided to die
Now I stand at the top of the falls.
I have no fear whatsoever.
For the first time in my life,
I have realized that
great pessimism is equal to great optimism.

</td>
</tr>
</table>

水の動脈　鬼怒川
the Kinu River

　鬼怒川は、日光国立公園北西部にある鬼怒沼に源をもち、湯西川、大谷川そして田川などの支流をあわせて、栃木県内を東に、南に、そして、南東に方向を変えながら、茨城県と千葉県との境界部で利根川に合流する。全長176.7kmの県内最長の一級河川である。

　鬼怒川の上流部は火山地帯で、深い渓谷を流れ、その奇岩・怪石は龍王峡や瀬戸合峡などの観光名所

　The Kinu River flows from Kinunuma Marsh in the north-western part of Nikko National Park. It joins rivers Yunishi-gawa, Daiya-gawa, and Ta-gawa, flowing east, sometimes south, and sometimes south-east, and joins the Tone River at the border of Ibaraki and Chiba Prefectures. The Kinu River is a Class A River with the length of 176.7 km. and is the longest river in Tochigi Prefecture.

　In its upper reaches, the river flows through deep valleys in the volcanic

鬼怒川 the Kinu River

となっており、自然の造形美を味わうための「鬼怒川ライン下り」は有名である。また、流域には、女夫渕温泉、川治温泉、湯西川温泉、鬼怒川温泉などの温泉地が点在する。

中下流部は平地に出て川幅が広がりその水は農業用水、工業用水、生活用水などに利用され、流域の住民の貴重な水源になっている。ちなみに、宇都宮市の上水道は鬼怒川から供給されている。

2012年2月には、鬼怒川の河原から約1,000万年前のクジラの化石が発見され、また、2013年1月にも板戸大橋の上流約2kmの地点でクジラの化石が見つかり、話題になった。

鬼怒川の呼称

鬼怒川の古い呼び名は「毛野河」であった。721年(養老5)ころ成立した「常陸風土記」の中にこの名がみえる。「毛野」の呼称は、草木の生い茂った地と解釈され、「下野」の古い言い方・「下毛野」に関係する。

平安時代(794-1185)の書物には「衣川」という表記がみえ、江戸時代 (1603-1867)の古地図には

zone. And the rocks of strange formation along the river, especially, at Ryu'okyo and Seto'ai-kyo Gorges attract a lot of visitors. Many people enjoy Kinu River Rhein Cruise (going down the Kinu River in a boat) and enjoy its natural beauty. Hot springs such as Me'oto-buchi, Kawaji, Yunishigawa, and Kinugawa are located along the river.

In its middle and lower reaches, the Kinu River becomes wider as it flows through level land. It supplies water to people along the river, and its water is utilized for irrigation, industry, and drinking. Drinking water for citizens of Utsunomiya comes from this river.

In February, 2012, a fossilized whale about 10,000,000 years old was found in the river bed of this river, and again in January, 2013, another fossilized whale was found about 2 kilometers upstream of the Itado-Ohashi Bridge. These fossil remains attracted attention of many people.

the Name of this River

According to *Hitachi Fudoki* ("a collection of reports of natural resources, geography, and traditions of the province of Hitachi") compiled about the year 721, the Kinu River was once called Keno River. 'Keno' probably means 'the land with dense vegetation,' and is related with the name Shimotsukenu, old name of the province of Shimotsuke.

In a book written during the Heian period (794-1185), Chinese characters

「絹川」の文字もみられる。これらの表記はこの川が穏やかな流れの川であるとの印象を与える。「鬼怒川」の表記が見られるのは明治時代以降である。「鬼が怒る川」という言い方は、この川が容易にコントロールできないとの印象を与える。

2015年（平成27）9月に、鬼怒川下流の茨城県常総市において堤防が決壊し、甚大な被害を与えたことはいまだに記憶に新しい。

利根川東遷事業

鬼怒川の歴史は、治水、利水の歴史でもある。江戸時代初期までの毛野河・衣川は、直接太平洋に注ぐ河川であった。一方、同じように関東平野を貫く利根川、渡良瀬川は、それぞれ個別に南に流れ、江戸湾（東京湾）に注ぐ河川であった。三つの河川ともに下流部は低湿地帯で、上流部の降雨はこの一帯にしばしば大きな洪水をもたらした。

江戸時代初期、徳川家康の命令により「利根川東遷事業」の大工事が行われた。江戸の排水性を高め、洪水から守ること、さらに、関東平野の新田開発の推進、江戸と関東以北との舟運の発展を図るためであった。利根川の水流を東に誘導し、渡良瀬水系と鬼怒川水系へとつな

衣川 were used for its name,and in an old map made during the Edo period (1603-1868), we also find characters 絹川. These characters give us the impression that the river is gentle. After the Meiji Era, Chinese characters 鬼怒川 ('the river of angry ogres') began to be used. The characters gives us the impression that the river is not easy to control.

In September, 2015, Joso City in the lower reaches of the Kinu River was greatly destroyed by the flood when the bank of the river collapsed. Its horrible scene is still fresh in our memory.

Improvement Work of Tone River

The history of the Kinu River has been the history of flood-controlling and irrigation works.The Kinu River used to flow directly into the Pacific Ocean until the Edo period. The Tone and Watarase Rivers, on the other hand, were flowing south through Kanto plain into low, damp area of the Edo Bay. Heavy rains in the upper reaches often inundated the surrounding area.

'Tonegawa Tosen Jigyo' (a large scale work to change the flow of the Tone River) started in the early days of the Edo period at the order of Tokugawa Ieyasu. Its purpose was to save Edo from floods by constructing a draining system, to promote reclamation of rice fields, and to develop the river transportation system between Edo and the Kanto Region. In the construction work,

ぐ工事で、元来の鬼怒川水系に利根川・渡良瀬川の水が流れるようになり、鬼怒川下流部の名称は「きぬ」ではなく「とね」とされた。

鬼怒川流域最大の災害の記録として、1723 年（享保 8）8 月 10 日からの「五十里洪水」がある。この洪水から遡ること約 40 年、日光地方は大地震に襲われ、その影響で男鹿川がせき止められ五十里湖が出現した。会津藩は何度かこの湖の水抜き工事を行なったが、工事が完成する前に、この地方は大雨に襲われ、五十里湖はついに決壊したのである。

鬼怒川の河岸

江戸時代には、五街道をはじめ陸上交通が発達していったが、河川を利用する舟運も盛んになっていった。小型の川舟でも船 1 艘に米 50 俵を積むことができ、これは馬 1 駄の約 25 倍であり、運賃も安く、舟運は大量輸送に有利であった。

下野国で舟運に利用されたのは、三つの水系、即ち鬼怒川、渡良瀬川（その支流には思川、巴波川、秋山川がある）、那珂川であり、このうち鬼怒川、渡良瀬川はいずれも、利根川、江戸川を経由して直接江戸へ到着することができる重要な内陸水路であった。

the flow of water of the Tone River was changed to flow east so that it may join the Watarase and the Kinu Rivers. The lower Kinu was now called Tone River.

The greatest natural disaster that befell the Kinu River area was the Ikari Flood of Aug. 10, 1723. The remote cause of the flood was a big earthquake that hit Nikko area about 40 years before the flood. The earthquake dammed up a river called Ojika and formed a new lake, Ikari. Aizu Domain tried to drain the water of the lake several times, but in vain. And at last, heavy rain caused the bank of the lake to collapse.

Riverbanks of the Kinu River

During the Edo Period, land transportation system along the Five Main Highways gradually developed, and with it, boat transportation on rivers became prosperous. Even a small boat could carry 50 bales of rice, which was about 25 times the amount a horse could carry. Charges for boat transportation were low, and it was convenient for mass transportation.

Three rivers in the province of Shimotsuke were utilized for boat transportation. They were Kinu, Watarase (with its tributaries Omoi,Uzuma and Akiyama) and Naka Rivers. Of the three rivers, Kinu and Watarase were important routes because they were directly connected with Edo (old name of Tokyo)

江戸時代初期の鬼怒川河岸は、阿久津（さくら市氏家）、板戸・道場宿（宇都宮市）、柳林（真岡市）、吉田（下野市南河内）、福良・中島（小山市）など10河岸であった。

なかでも、阿久津河岸は、奥州街道と鬼怒川が交わるところで地理的に恵まれており、大いに賑わった。

この河岸から下野国の産物（諸藩の廻米や御用材、商人米、大豆、小豆、大麦、煙草等）が大量に輸送され、江戸からは、諸藩あて物資や茶、塩、さとうなどの日用品, 干鰯などが送られてきた。

また、この阿久津河岸には会津藩の御用蔵があり、会津藩の物資輸送ばかりでなく、奥州諸藩の廻米や御用物資の輸送の役割も果たした。

現在、阿久津河岸には船玉神社が残っており、当時の河岸問屋の人々や船頭・人足が水上交通の安全と河岸の繁栄を祈ったあとがしのばれる。

via Tone and Edo Rivers.

During the early days of Edo, there were 10 riverbanks along the Kinu River: Akutsu, Itado, Dojojuku, Yanagibayashi, Yoshida, Fukura, Nakajima and two others. The riverbank at Akutsu was favorably located at the place where the Oshu Highway crosses the Kinu River and enjoyed great prosperity. Products (rice, beans, barleys and tobacco) of Shimotsuke domain as well as products of other domains were transported from here to Edo, and, on the way back, goods for various domains and daily goods (like tea, salt, sugar, and dried sardines) were carried from Edo.

At Akutsu Riverbank, there was an official storehouse of Aizu Domain and played an important role in transporting Aizu goods. It was also an important riverbank for other domains in Ōshu district to transport rice and other goods for the Shogunate.

There is a shrine called Funadama in Akutsu. This is where people working in the riverbank prayed for safe transportation and the prosperity of the riverbank.

船玉神社 Funadama Shrine

鮎おどる那珂川　やな
the Nakagawa River that Abounds in Ayu

　栃木県の観光資源として、アユ漁は見逃すことができない。1879年に国賓として元米国大統領ユリシーズ・グラント将軍（1822-1886）が日本を訪れた折、日光の帰り、絹織物工場、大嶹商舎を見学に宇都宮の石井村にやってきた。その時、その饗応に使われたのもアユ漁（投網漁）であった。

　県内のアユ漁では、特に那珂川が盛んで、黒羽から小川、馬頭、烏山、茂木の間がアユの本場である。6月初めにアユの解禁となると、釣り人で賑わう。

　8月に入るとアユは産卵のため川を下り始めるので、これを捕るために川中に簗を掛ける。簗は木や竹で

　Ayu fishing (sweet fish fishing) can not be overlooked as one of Tochigi Prefecture's tourist attractions. In 1879, when the former US president Ulysses S Grant (1822-1886) came to Japan as a state guest, he visited Oshima Shosha (a silk factory) in Ishii, Utsunomiya, on his way back from Nikko. Ayu fishing (a method of catching ayu-fish by casting a net) was chosen as an entertainment for General Grant at the time.

　Ayu fishing in Tochigi Prefecture is most prosperous in the Nakagawa River, especially in the areas from Kurobane to Ogawa, Bato, Karasuyama, and Motegi. In early-June, when the fishing season of ayu opens, the river is crowded with people who enjoy fishing.

　In August, Ayu start coming down the river to spawn. And in order to

やな　yana

出来ていて、作るのに多額の費用が
かかる。このアユ漁は「落ちアユ拾い」
と言われ、9月・10月がその最盛期
となる。

　「やな」の近くにはたいてい食事
処があり、人々は川を渡る涼風を受
けながら、捕れたての新鮮な鮎料
理に舌鼓を打つ。料理としては、鮎
塩焼、鮎みそ焼、鮎から揚げ、鮎刺
身、鮎めし、うるか、などである。

　農林水産省調べ、2010年のアユ
の河川別漁獲量を見ると、那珂川が
1位（684 t）で、2位が相模川（318
t）、4位が長良川（154 t）、四万十
川（20 t）は12位となっている。

　また、2013年時点における全国
の主な「やな」47か所（小規模で
無許可のものを除く）の中で、27か
所が那珂川水系と利根川水系に存
在している。

　アユは環境のバロメーターと云わ
れている。那珂川は自然災害、ダム・
堰などの建設、環境破壊など、様々
な障害を乗り越え、生き残った全国
でも数少ないアユの清流である。そ
して、その中で生き残った「やな」も
栃木県には、まだ数多く存在し、今
でも多くの観光客を魅了し続けてい
る。

catch them, people build fish traps
called 'yana' in the stream. Yana is made
of timbers and bamboos and it costs a
lot to build one. This method of catching ayu is called "ochi ayu hiroi" (catching ayu which are coming down the
stream). The best season is in September
and October.

Near yana, there is usually a restau-
rant where they serve ayu dishes. There
we can enjoy eating variety of ayu dishes
such as salt-grilled ayu, miso-grilled ayu,
deep-fried ayu, ayu tempura, ayu sashi-
mi, ayu rice, uruka (pickled ayu-roe),
and so on.

According to the Report given by
the Ministry of Agriculture, Forestry,
and Fisheries, the Nakagawa River is
ranked 1st (684 t) in the amount of ayu
catch in 2010. The Sagami River comes
2nd (318 t). The Nagaragawa River
comes 4th (154 t) and the Shimanto
River 12th (20 t).

As of the year 2013, 27 out of 47 major yana in Japan (excluding small-sized,
license-less yana) are along the Nakagawa River or the Tonegawa River in
Tochigi Prefecture.

Ayu is said to be a barometer of environmental quality. The Nakagawa River
is one of the most precious and rare rivers that have survived various difficul-
ties such as natural disasters, dam-and-
barrier constructions, environmental
destructions and so on. In Tochigi Prefecture, there are still many yana which
keep on attracting many tourists.

荒野を潤す那須疏水
Nasuno-ga-hara Canals
那須塩原市、大田原市

　栃木県北部に広がる那須野が原は、東は那珂川、西は箒川に挟まれた木の葉の形をした約4万haの広大な扇状地で、その中央を蛇尾川、熊川が伏流水となって南下している。

　那須野が原は江戸時代までは、水の確保ができなかったためほとんど人の手の入らない広大な原野であった。火山灰と砂礫が積み重

Nasuno-ga-hara is a leaf-shaped alluvial fan extending in northern Tochigi Prefecture. It covers a vast area of about 40,000 ha. It is bounded by the Naka River on the east and by the Hoki River on the west, and two rivers, Sabi and Kuma, flow underground toward south in the center of the fan.

Nasuno-ga-hara remained largely undeveloped due to lack of water until the Edo period (1603-1867). Here, water

西岩崎取水口 Sluice Gate at Nishi-Iwasaki

なった扇状地で地下水位が著しく低く、北部では20m以上掘らなければ地下水に届かないほどであった。そんな那須野が原を人が住めるようにし、農耕が可能な土地にするには、まず、水を確保することが必要であった。

　那須野が原の本格的な開拓が始められたのは明治時代(1868-1911)に入ってからである。1876年(明治9)、時の若き栃木県令鍋島幹(なべしままつよし)(1844-1913)は那須野ヶ原に「大運河構想」を打ち出した。この構想に大きな影響を受けたのが、地元の有力者印南丈作(じょうさく)(1833-1888)と矢板武(1849-1922)であった。彼らは鍋島県令の構想を受けて、那須野が原に飲用、灌漑を目的とした疏水を造る計画を立てた。

1881年(明治13)10月、那須開墾社の 印南丈作・矢板武、肇耕社(ちょうこうしゃ)の三島通庸(みちつね)などが中心となって飲用水路の開削が始められ、翌年11月、工事は完成した。しかし、飲用水路だけでは水不足は解消されなかった。このため、両氏は、灌漑用を兼ねた大運河を造ることの急務を政府にねばり強く訴え続けたが交渉は難航し、両氏はついに1884年(明治17)7月、私費による試削を開始した。

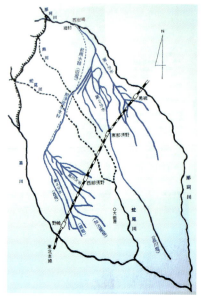

那須疏水 Nasu Canals

flows deep under the piles of volcanic ashes and gravels, and in the northern part of the fan it was impossible to get water if they did not dig 20 meters deep. Getting water was most necessary in order to make Nasuno-ga-hara a place where people could live and to make farming possible.

　Full-scale reclamation work of Nasuno-ga-hara started in the Meiji period (1868-1911). In 1876, Nabeshima Tsuyoshi (1844-1913), young governor of Tochigi Prefecture at that time, announced "a grand plan to build canals in Nasuno-ga-hara." This grand plan moved two influential people of the district, In'nami Josaku (1833-1888) and Yaita Takeshi (1849-1922). In accor-

那須疏水開削工事が国営事業として起工されたのは1885年（明治18）4月のことであった。西岩崎の那珂川右岸を取水口として、千本松までの約16.3kmの本幹水路の開削が進められ、起工式からわずか5ヶ月で完成した。本幹水路は西岩崎から那須野が原を南西方向に流れ、その途中に第一から第四までの分水が設けられた。それぞれの分水は更に何カ所かで枝分かれをし、広大な那須野が原に水が行き渡るように工夫された。

全ての支線を含めるとその総延長は300km以上になった。そして、最終的には約4,300haもの土地を潤す那須疏水が完成した。那須疏水によって那須野が原の開拓は急速に進展したのである。

西岩崎の取水口（第一次取水口）は那珂川の絶壁にトンネルを掘って造られたもので、水量を調節したり、土砂の流入を防ぐ開閉施設がなかったため、しばしば、大水などによって使用できなくなることがあった。そのため、1905年（明治38）11月に約200m上流に新たな取水口が造られた（第二次取水口）。

しかし、その後、那珂川の流れが変わった為、1915年（大正4）には元の第一次取水口に戻されている

dance with the grand plan, they made a plan to build canals in Nasuno-ga-hara to get water for drinking and irrigation.

Construction work of canals to secure drinking water started in October, 1881. Its chief leaders were In'nami and Yaita of Nasu Reclamation Work and Mishima Michitsune (1835-1888) of Chokosha Farm. The work was completed in November in 1882. Building the canals, however, did not solve the problem of water shortage. In'nami and Yaita persistently petitioned the Japanese Government to build larger canals that could supply water for both drinking and irrigation. The petition, however, was not granted. At last, they decided to build canals at their own expenses in July, 1884.

The construction work of Nasu Canals by the Japanese Government began in April, 1885. The canal was built for about 16.3 km from the sluice gate at Nishi-Iwasaki to Senbonmatsu. Water was taken from the right bank of the Naka River. It took only 5 months to complete. The canal flows south-west from Nishi-Iwasaki, and it branches out at four points on the way. It further branches out at several points so that the water from the canal would reach every part of Nasuno-ga-hara.

The total length of the canal was more than 300 km if every branch stream was added. Thus, Nasu Canal, which waters 4,300 ha of land, was completed. With the completion of Nasu Canal, the rec-

（第三次取水口）。

　そして、1976 年（昭和 51）4 月には那須野が原総合開発の一環として新しい取水口が造られ（第四次取水口）、古い取水口は使われなくなった。

　旧取水施設は、那須野が原に飲用、水田灌漑等を目的に建設された施設で、明治期有数の規模を誇る土木遺産で、2006 年（平成 18）7 月に国指定重要文化財に指定された。

　那須疏水は福島県の安積疏水、滋賀県の琵琶湖疏水と共に日本三大疏水の一つに数えられている。

lamation of Nasuno-ga-hara was greatly accelerated.

The sluice gate at Nishi-Iwasaki (the First Sluice Gate) was built by cutting out a tunnel through the river bank. It had, however, no facilities to control the flow of water and to prevent earth and sand from clogging the gate. So, a new sluice gate (the Second Sluice Gate) was built in 1905 about 200 m up the stream.

After that, however, since the Naka River started to flow differently, the First Sluice Gate was in use again instead (the Third Sluice Gate)in 1915.

And in April, 1976, a new sluice gate was built as part of Overall Development Plan of Nasuno-ga-hara (the Fourth Sluice Gate), and the old gate fell into disuse.

The old gate was built for the purpose of supplying water for drinking and irrigation. It is one of the greatest engineering works of the Meiji period and it was designated as National Important Cultural Property in July, 2006.

Nasu Canal, together with Asaka Canal in Fukushima and Biwako Canal in Shiga, is one of the three great canals in Japan.

那須七湯
Seven Hot Springs in Nasu

那須町

　那須温泉郷には、那須湯本（鹿の湯）、大丸、弁天、北、八幡、高雄、三斗小屋の七つの温泉があり「那須七湯」として知られている。七つのうち「鹿の湯」の開湯が一番古く、その歴史は舒明天皇（593-641）の御代の630年まで遡ることができ、その発見について次のような伝説が伝えられている。

　In Nasu area, there are 7 hot-spring resorts: Nasu-yumoto (Shika-no-yu), Omaru, Benten, Kita, Yahata, Takao, and Sando-goya. They are popularly known as "Seven Hot Springs of Nasu." Shika-no-yu is the oldest of them and its history goes back to 630 in the reign of Emperor Jomei (593-641). A legend goes as follows:

鹿の湯　Shika-no-yu Hot Spring

伝説：鹿の湯

　那須山麓の茗荷沢に　狩野行広という一人の猟師が住んでいた。ある日、行広は狩りに出て一匹の白い大きな鹿を見つけ、その鹿めがけて矢を放った。矢は狙い違わず鹿に命中したが、手傷を負った鹿はどんどん山奥に逃げ込んでいき、行広は遂にその鹿を見失ってしまった。

　呆然と佇んでいると、行広の目の前の岩の上に白髪の老人が立っていた。その老人が言うには、「私は温泉の神である。お前の探している鹿は、傷を癒すために谷間の温泉に浸かっている。この温泉は万病に効く温泉である。お前は早くこのことを人々に教えて彼らの病苦を救ってあげなさい。」こう言うと、老人はいずこともなく消えうせた。

　行広は不思議に思いつつも、老人の言った谷間を探してみると、確かに、先ほどの鹿が温泉に浸かって傷を癒している様子であった。この温泉が現在の「鹿の湯温泉」である。行広はこの鹿を射止め、温泉のそばに祠を建てて神霊を祀ったという。これが那須温泉神社のはじまりと言われる。

駿河国正税帳

　正倉院の古文書「駿河国正税帳」

Legend: Shika-no-yu

There once lived a hunter named Karino Yukihiro in Myogazawa, at the foot of Nasu mountains. One day he went hunting and found a big, white deer. He shot an arrow at the deer. The arrow hit the deer. The wounded deer, however, ran deep into woods and, finally, Yukihiro lost sight of it.

He stood in utter disappointment for a while, when he saw a white-haired old man standing on a rock in front of him. The old man said to him, "I am the god of hot springs. The deer you are looking for is bathing in a hot spring in the valley to cure the arrow-wound. The hot spring cures every kind of diseases. Go and tell people about the hot spring and relieve their sufferings." No sooner had he said so than the old man disappeared.

Yukihiro could hardly believe what the old man told him, but he went down to the valley to look for the deer. Sure enough, the deer was bathing in the hot spring as if it were healing its wound. This is the beginning of Shika-no-yu Hot Spring. Yukihiro shot the deer dead. He built a small shrine near the spring to enshrine its holy spirit. They say this is the beginning of Nasu Yuzen Shrine.

the Statement of Accounts of Suruga Province

The Statement of Accounts of Suru-

には、奈良時代の738年（天平10）にある貴人が都から那須温泉に湯治にやって来たことが記されており、那須温泉がすでに奈良時代から湯治場として日本全国に知られていたことがうかがわれる。

那須与一と那須温泉神社

　1185年（文治元）、源氏と平氏が屋島において戦った時、源氏は陸に、平家は海に陣取った。夕闇がせまっていて、その日のうちに戦いの決着をつけるのは不可能に思えた。その時、平家方から一艘の船が現れた。その船には若い女性が乗っていて、先端に扇を結びつけた竿をかかげ、源氏方に向かってこの扇を射落としてみよと言っているようであった。

　この扇を射落とすようにと源氏の大将義経から命じられたのが那須与一であった。与一は矢を射る前に心の中で祈った。

　「南無八幡大菩薩、我が国の神明、日光の権現、宇都宮、那須の温泉大明神、願はくは、あの扇の真ん中射させてたばせたまへ。これを射損ずるものならば、弓切り折り自害して、人に二度面を向かふべからず。いま一度本国へ迎へんとおぼしめさば、この矢はづさせたまふな。」

（平家物語巻11）

ga Province, an old document kept in Shosoin (the wooden storehouse at the Todaiji Temple in Nara), tells us that a nobleman came all the way from Nara to Nasu Hot Spring in 738 to recover his health. This shows that Nasu Hot Spring resort has been widely known to all over Japan ever since Nara Period.

Nasu-no-Yoichi and Nasu Yuzen Shrine

When the Minamoto Clan and the Taira Clan fought at Yashima in 1185, the Genji took up their position on the land and the Heike in the sea. Night was falling and it seemed impossible to continue the fight on that day, when a boat appeared suddenly from the Taira side. There was a young lady standing on the bow. She produced a pole with a fan on its top and seemed to invite the Minamoto to shoot the fan.

It was Nasu-no-Yoichi who was told by Yoshitsune to shoot the fan. Before he shot an arrow, Yoichi prayed:

"Hail, Great Bodhisattva Hachiman and ye gods of my province at Nikko, Utsunomiya and Nasu Yuzen! Vouchsafe that I may hit the center of that fan. If I miss, I will smash my bow and kill myself; I will never show my face to others again. If it is your will that I return home, keep my arrow from straying." (Chap. 11, *the Tale of the Heike,* transl. by Helen Craig McCullough)

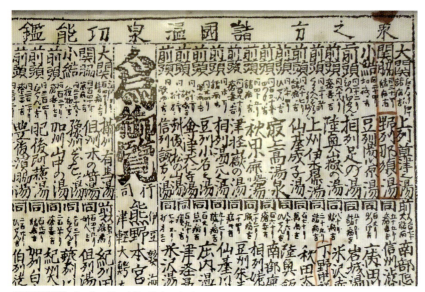

諸国温泉効能鑑　Ranking List of Hot Springs in Japan

諸国温泉効能鑑

　1851年（嘉永4）に書かれた「諸国温泉効能鑑」によると、東の最高位である大関*の地位には群馬県の草津温泉、次いで関脇の地位には那須湯本温泉が、そして、西の大関には兵庫県の有馬温泉、関脇には同じく兵庫県の城崎温泉が挙げられている。

＊大関：相撲番付の最高位。本来は称号であった「横綱」が地位として考えられるようになり、現在では横綱に次ぐ地位とされる。

　那須ロープウェイ山麓駅近くの大丸温泉には小川の流れ全体が天然の温泉となっている川の湯があり、乃木希典夫妻がよく訪れたと言われる。

Ranking List of Hot Springs in Japan

　According to 'Ranking List of Hot Springs in Japan,' which was printed in 1851, Kusatsu Hot Spring in Gunma Prefecture was given the first place (Ozeki) in East Japan and Nasu Hot Spring the second (Sekiwake). In West Japan, Arima Hot Spring in Hyogo Prefecture was given the first place and Kinosaki Hot Spring the second.

　In Omaru Hot Spring, Nasu, near Sanroku Ropeway Station, we can enjoy an open-air river-bath. The river itself forms a natural hot spring. It is said that General Nogi and his wife often visited this hot spring.

塩原温泉郷
Shiobara Hot Spring Resort
那須塩原市

塩原温泉郷の歴史は古く、806年（大同元）に元湯温泉が発見されたと言われる。承平年間（931-938）に書かれた「倭名類聚抄」には「八塩之里」という名称が見え、そこには現在の塩原温泉郷の「塩原」「塩の湯」の名が見える。

塩原温泉郷には、箒川に沿って11の温泉地が点在し、これらは「塩原十一湯」と呼ばれている。大網、福渡、塩釜、塩の湯、畑下、門前、古町、中塩原、新湯、上塩原、元湯がそれである。

塩原温泉郷で一番古い「元湯」は箒川源流の一つ赤川河畔に湧く温泉地で、かつては、多くの宿が立ち並び繁栄していた。しかし、1659年（萬治2）2月の地震による山津波で埋没、廃業を余儀なくされた。現在は三軒の旅館が営業している。濁り湯の魅力が堪能でき、山奥にひっそりと佇む秘湯の趣が魅力である。

塩原温泉郷では、地区により、また、その日の温泉の状況によって「乳白色」「茶褐色」「黒色」「黄金色」「緑

The history of Shiobara Hot Spring Resort goes back to 806 when Motoyu Hot Spring was discovered. In an old book named *Wamyoruijusho* written during the Johei period (931-938), we find a name Yashio-no-sato, which includes Shiobara and Shio-no-yu of Shiobara Hot Spring Resort.

In Shiobara Hot Spring Resort, there are 11 hot springs spotted along the River Hoki. They are Oami, Fukuwata, Shiogama, Shio-no-yu, Hataori, Monzen, Furumachi, Naka-Shiobara, Arayu, Kami-Shiobara and Motoyu. They are called the 11 Hot Springs of Shiobara.

The oldest hot spring, Motoyu, is located along the Aka-gawa River, one of the branch streams of the Hoki-gawa River. There once were many inns in Motoyu, but when the area was hit by a landslide caused by the earthquake of February, 1659, many inns were buried under the debris and were forced to close down. There are only three inns in Motoyu today. Here we can enjoy the splendor of opaque hot-spring bathing and the wonder of hot springs in deep mountains.

In Shiobara Hot Spring Resort, you can enjoy hot springs of Seven Colors,

白色」「薄墨色」「透明」など「七色の温泉」を楽しむことができるという。

妙雲寺

　那須塩原市塩原（門前）にある妙雲寺の創建は1184年（寿永3）で、小松内府平重盛（こまつのないふたいらのしげもり）（1138-1179）の妹君である妙雲尼（みょううんに）の開創になる寺である。ご本尊は重盛公が生存中に念持仏（ねんじぶつ）としていた釈迦牟尼仏（しゃかむにぶつ）で、インド、中国、日本と渡ってきたいわゆる三国伝来の仏像で、京都市嵯峨の清涼寺（せいりょうじ）にある仏像と同工同木であると言われる。

　源氏との戦いに敗れた平氏一族は日本全国に落ち延びていった。妙雲尼は平貞能（さだよし）を伴ない、重盛公の念持仏を笈（おい）に納めて東国に下った。妙雲尼一行は栃木県北部にある釈迦ケ岳の山中に一時身をひそめたが、源氏による平家残党探しが厳し

depending on conditions of the day: milky-white, brownish, blackish, golden, greenish, grayish and clear.

the Myoun-ji Temple

　The Myoun-ji Temple in Shiobara, Nasu-Shiobara City, was founded in 1184 by Myoun-ni, sister of Taira-no-Shigemori (1138-1179). The principal object of worship of this temple is the Statue of Shakyamuni, which was once Shigemori's 'nenjibutsu' (a Buddhist image that is always kept close at hand). The statue is said to have been made of the same tree and in the same way as the Statue at the Seiryo-ji Temple in Saga, Kyoto. It came from India, through China, to Japan.

　After the defeat in the battle with the Minamoto Family, members of the Taira Family escaped to various places in Japan. Myoun-ni came down to Eastern Japan accompanied by Taira-no-Sadayoshi, with the Statue of Shakyamuni in a wooden box. They hid themselves in

妙雲寺　Myōun-ji Temple

くなったため、塩原にやってきて、この地に永住の草庵を結び、念持仏を安置し平家一門の菩提を弔った。妙雲尼は 1194 年（建久 5）入寂し、貞能は寺域に九層の石塔を建て妙雲尼の供養をした。

　1868 年（明治元）の戊辰の役の際には、妙雲寺は会津軍に一時占拠され、彼らが退去する際すんでのところで焼き打ちにされるところであったが、檀徒渡邉新五衛門の必死の嘆願によりその難を逃れることができた。

　妙雲寺は「ぼたん寺」としても有名で、毎年 5 月には 2,000 株以上ある牡丹が美しい花を咲かせ訪れる人々の目を楽しませている。

源三窟

　塩原古町温泉地区には源三窟とよばれる全長 50m ほどの鍾乳洞がある。洞窟の中の年平均気温は 15°C 〜 20°C。この洞窟はかつて源有綱（? -1189）が隠れ棲んでいたところと伝えられている。源有綱は源三位頼政（1104-1180）の孫で、源義経腹心の家来として 1185 年（文治元）の壇ノ浦の戦いで活躍した武将である。しかし、その後、義経と兄源頼朝との間に不和が生じ

the mountains of Shaka-ga-dake for a while, but, as the search by the Minamoto grew exhaustive, they fled to Shiobara. They built a thatched hut there and settled down. They installed the statue in the hut and prayed for the repose of the deceased of the Taira Family members. Myoun-ni died in 1194. Sadayoshi built a nine-storied pagoda in the precincts and prayed for her repose.

Years later, during the Boshin Civil War in 1868, the Myoun-ji Temple was occupied by the Aizu army for a while. When the army retreated from the temple, they decided to set a fire to the temple. However, thanks to Watanabe Shingozaemon's earnest entreaties, it was saved from burning down.

The Myounji Temple is well-known as a temple of peonies. It attracts a lot of visitors when more than 2,000 peonies bloom in May every year.

Genzan-kutsu

Genzan-kutsu is a limestone cave, about 50 meters in length, in Furumachi Onsen District. The temperature inside is 15°C〜20°C all the year round. It is said that Minamoto no Aritsuna, grandson of Minamoto no Yorimasa (1104-1180), was once hiding in this cave. He served Minamoto no Yoshitsune and was a warrior most trusted by him. He distinguished himself in the Battle at Dan no Ura in 1185. After Yoshitsune became on bad terms with his brother, Yoritomo, however, Aritsuna

たため有綱は頼朝から追われる身となり、これを逃れるために陸奥に向かった。その途中、有綱はしばらく洞窟の中に隠れていたが、米をといだ白い水が洞窟の外に流れ出しているのを見つけられ捕らえられた。

なお、源三窟の入口近くには「源有綱公墓碑」が建てられているが、これは、以前、中塩原の「小田ケ市」にあったものをここに移設したもので、「小田ケ市」とは「御他界地」が訛ったものであると言われる。

was forced to run away from Yoritomo's pursuers, and came as far as Shiobara. He was hiding in the cave for a while. Unluckily, he was found by them because white water from rice-washing, which was flowing out of the cave, was spotted by them.

Near the entrance to Genzan-kutsu Cave, there is a grave stone erected in memory of Aritsuna. The grave stone was once at Oda-ga-ichi in Naka-Shiobara, and later it was moved to the present place. It is believed that Oda-ga-ichi is a corrupted form of 'Otakai-chi' meaning 'death place.'

源有綱公墓碑　Tomb Stone of Minamoto-no-Aritsuna

高尾太夫

塩釜温泉地区にあるホテル明賀屋前の駐車場には「高尾塚」という三文字が刻まれた石碑が建っている。高尾というのは、江戸吉原の三浦屋お抱えの遊女のことで、萬治高尾として著名なのが塩原生まれの第三世（第二世とも）高尾（1641-1659）である。

Takao-Tayu

There is a stone monument in the parking lot of Hotel Myogaya in Shiogama Onsen District. Three characters "高尾塚" (Takao-zuka) are inscribed on the monument. Takao was one of the hereditary titles for ladies of pleasure of the highest rank. Takao belonged to Miura-ya. The third Takao (1641-1659) named Manji Takao is the most famous. She was a native of Shiobara.

高尾塚　Monument to Takao

　この石碑は「萬治高尾」を偲んで、死後150年余を経た1802年(享和2)に建てられたものである。撰文は漢学者山本北山(ほくざん)によるもので、高尾の生い立ち、遊女としての名声を記し、若くして病に倒れた高尾を供養したものである。

　「萬治高尾」は幼名を安幾(あき)といい、父は君島勘解由(かげゆ)、母は「はる」といった。1650年(慶安3)、安幾は江戸の三浦屋に養女として引き取られて江戸に行き、学問や芸事などの教養を身につけた。1657年(明暦3)江戸で大火事、いわゆる「振袖(ふりそで)火事」(明暦の大火)が起き、三浦屋は灰燼(かいじん)に帰してしまった。すでに、16歳になっていた安幾はそれまでの養父母の恩義に報いるため三浦屋を再興しようと、両親の反対を押

This stone monument was built in 1802 after 150 years of her death. The epitaph on the monument was written by Yamamoto Hokuzan, a scholar of Chinese classics. It tells us about her early life and her fame as a lady of pleasure. It is for the repose of Takao's spirit who fell ill and died young.

Takao was called Aki in her childhood. Her father's name was Kageyu Kimijima and her mother was called Haru. Aki was adopted into Miura-ya in Edo in 1650 when she was 9 years old. She was given good education and acquired various accomplishments necessary for a woman. Miura-ya, however, was reduced to ashes in a big fire called Furisode Fire in 1657. Aki, who was now 16 years old, decided to be a lady of pleasure against the strong objection of her adoptive parents. She wanted to repay them for bringing her up so far. She succeeded to the name of Takao

し切って遊女になり、三代目「高尾」を襲名した。才色兼備の名妓であったため、高尾はたちまち江戸中の評判となったがまもなく肺を患い、一年余で離籍し、浅草山谷の別荘で療養につとめたが、1659年(萬治2)12月、19歳を一期としてこの世を去り、浅草の春慶院に葬られた。高尾の遺詠：

　　寒風にもろくもくつる紅葉かな

尾崎紅葉と「金色夜叉」

　湾曲した箒川に抱かれるようにある畑下は、尾崎紅葉が「金色夜叉」の舞台に選んだゆかりの温泉地である。尾崎紅葉は、1899年(明治32)6月9日上野発午前5時の汽車に乗って、午前10時に西那須野駅に着き、そこから古町の「米屋」に向かって人力車を走らせた。「米屋」では三階の左端の部屋に案内された。彼はこの日の日記に「此舎眺望に乏し」と書いている。

　小説「金色夜叉」では、主人公の貫一が悶々たる気持ちを抱いて西那須野駅に降り立ち、「清琴樓」という架空の宿屋に向かう形で書かれている。そこには、塩原の美しい自然が美文で描写されていて、明治時代の塩原の様子が彷彿とさせられる。

and became the Third Takao. She soon became known all over Edo because she was endowed with both beauty and intelligence. But she soon suffered from tuberculosis and retired one year later and spent her days in recuperation at a detached house in Sanya, Asakusa, and, died at the age of 19 in December, 1659. She was buried at Shunkei-in Temple, Asakusa. The last poem she composed on her deathbed was:

> A maple leaf
> Frailly falling
> Blown by the cold wind

Konjiki-Yasha by Ozaki Koyo

　Hataori Onsen District is the place which was chosen by Ozaki Koyo as a scene of his novel *Konjiki-Yasha*. On June 9, 1899, Koyo took the train leaving Ueno Station at 5 in the morning and arrived at 10 at Nishi-Nasuno Station. Then he headed for Hotel Komeya in Furumachi on a rickshaw. His room in the hotel was a corner room on the third floor. He wrote in his diary on that day: "the view from the hotel is poor."

　In *Konjiki-Yasha,* Hazama Kan'ichi, hero of the story, gets off the train at Nishi-Nasuno Station with great mental anguish and heads for a fictitious hotel named Seikinro. Speculacular scenery of Shiobara is described in luxuriant prose of the story and when we read it, we can easily imagine how Shiobara looked like during the Meiji Period.

逆杉

　逆杉は古町温泉地区にある杉の古木である。源頼義(988-1075)、義家(1039-1106)父子は、「前九年の役」(1051-1062)の際、安倍貞任(1019-1162)・宗任(?-?)兄弟を討つために奥州に向かう途中、ここ塩原の地を過ぎた。

　その時、一行はこのあたりの山川一帯に神気を霊感して、戦いに勝った折にはこの清浄の地に社殿を奉献すると誓い、武運長久を願って奥州に向かったのであった。

　1062年(康平5)、安倍一族を衣川関に破った頼義、義家父子は、その帰途、再びこの地を訪れて社殿を建てるという約束を果たした。これが塩原八幡宮である。この八幡宮には義家の守護神である譽田別命が祀られている。

Sakasa-sugi

　Sakasa-sugi is an old cryptomeria tree in Furumachi Onsen District. Minamoto no Yoriyoshi (988-1075) and his son, Minamoto no Yoshi'ie (1039-1106), passed Shiobara on their way to Oshu (northeastern region of Japan) to crush Abe no Sadato (1019-1062) and his brother, Abe no Muneto (? - ?), in the Earlier Nine Years' War (1051-1062).

　When they came to Shiobara, they felt some holy atmosphere. So they prayed for victory in the coming war and pledged to build a shrine if they succeeded in crushing their enemy. And they left for Oshu.

　They succeeded in defeating the Abe brothers at Koromogawa in 1062. They kept their promise and built a shrine which is now called the Shiobara Hachiman Shrine. Enshrined here is Homudawake no Mikoto, guardian god of Yoshi'ie.

逆杉　Sakasa-sugi

この神社の境内には逆杉と呼ばれる杉の大木がある。この杉はその枝ぶりから逆杉と呼ばれ、「連理の御神木」とか「夫婦杉」とも言われる。かつて、源義家が戦勝祈願をした際に植えた2本の杉の苗が成長したものである、とか、義家が箸がわりに使った2本の杉の小枝を地面に逆さに指したものが根付いて成長したものであるとか伝えられている。

逆杉の実際の樹齢は義家の時代よりは約100年若く、800歳前後と推定されている。1937年（昭和12）に国の天然記念物に指定されている。

一夜竹

源頼義、義家父子がこの地に立ち寄った際、弓に用いる矢が不足していることに気づき、矢の材料である篠竹を探したが、見つけることが出来なかった。ところが、一夜明けて、当境内に篠竹が群生しているのを発見し、これにより東征に必要な矢を手にすることができた。このことからこの篠竹は「一夜竹」と呼ばれるようになったと言う。

In the grounds of this shrine, there are two tall cedar trees called Sasaka-sugi (Up-side down Cedars). The trees are so called because their branches grow downward instead of upward.

Some people say that the two trees were planted by Minamoto no Yoshi'ie when he prayed for the victory in the coming battle. Others say that the gigantic trees grew up from chopsticks that were planted upside-down into the ground by Yoshi'ie.

It is estimated that the trees are about 800 years old, which means Yoshi'ie came to Shiobara 100 years before the trees were born. The trees were designated as National Natural Treasure in 1937.

Ichiya-dake

Minamoto no Yoriyoshi and his son, Yoshiie, visited the shrine on their way to Ohshu to subjugate the Abe brothers. They noticed that they were running short of shino (a small kind of bamboos) to be used for arrows. They sought here and there for suitable shino, but in vain. When it dawned the next day, they were rejoiced to find a lot of shino growing in the precincts of this shrine. Thus, they could secure a lot of shino needed for the coming battle. That is why the shino came to be called ichiya-dake (lit. one night bamboo).

日光湯元温泉
Nikko Yumoto Hot Springs
日光市湯元

　日光湯元温泉の歴史は古く、788年（延暦7）に日光開山の祖勝道上人が発見したものと伝えられる。上人は温泉の背後にある山を温泉ヶ岳と名付け、その頂上に人々の病苦を救う薬師瑠璃光如来を祀り、湧出する温泉を薬師湯（瑠璃湯）と名付けた。

　江戸時代（1603-1867）になると、湯元温泉は聖なる温泉として、日光山輪王寺の直轄となり、輪王寺が温泉の湯の使用法や入浴の掟を設け、湯守を置いて管理に当たった。現在残っている1687年（貞享4）の「掟高札には入湯者が守るべきルールが細かに記されている。例えば、「湯

The history of Nikko Yumoto Hot Springs goes back to 788 when Priest Shodo, founder of Nikko, found a hot spring there. Shodo built a temple on the top of Mt. Yuzen-ga-dake and enshrined an image of Yakushi-Nyorai (Buddha of Healing) there. And he named the hot spring Yakushi-to (hot springs of healing).

During the Edo period (1603-1867), Yumoto Hot Springs came to be regarded as holy springs and began to be directly controlled by the Rin'no-ji Temple. The temple made rules how to take a bath and appointed 'yumori' (hot-spring manager) in each hot spring. The Bulletin Board Regulations written in 1687 say: "Don't sit on the bath-tab." "Don't wash your hair in the bath." "Don't gamble." "Don't cut down trees in areas about 800 m around hot springs." Ancestors of Itaya and Kamaya Hotels in Yumoto were once 'yumori.'

It is said that there were 9 hot springs in Yumoto in 1836. They were Gosho-yu, Sasa-yu, Uba-yu, Taki-no-yu, Kawara-yu, Yakushi-yu, Naka-yu, Ara-yu, and Jizai-yu. Kogakubo* Ashikaga Haruuji (1508-1560), came to Yumoto and took a bath at a hot spring. After this, the hot spring came to be called

湯元温泉源　the Source of Hot Spring Water in Yumoto

船に腰掛けてはいけない」「湯船の中で髪を洗ってはいけない」「博奕や賭けごとをしてはいけない」「温泉場の八丁四方は立木を伐採してはいけない」などである。現在の「湯元板屋」ホテル、「湯守釜屋」ホテルの先人はかつて湯守を務めていた。

　1836年（天保7）頃には、御所湯、笹湯、姥湯、滝湯、河原湯、薬師湯、中湯、荒湯、自在湯の9湯があったと言う。御所湯という名前は、1544年（天文13）に古河公方足利晴氏（1508-1560）が入湯したことに由来すると言われる。

　以前、温泉街の東側高台には湯元薬師堂があり、境内には1513年（永正10）の銘のある銅祠があったが、この祠は国の重要文化財の指定を受け、現在は二荒山中宮祠の宝物館に保存されている。

　湯元薬師堂は1868年（明治元）の「神仏判然令」によって温泉神社と薬師堂に分けられた。大己貴命を祀る温泉神社は現在も温泉街東の高台の上に建っている。薬師堂は1972年（昭和47）の台風で倒壊したため、輪王寺は温泉街の北側に広がる湯の平湿原そばに新たに堂宇を建立し、そこに薬師瑠璃光如来仏を祀った。これが、現在ある輪王

御所湯跡　Gosho-yu

Gosho-no-yu.

＊koga-kubo: a shogunate deputy in Koga

　There once was a building of Yumoto Yakushido on a low hill in the east of the hot spring resort and, in its one corner, there was a small shrine made of copper which bore an inscription of the year 1513. The shrine was designated as a national important cultural asset and is presently kept in the Treasure House of Futarasan Shrine Chugushi.

　Yumoto Yakushido became separated into two independent entities, Onsen-jinja Shrine and Yakushido Temple in accordance with the decree of separating Shinto and Buddhism in 1868. The Onsen-jinja Shrine which is dedicated to Onamuchi no mikoto is still on the low hill. The Yakushi-do Temple, however, collapsed in the typhoon of 1972 and was rebuilt near Yunodaira marsh in the north of the spring resort. It is now called Onsen-ji Temple, a branch temple of Rin'no-ji. An image of Yakushi-Nyorai (Buddha of Healing) is enshrined there.

寺別院の温泉寺である。

尚、日光湯元温泉は1954年（昭和29）に青森県酸ケ湯温泉および群馬県四万温泉と共に国民保養温泉地の第一号に指定されている。

植田孟縉著：日光山志

植田孟縉（1757-1843）はその著「日光山志」の中で、「中禅寺温泉八湯」という表現で奥日光湯元温泉の八湯（河原湯、薬師湯、姥湯、滝湯、中湯、笹湯、御所湯、荒湯、自在湯）を挙げ、それぞれの湯についてコメントを書いている。例えば、河原湯については「湯は非常に熱く、湖水の水位が高い時ほど熱く、低い時ほど温い。」とか、また、自在湯については、「混じり気が無い。この湯でご飯を炊いても匂いがしない。」などと書いている。

イザベラ・バード

1878年（明治11）には、イギリスの女性旅行家 イザベラ・バード（1831-1904）が来日して、奥日光の湯元まで足を延ばしている。彼女は Unbeaten Tracks... の6月22日の項で、湯元のヤシマ屋という宿に泊まった際の印象を次のように書

Nikko Yumoto Hot Spring Resort was designated as one of the first three People's Hot Spring Health Resorts in Japan together with Sukayu Hot Spring Resort in Aomori and Shima Hot Spring Resort in Gunma.

Nikkosanshi by Ueda Moshin

Nikkosanshi written by Ueda Moshin (1757-1843) gives names of 8 hot springs in Nikko Chuzenji.* They are Kawara-yu, Yakushi-yu, Uba-yu, Taki-no-yu, Naka-yu, Sasa-yu, Gosho-yu, Ara-yu and Jizai-yu. And he gives some comments about each hot spring. His comment about Kawara-yu, for example, says: "The spring water is very hot. When the water level of the Lake Yunoko rises, it reaches higher temperatures, and when the water level goes down, its temperature also goes down." He writes about Jizaiyu: "The spring water is almost pure and without unpleasant smell. Rice can be cooked using this water."

＊Moshin uses the name 'Nikko Chuzenji' instead of 'Nikko Yumoto.'

Isabella Bird

Isabella Bird (1831-1904), a British traveller and writer, came to Yumoto and stayed at Yashima-ya. She wrote in her diary on June 22nd as follows:

"The hard day's journey ended in an exquisite yadoya, beautiful within and without, and more fit for fairies than for travel-soiled mortals. The fusuma are light planed wood with a sweet scent,

いている。

　「きびしい一日の旅が終り、素晴らしい宿屋に着いた。宿は内外ともにきれいで、旅で泥まみれになった人間よりも妖精にふさわしい宿であった。なめらかに鉋がかけられた襖は心地よい香りを放ち、畳はほぼ真っ白で、バルコニーは磨かれた松でできていた。私が部屋に入ると、間もなく、一人の女性が笑みを浮かべながらやってきて、梅の花の入ったアーモンドの香りのするお茶、豆の砂糖菓子、そして、氷状になった雪を漆塗りの器にいれて持ってきてくれた。……大きな温泉は村の裏手にあり小高く盛土をした中に四角い浴槽がある。お湯がすごい勢いで沸き出し強烈な臭いをさせている。浴槽には広い板が一定の間隔をおいて渡されていてリューマチを患っている人達が硫黄の蒸気を浴びるために終日その板の上に横になっている。温泉の温度は華氏130度（摂氏約54度）ある。このお湯が木製の樋を通して村に至る頃には華氏84度（摂氏約29度）になっている。」

アーネスト・M・サトウ

　1872年、アーネスト．M．サトウ（1843-1929）はその著「中部及び北日本旅行者のための案内書」

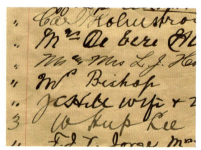

金谷ホテル宿帳に残るI.Bird（Mrs Biship）のサイン
Signature by I. Bird registered in the Kanaya Hotel book

the matting nearly white, the balconies polished pine. On entering, a smiling girl brought me some plum-flower tea with a delicate almond flavor, a sweetmeat made of beans and sugar, and a lacquer bowl of frozen snow. The great spring is beyond the village, in a square tank in a mound. It bubbles up with much strength, giving off fetid fumes. There are broad boards laid at intervals across it, and people crippled with rheumatism go and lie for hours upon them for the advantage of the sulfurous steam. The temperature of the spring is 130 degrees F. but after the water has traveled to the village, along an open wooden pipe, it is only 84 degrees." [*Letter 9, Unbeaten Tracks in Japan*, by Isabella L. Bird]

Ernest M. Satow

　Ernest M. Satow (1843-1929) wrote in his book *A Handbook for Travellers in Central and Northern Japan* (1884) about Yumoto in Nikko as follows:

（1884）の中で、日光湯元について次のように書いている。

「湖の東側の木々の間をぬかるんだ小道が通っていて、終着点の湯元の小さな村へと続いている。ここでは、湖の水は硫黄泉の為に変色していて、慣れるまではその臭いは堪え難い。道の右側一軒目の吉見屋という新しい宿は眺望は最高で、風呂の設備もあるが、法外な料金をふっかけるし、主人は無礼なので注意を要する。これより少し先で、やや道から離れたところにある宿のほうがいいであろう。この宿のすぐ下には薬師湯があり、お湯の温度も西欧人にも熱すぎることはない。この他に、八つの温泉があり、屋根付きのものもあれば露天の湯もある。これらの温泉に人々は自由に入ることができ、混浴であった。」

"A muddy path winds through the wood along the E. side of the lake to the small vill of Yumoto at its upper end. Here the water is particularly discoloured by the sulphur springs, and the smell at first is anything but agreeable. A new inn, called Yoshimi-ya, the first house on the right enjoys the best view and has baths on the establishment, but visitors are warned against the extortionate charges made and the rudeness of its landlord. The inn beyond, a little off the road, will be found preferable. Immediately below is the bath called Yaku-shi yu, the temperature of which is not too high for Europeans. Besides this spring, there are eight others, some under cover, others exposed to the open air, all free to the public and frequented by both sexes promiscuously."

日本列島のへそ　たぬま
Tanuma, Center of Japan
佐野市田沼地区

　佐野市（旧田沼町）の県道16号線と県道270号線が交差するところに「どまんなか　たぬま」というちょっと変わった名前の「道の駅」がある。「どまんなか」とは日本列島の「ど真中」ということである。何故この様な名前がつけられているのであろうか。日本列島の「ど真中」は次の様にして求められるという。

　1. 北海道北端の宗谷岬から九州南端の佐多岬までの距離の日本海側中間点と太平洋側中間点を求める。

　2. それら二つの中間点を結ぶ直線の中間点を求める

　その中間点が田沼町で、まさに、日本列島の「へそ」に当たるということになる。作原町蓬山（よもぎやま）ログ・ビレッジの前には「日本列島中心の地」という大きな碑が立っている。

　日本国内には「日本のへそ」と称する場所が田沼町以外にもいくつかある。その一つが兵庫県西脇市である。日本国の東の端は択捉島（えとろふ）で東経147度、西の端は与那国島で東経123度、北の端の宗谷海峡は北

There is a michi-no-eki (roadside station) where Prefectural Route 16 crosses Prefectural Route 270 in Sano City. The station has a very unique name, Domannaka Tanuma. 'Domannaka' means 'the very center' of the Japanese Archipelago. How does it come to be called 'Domannaka' of Japan? The center of Japan can be obtained in the following way:

1. Measure the distances from Cape Soya (northernmost point of Hokkaido) to Cape Sata (southernmost point of Kyushu) on both the Japan Sea coast line and the Pacific Ocean coast line and get the middle points of the two distances.

2. Draw a straight line between the two middle points and get the middle point of the straight line.

That is where Tanuma is situated. It can be said that Tanuma is the very "navel" of Japan. There is a big monument in front of Yomogiyama Log-village in Sakuhara, Sano. It says: "the Center of Japanese Archipelago."

There are other "navels" in Japan. Nishiwaki City in Hyogo Pref. is one of them. Etorofu Island is the easternmost point in Japan at 147° E longitude and Yonaguni-jima is the westernmost point at 123° E longitude. The cape Soyami-

日本列島中心の碑　Monument at the Center of Japanese Archipelago

緯46度、南の端の沖縄県八重山諸島の波照間島は北緯24度である。従って、日本の真中は東経135度、北緯35度となりこれら二つの線が交差するところに「日本のへそ」西脇市があるというのである。なお、明治19年7月12日に日本標準時が制定され、「東経135度ノ子午線ノ時ヲ以ッテ本邦一般ノ標準時ト定ム」とされたことは周知のことである。

　岐阜県関市も「日本のへそ」の一つとされる。2005年の国勢調査によると、日本の人口重心は北緯35度36分20.65秒、東経137度00分27.43秒にあるとされ、関市が丁度そこに位置するという。

saki is the northernmost point at 46° N latitude and Hateruma-jima in Okinawa is the southernmost point at 24° N latitude . This means that the center of Japan, Nishiwaki City can be said to be at the crossing point of 135° E longitude and 35° N latitude. As is well known, 135° E longitude (Akashi) was designated as Japan Standard Time on July 12, 1886,.

　Seki City in Gifu Pref. is also said to be another "navel." According to the Census conducted in 2005, the center of the population of Japan is at the crossing point of 35° 36'20" N altitude and 137° 00'27" E longitude, where Seki City lies.

奇岩　御前岩
Gozen-iwa

那珂川町大山田

　那珂川町（旧馬頭町）の大山田下郷地区を流れる武茂川の東岸には、御前岩と言われる高さ約10m、幅8mの奇岩がある。

　かつて、この地を訪れた徳川光圀公はこの岩をご覧になって、「これは誠に天下の奇岩じゃ。かかるものを衆目に曝すことはよろしからず。」と言い、岩の対岸に竹を植えさせて道路から直接見えないようにした。この竹は「腰巻竹」と言われる。

　以前、御前岩の上には小さな祠があって土地の人達は木や石で作った男根を奉納したという。

　There is a rock called Gozen-iwa on the left bank of the Mumo River which flows through Oyamada-Shimogo in Nakagawa Town. It is about 10m in height and 8m in width.

　Once Tokugawa Mitsukuni visited this area and saw the rock and said, "This is really a rare rock. It is not good that it is exposed to public view." He told people to plant bamboos on the opposite bank so that it could not be seen by passers-by. The bamboos are called 'waistcloth bamboos.'

　Once there was a small shrine on the rock. Many local men made wooden or stone phalluses and offered them to the god of the shrine.

御前岩　Gozen-iwa

明治のはじめの頃、この地方に赴任してきた一人の巡査が祠に行って驚いた。そこには沢山の男根が奉納されていて、中でも一番大きなものには奉納者の名前がはっきりと書いてある。1872年（明治5）の太政官布告で、色々なところに祀ってある男根は即刻取り壊すようにとの命令が出ていたので、その巡査は早速その男を逮捕した。男は自分で作った男根を背中にくくりつけられ、警察に連れていかれた。沿道には野次馬が集まってこの奇妙な見せ物を見て喜んだという。幸い、男はたいしたおとがめもなく帰宅を許されたという。

A police officer who was newly assigned to this district was greatly surprised when he went to the rock and found a lot of phalluses there. The largest of them clearly bore the name of the man who made it and offered it to the shrine. It had been decreed by the Order of the Grand Council of State of 1872 that such phalluses should be removed from shrines and temples. The man was arrested at once and was taken to the police office. A lot of people gathered to see the man taken to the police with the phallus tied on his back. They were greatly rejoiced at the queer sight. Fortunately, the man was soon set free without serious charge.

ナスヒオウギアヤメ（那須檜扇綾目）
アヤメ科アヤメ属

那須町の水田用水路から採取された標本をもとに昭和天皇が研究され、命名発表されたもの。

第3章
史跡・城跡・街道
Historic Sites, Castle Ruins and Highways

唐沢山城跡　The ruins of Karasawayama Castle

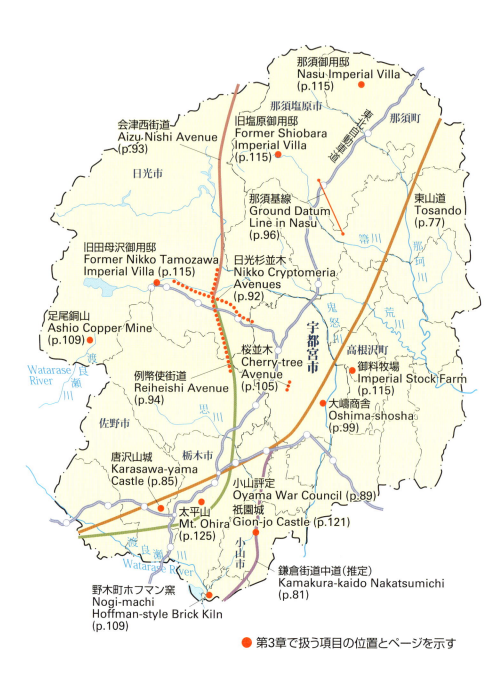

古代の道　東山道
Ancient Highway: Tosando

下野国府跡　The Ruins of Shimotsuke Kokufu

　律令時代 (700年～800年) には、日本全国は大きく「畿内」と「七道」に分けられていた。「五畿七道」と言い、「五畿」すなわち五つの「畿内」地域は、山城国、大和国、摂津国、河内国、和泉国の5国で、現在の京都府、大阪府、奈良県に当たる地域である。これ以外の諸国は東海道、東山道、北陸道、山陰道、

Under the Ritsuryo System (700-800), Japan was divided into two administrative units:Kinai (Goki) and Shichido. Goki referred to Five Provinces (Yamashiro, Yamato, Settu, Kawachi, and Izumi) around the old capitals of Nara and Kyoto. They roughly correspond to Kyoto, Osaka and Nara Prefectures of present-day Japan. Other provinces belonged to one of Shichido.

山陽道、南海道、西海道という「七道」のいずれかに属した。

道としての「東山道」

　「七道」は行政上の区分であったが、それと同時にそこを通る街道を意味していた。すなわち、下野国が属していた東山道は、近江国（現、滋賀県）、美濃国（現、岐阜県南部）、飛騨国（現、岐阜県北部）、信濃国（現、長野県）、上野国（現、群馬県）、下野国（現、栃木県）、陸奥国（現、福島県、宮城県、岩手県など）、出羽国（現、山形県、秋田県）の八つの国を通っていた。

　栃木県内では、これまでに東山道の遺構が17か所見つかっている。そのうちの一つ宇都宮市の杉村遺跡では、幅12〜15mの広い道路が直線的に造られ、その両脇には断面が箱型の側溝が設けられていたことが見てとれる。

　「七道」が通る国々には「国府」（その国の行政を司る政庁）が置かれ、中央政府と地方を結ぶ重要な役割を果していた。下野国の場合、国府は栃木市田村町の思川西岸にあったことが判明している。

　街道としての「七道」には、30里（約16km）ごとに駅家が設けられ、街道を行き来する役人に馬や宿

Tosando as a Highway

Shichido referred to Seven Regions other than Goki, and at the same time, it referred to Seven Highways. In other words, Shichido meant seven administrative units as well as seven highways that ran through them. Seven Highways were Tokaido, Tosando, Hokurikudo, San'indo, San'yodo, Nankaido, and Saikaido. Shimotsuke Province belonged to Tosando, which ran through Provinces of Omi, Mino, Hida, Shinano, Kozuke, Shimotsuke, Mutsu, and Dewa.

So far, 17 sites of Tosando have been discovered in Tochigi Prefecture. The Sugimura Site in Utsunomiya shows that the highway was 12 to 15 meters wide and straight and had U-shaped gutters on both sides.

Shichido played an important role in connecting the central government with provincial governments ("kokufu"). The kokufu of Shimotsuke Province was located at Tamuracho, Tochigi City, on the western bank of the Omoigawa River.

Shichido had post stations at every 30-ri (about 16 km), which provided horses, lodgings and food to traveling government officials. There were 7 post stations in Shimotsuke Province. They were (from south to north): Ashika-

舎、食事の提供をした。下野国には東山道沿いに、南から北に、足利、三鴨、田部、衣川、新田、磐上、黒川の七つの駅家が設けられていた。

「延喜式」によると、平安時代に役人が平安京（京都）から下野国に下るには17日を要した。逆に、上りは税としての調と庸等を運んだため、下りの2倍の34日を要したとされる。

「東山道」は、都と東北地方とを結ぶ重要な道路で、陸奥国に赴く役人たちが通った道であり、蝦夷地域における不穏な動きを中央に伝える早馬の駆け抜けた道であった。

ga, Mikamo, Tabe, Kinugawa, Nifuta, Iwakami, and Kurokawa.

Incidentally, according to *Engi Shiki** it took 17 days for government officials to travel from Kyoto to Shimotsuke. But it took 34 days to return to Kyoto because they had to carry back cho and yo ("payment in kind").

* Engi Shiki: a collection of books of early-10th century governmental regulations

Tosando was a very important highway which connected the capital in Kyoto and Tohoku District. Government officials took this highway when they were assigned to Mutsu Province. Mounted messengers dashed along this highway to report to the central government any disorderly movements among Ezo people. And soldiers took this high-

東山道跡：さくら市将軍桜附近　Tosando near Shogun-zakura, Sakura City

かつて、坂上田村麻呂（751～811）は蝦夷征討に向う際にこの道を通り、源頼義（988～1075）・義家（1039～1106）父子も「前九年の役」「後三年の役」の際にここを通っている。

義経伝説の道

1180年（治承4）8月17日、奥州平泉の藤原秀衡（？～1187）の許に身を寄せていた源義経（1159～1189）は、兄源頼朝（1147～1199）の挙兵に呼応して、平泉から一路鎌倉に向かった。「義経記」*によると、義経一行は白河関址から現在の県道76号線を南下して、那須町伊王野を通って「きつ川（喜連川）」を過ぎ、「さげはし（下ヶ橋）」、宇都宮、室の八島を経て武蔵国に入った、とされる。

＊「義経記」：源義経の生涯を書いた軍記物

県道76号線の杳石から伊王野までの間には、義経にまつわる伝説が多く伝えられていて、「義経伝説の道」と言われる。数例を挙げるなら、「追分明神」、「月夜見山」、「具足岩」、「杳石」等である。

way on their way to subdue Ezo.

Sakanoue-no-Tamuramaro (751-811) once passed along Tosando on his way to northern Japan to subdue the Ezo people. Minamoto no Yoriyoshi and his son Yoshiie also passed along this highway when they fought Earlier Nine Year's War and Later Three Year's War.

Road of Yoshitsune Legends

Minamoto no Yoshitsune (1159-1189) was in Hiraizumi in northern Japan under the protection of Fujiwara no Hidehira (? -1187), when the news reached him that his brother Yoritomo (1147-1199) raised an army against Taira rule. He at once rushed to Kamakura to join his brother. According to *Gikeiki**, Yoshitsune and his followers passed through the Barrier Station at Shirakawa, went straight south along Tosando Highway, passed Iono, Kitsukawa (Kitsuregawa), Sagehashi, Utsunomiya, Muro-no-Yashima, and into Musashi Province.

＊Gikeiki :an account of the life of Minamoto no Yoshitsune

The part of the highway between Kutsuishi and Iono is often called "Road of Yoshitsune Legends" because there are a lot of places with legends woven around Yoshitsune. Oiwake Myojin, Mt. Tsukiyomi, Gusoku-iwa, Kutsuishi, just to mention a few.

鎌倉街道中道
Kamakura-kaido Nakatsumichi

　鎌倉時代、関東地方には鎌倉と地方を結ぶ4つの主要街道があった。「京鎌倉往還」（京都～鎌倉）、「鎌倉街道上道」（鎌倉～上野～信濃）、「鎌倉街道中道」（鎌倉～武蔵～下野～陸奥）、「鎌倉街道下道」（鎌倉～常陸～陸奥）である。鎌倉幕府の御家人達が、有事の際に「いざ鎌倉」と鎌倉に馳せ参じたのはこの道であった。「鎌倉街道」という名称は鎌倉幕府の記録である「吾妻鏡」には見えておらず、この名称が使われるようになったのは江戸時代以降のことのようである。

　4つの街道のうち最も下野国と関係が深い「鎌倉街道中道」は、「奥大道」とも言われ、下野国を南北に縦断し陸奥に通じていた。

　下野国内における「奥大道」の正確なルートについては不明な点も残されているが、おおよそ次のようであったと考えられている。（茨城県古河）→小山→下古館→児山（下野市）→宇都宮→氏家→喜連川→福原（大田原市）→黒羽→芦野（那須町）→（福島県白河）

　この道は1189年（文治5）奥州

During the Kamakura period (1185-1333), there were four main highways that radiated from Kamakura (the seat of the central government). They were Kyo-Kamakura Okan (Kyoto ~ Kamakura), Kamakura Kamitsumichi (Kamakura ~ Kozuke ~ Shinano), Kamakura Nakatsumichi (Kamakura ~ Musashi ~ Shimotsuke ~ Mutsu) and Kamakura Shimotsumichi (Kamakura ~ Hitachi ~ Mutsu). These were the highways that "Gokenin" (direct vassals of the Kamakura shogunate) hurried along to Kamakura in the case of emergency. The names of these highways were used without "Kamakura" attached to them before the Edo period. *Azumakagami* (a historical account of the Kamakura shogunate) gives no instance of attaching "Kamakura" before the names of these highways.

Of the four highways, Shimotsuke Province lay along "Nakatsumichi," which was also called "Oku no Daido." The highway ran through Shimotsuke from south to north leading to Mutsu Province.

The exact route of "Oku no Daido" is still unknown, but it was roughly as follows.

(Koga, Ibaraki) → Oyama → Shimo-Furudate → Koyama → Utsunomiya

合戦の際に源頼朝 (1147-1199) が通った道である。頼朝は、奥州の藤原泰衡 (?-1189) を討つため1189年7月19日に鎌倉を発ち、7月25日に宇都宮に到着している。一日平均約25kmから30kmのペースである。頼朝は宇都宮に到着すると、早速、宇都宮明神に詣でて戦勝祈願をし、奥州藤原氏を倒すことができた暁には生虜を神職として献上すると誓っている。

頼朝は10月19日奥州からの帰路、再び、宇都宮明神に立寄り、捕虜として連れてきた奥州の豪族樋爪季衡・経衡父子を明神の神職に献

→ Ujiie → Kitsuregawa → Fukuwara → Kurobane → Ashino → (Shirakawa, Fukushima)

This was the highway that Minamoto no Yoritomo (1147-1199) passed on his way to Oshu to fight against the Fujiwaras. He left Kamakura on July 19, 1189, and arrived at Utsunomiya on July 25. The average distance he covered in a day was from 25 km to 30 km. As soon as he arrived at Utsunomiya, he visited Utsunomiya Shrine to pray for the victory in the coming battle, and pledged that if he could successfully defeat the Fujiwaras, he would offer captives to the shrine as Shinto priests.

On his way back, Yoritomo visited Utsunomiya Shrine again on Oct. 19

三峰山神社　Mitsumine-san Shrine

じている。宇都宮市内を流れる田川にかかる幸橋近くに三峰山神社という小さな神社があるが、樋爪父子はここに葬られている。

1258年（正嘉2）頃に成立したと考えられる「新○和歌集」に

あづまぢや　おほくのゑびす
たいらげて　そむけば
うつのみやとこそきけ

という歌が載っており、「宇都宮」は「討つの宮」に通じ、頼朝は奥州の蝦夷を「討つ」ことを願って宇都宮明神に詣でたものと想像される。

「鎌倉街道中道」は、また、1590年（天正18）に奥州仕置の際に豊臣秀吉（1536－1598）が通った道でもある。7月19日、鎌倉を出た秀吉は、7月26日に宇都宮に入城している。興味深いことに、豊臣秀吉が鎌倉を出て宇都宮に至る日程が、約400年前に源頼朝が奥州合戦に向かった時の日程とほぼ同じであることで、天下統一を目指す秀吉が頼朝を強く意識していたことが想像される。

秀吉は、宇都宮で8月4日までの8晩を過ごして会津に向かい、会津からの帰路にも1泊しているので延べ11日間を宇都宮で過ごしたこ

and offered two members of a powerful clan in Oshu, Hizume Suehira and his son Tsunehira. There is a small shrine, Mitsumine-san Shrine, near Saiwai Bridge on the Tagawa River. The Hizumes lie buried there.

In an anthology, *Shin-maru-waka-shu*, which was compiled in about 1258, there is a waka poem:

O Utsunomiya in the East,
It conquers many ebisu
And defeats them if they rebel

We can easily imagine that Yoritomo visited Utsunomiya Shrine because "Utsunomiya" implied "Utsu-no-miya," meaning "defeating the enemy."

Toyotomi Hideyoshi (1536-1598) also passed Nakatsumichi in 1590 on his way to Oshu (northern Japan). He left Kamakura on July 19, 1590, and arrived at Utsunomiya on Juy 26. It is interesting to note that Hideyoshi traveled almost on the same dates as Minamoto no Yoritomo when he went to Oshu about 400 years before. We can imagine that Hideyoshi, who had an intention of bringing the whole Japan under his control, was intensely conscious of this fact.

Hideyoshi stayed in Utsunomiya for 8 nights until Aug. 4 and headed for Aizu. He spent one more night there on his way back. Thus, he spent a total of 11 days in Utsunomiya. While he was in Utsunomiya, powerful local lords like Tokugawa Ieyasu (1542-1616), Date

とになる。その間、宇都宮には徳川家康（1542－1616）、伊達政宗（1567－1636）、最上義光（1546－1614）などの諸大名が集まり秀吉への忠誠を誓ったのである。宇都宮は秀吉が東国の支配体制を確固たるものにした重要な場所であった。

鎌倉街道中道（奥大道）の面影を偲ぶことのできる場所が県内にはいくつか残っている。例えば、小山市安房神社と鷲城趾を結ぶ道、下野市龍興寺北西側の道、宇都宮市常念寺前の「亀井の水」の側を通る道などである。

Masamune (1567-1636) and Mogami Yoshimitsu (1546-1614) came to Utsunomiya and pledged their loyalty to Hideyoshi. Utsunomiya played an important role for Hideyoshi to make his control of Eastern Japan secure.

In some places in Tochigi Prefecture, we can see some traces of Nakatsumichi (Oku no Daido) in such places as the road that connects the Awa Shrine in Oyama City and the site of Washi Castle, the road that runs in the north-west of the Ryuko-ji Temple in Shimotsuke City, and the road along Kamei Fountain near the Jonen-ji Temple in Utsunomiya City.

亀井の水　Kamei Fountain

なるほど名城・唐沢山
A Renowned Castle on Mt. Karasawa
佐野市

　2014年（平成26）3月18日、関東七名城の一つに数えられた唐沢山城跡は国指定史跡となった。削平されたいくつもの曲輪（くるわ）、土を盛り上げた土塁、堅牢な高石垣や空堀が、本丸跡に建つ唐沢山神社本殿を取り囲んでいる。国指定史跡としては関東最大の面積である。

　唐沢山城は940年（天慶3）下野国押領使（おうりょうし）に任じられていた藤原秀郷が築城を始め翌々年に落成したという伝承があるが、史実としての確認はできていない。平将門の

唐沢城跡　Karasawa Castle Site

　The ruins of Karasawayama Castle, which once was called one of the Top Seven Castles in Kanto Area, was designated national historic site. The main building of Karasawayama Shrine was built at the place where the inner citadel of the castle once stood. It is surrounded by 'kuruwa' (flat area enclosed by earthwork), earthen walls, high stone walls and moats without water. The ruins of the castle cover largest areas in Kanto area.

　It is popularly believed that this castle was built by Fujiwara-no-Hidesato, local military commander of Shimotsuke Province, around 940, but there is no reliable record to prove it. However, this popular belief can be supported by such facts as (a) he was appointed governor of Shimotsuke and Musashi Provinces soon after he put down the rebellion of Taira-no-Masakado (?-940) in 940, (b) his tomb is at Yoshimizu in Tanuma, and (c) the castle is on a mountain that commands a panoramic view of the Kanto Plain. It is quite natural that Hidesato chose this place for his castle. On a fine day, we can see the Sky Tree and the Tokyo Tower from the castle site.

　During the late years of Heian Peri-

乱を平定した秀郷が、その後 (a) 下野守さらに武蔵守を兼任したこと、

(b) 佐野市吉水町に藤原秀郷の墳墓が現存すること、そして何よりも (c) 関東平野を一望できる眺望を考慮するならば、秀郷ならずとも唐沢山に拠点、少なくとも物見櫓を設置することは当然のことと思われる。現在も、東京スカイツリー・東京タワー・高層ビル群を肉眼ではっきりとらえることができる。

平安時代末期、下野国佐野は左大臣藤原頼長 （1120-1156）の荘園であった。頼長は 1156 年（保元1）の保元の乱で崇徳上皇に与し敗れて傷死した。頼長の佐野庄は没収された。

その後の源平の争乱を経て、佐野は足利氏の領有となり一族から佐野氏が成立した。佐野氏は唐沢山城を居城とした。この佐野氏の一派が田沼地域を領有し、田沼氏を名乗る。この田沼氏の末裔の一人が江戸幕府の老中田沼意次 (1719-1788) である。積極財政を推進した田沼意次の姓は佐野市田沼町に由来する。

戦国時代(1467-1568)になると、唐沢山城はその地理的位置と眺望により、関東支配を目指す小田原の後北条氏と越後の上杉氏がその

od. Sano in Shimotsuke Province was a manor of Sadaijin (Minister of the Left) Fujiwara-no-Yorinaga (1120-56), but the manor was confiscated after his death during the Hogen Disturbance in 1156. In the war, Yorinaga sided with Retired Emperor Sutoku.

Sano came to be governed first by the Ashikaga Family and later by the Sano Family which had branched off from it. Karasawayama Castle was the residence castle of the Sano Family. Tanuma Okitsugu (1719-1788), a senior official of the Tokugawa shogunate, was a descendant of the Tanuma Family which branched off from the Sano Family. Okitsugu tried to expand the commercial economy of the shogunate. The name, Tanuma Machi came from his family name.

During the Warring States period (1467-1568), both the Go-Hojo family in Odawara and the Uesugi family in Echigo tried to gain control over the castle because it was located at a strategically ideal position and commanded a very good view. The Sano family took sides with the Go-Hojo family at one time and with the Uesugi family at the other. In 1567, when it was taking sides with the Uesugi family, the Go-Hojo attacked the Karasawayama Castle with a force 35,000 strong. The Sano family succeeded in driving it away with the help of the Uesugi. After it took sides with the Go-Hojo family in 1561, it was attacked by Uesugi Kenshin 9 times but

争奪に鎬を削ることになる。佐野氏は後北条氏に帰属することもあれば上杉氏に帰属することもあった。上杉氏に帰属している1567年（永禄10）、後北条氏が3万5千の大軍で唐沢山城を攻撃したが、上杉氏の援軍もあってこれを撤退させている。ことに後北条氏に帰属した1561年（永禄4）以降1572年（天正2）まで、上杉謙信に9回の攻撃を受けるが、ことごとく退けた。それほどに唐沢山城は難攻不落の城だったのである。

　佐野氏は小田原城攻めの案内役を務めるなど、豊臣秀吉（1536 - 1598）とは良好な関係を保った。1592年（天正20）佐野家当主となった信吉の名は秀吉から「吉」の字を賜ったものである。1600年（慶長5）佐野信吉は徳川家康より小山城普請を命ぜられ、会津の上杉景勝に備えた。江戸時代初期、信吉は唐沢山城から江戸の火災を発見、早馬で江戸に急報、これが家康の不興を買い春日岡に移城を命ぜられたという。家康は江戸20里以内の山城をすべて廃城にすることにした。唐沢山城の廃城が1602年（慶長7）か1607年（慶長12）かは確定していない。1614年（慶長19）信吉は所領没収、信州松本へお預

it drove away all of them. This shows how the Karasawayama Castle was impregnable.

The Sano family had good relations with Toyotomi Hideyoshi (1536-1598) and served him as a guide when Hideyoshi attacked the Odawara Castle. One of the Chinese characters (吉) that consisted the given name of the lord of the Sano family Nobuyoshi (信吉) was given by Hideyoshi (秀吉). In 1600, Tokugawa Ieyasu ordered Sano Nobuyoshi to build a castle in Oyama against the attack by Uesugi Kagekatsu in Aizu (now, Fukushima Prefecture). During the early days of Edo period, Nobuyoshi happened to see raging flames of a conflagration in the direction of Edo from his castle on a high mountain. He at once dispatched a messenger to Edo to express his sympathy. This, however, incurred Ieyasu's displeasure and Nobuyoshi was ordered to move his castle from the mountain to level land in Kasugaoka. Ieyasu ordered that all the mountain castles within 20-ri (about 80 km.) of Edo be demolished. The Karasawa Castle became abandoned either in 1602 or in 1607. In 1614, Nobuyoshi had his domain confiscated and was left under the care of Matsumoto domain in Shinshu (now, Nagano Prefecture). This was the end of the Sano family as daimyo.

Nobuyoshi's two sons enjoyed the favors of the third shogun Tokugawa Iemitsu and succeeded in reviving the Sano family as a retainer of the shogun.

けの身となり、大名としての佐野家は滅亡した。

　信吉の二人の子供は三代将軍徳川家光の恩命に浴し、旗本として佐野家を再興した。明治になって佐野家一族、旧臣が沢英社と東明会を組織し、1883年（明治16）唐沢山城本丸跡に藤原秀郷を祀る唐沢山神社を創建した。

　今、私たちが唐沢山神社に参詣すると、高さ8mに及ぶ苔むす高石垣に古城の風格を感じ取る。また、天狗岩や南城からの眺望に、思わず「絶景！」と感嘆する。その眺望こそが唐沢山城を難攻不落の名城とし、また廃城へと追い込んだのである。

Descendants of the Sano family and of its former retainers formed an organization Takueisha and Tomeikai, respectively, and, in 1883, built the Karasawayama Shrine at the fomer site of the inner citadel of the Karasawayama Castle. And Fujiwara no Hidesato was enshrined there.

When we visit the Karasawayama Shrine today, we feel the grandeur of the old castle in the tall stone walls 8 meters in height and at Tengu-iwa we shout "Beautiful!" in spite of ourselves at the sight expanding below our eyes. It was this beautiful sight that made the Karasawayama Castle impregnable and forced it to be demolished.

天下を決めた小山評定
War Council at Oyama
小山市中央町

　1600年（慶長5）天下分け目の関が原合戦の前夜である。豊臣秀吉の死後、五大老の筆頭にあった徳川家康の地位が強まるにつれて、家康と、同じく五大老の一人である上杉景勝（会津藩主）や、秀吉子飼いの石田三成（五奉行の一人）との対立が深まっていった。

　家康は、景勝が会津に帰国し、三成らと諮って会津城をかためたまま上洛を拒否していることに対し、慶長5年5月ついに諸大名に会津出陣を命じ、自らも大坂を出発した。それに対し三成は、景勝と通じ、7月毛利輝元や島津家久と諮って兵を

　It was a little before the decisive Battle of Sekigahara in 1600. after the death of Toyotomi Hideyoshi. A deep confrontation heated up between Tokugawa Ieyasu (Chief of Five Great Elders) on the one hand and Uesugi Kagekatsu (one of Five Great Elders, Lord of Aizu Province) and Ishida Mitsunari (one of Five Commissioners whom Hideyoshi most trusted) on the other.

　In May, 1600, Ieyasu ordered his supporters to attack Uesugi Kagekatsu at Aizu Castle because Kagekatsu conspired with Ishida Mitsunari and would not come up to Osaka. Ieyasu himself also left Fushimi Castle for Aizu. In July, Mitsunari together with Mori Terumoto and Shimazu Iehisa began to

小山評定跡　Site of War Council at Oyama

挙げ、家康の留守となった伏見城を攻撃した。

　三成の行動を予期していた家康は、下野国の小山に着陣してすぐの7月25日、会津討伐のため陣に加わっていた諸大名を集め、軍議を開いたのである。これが小山評定である。

　「徳川実記」によると、その軍議の最中、家康は「諸将の中には妻子を人質にとられている者もある。去就は各々の自由に任せる。三成方に加勢されるもよし、陣を払って引き返してもよし」と言ったという。一瞬、武将の間に動揺が広まったが、清洲城主福島正則は「余人はともかく拙者は妻子を捨てても内府殿（家康のこと）にお味方申す」と叫んだ。これで衆議は一決したという。

　この軍議では、周到な準備のもと「このまま上杉景勝を討つべきか、引き返して石田三成と戦うか、それとも三成に味方するか」、各武将の意向を聴き、家康のもと結束を図ろうとしたものである。軍議は、家康の期待通り会津の上杉討伐を中止し、西上して三成と戦うことに決まった。

　山岡荘八の「徳川家康」巻9の中、「突風前夜」の項にも史実に即して詳しい記述がある。

　小山評定は、かつて小山氏の居

attack the masterless Castle of Fushimi.

Ieyasu had expected how Mitsunari would move when he left Osaka. On July 25, soon after he arrived at Oyama in Shimotsuke Province, he gathered his supporters and held a meeting. This meeting is popularly called Oyama Hyojo.

According to *Tokugawa Jikki* (an official record of Tokugawa Shogunate), Ieyasu said at the meeting: "Some of you may have your wife or children held as hostages. It is up to you to decide whether to stay with me or to leave me and work with Mitsunari." What he said threw commotion among the attendants. At that moment, Fukushima Masanori, Lord of Kiyosu Castle, declared that he would work with Ieyasu even if he sacrificed his wife and children. All the others present agreed.

At this meeting, Ieyasu intended to learn what each lord was thinking and to solidify his party. He wanted to know whether he should fight with Kagekatsu or to go back and fight with Mitsunari. They agreed to stop fighting with Uesugi and to return west to fight with Mitsunari.

In the story "*Tokugawa Ieyasu*" (vol. 9, 'the Night before the Fight') by Yamaoka Sohachi, there is a detailed description about the meeting.

The Oyama War Council was held in Ieyasu's headquarters (a hut about 7m by 7m) somewhere around the present Oyama City Office or the Suga Shrine.

城であった小山城内の南の領域に、家康が急造した仮御殿（3間四方の仮屋）で行われた。今の小山市役所から須賀神社のあたりである。この評定の後、ただちに諸将は陣を引き払い、日光街道を南下していった。

　家康は、上杉景勝の備えとして次男結城秀康の軍勢を残し、各武将への画策を十分行いながら（約1週間の間に、108人の武将に180通の手紙を書いたという）、8月5日に江戸に帰った。

　9月15日、「東軍」「西軍」二つの軍隊は、関ヶ原（美濃国関ヶ原、現岐阜県関ヶ原町）で対決した。「東軍」は徳川家康率いる七万人余の軍隊で、「西軍」は石田三成方の軍隊の八万人余である。この戦いは、一般に「天下分け目の関ヶ原」と言われている。関ヶ原は、古代の関所・「不破の関」のすぐ近くであり、京都と江戸を結ぶ「中山道」、敦賀方面からの「北国街道」、伊勢・松坂方面からの「伊勢街道」が接続する要衝の地である。早朝から始まった合戦は、その日の昼ごろに「東軍」勝利のうちに終結した。家康の天下支配が確定したわけである。

　家康は、関ヶ原で勝つ前に、小山評定で勝ち、天下人への方向性を決めていたと言ってよいだろう。

Soon after the meeting, daimyos went down the Nikko Avenue for Kansai region.

Ieyasu went back to Edo on Aug. 5, leaving the army of Yuki Hideyasu, his second son, as defense against Uesugi Kanekatsu. It is said that Ieyasu wrote 180 letters to 108 warriors in a week.

On Sep. 15, two armies confronted with each other at Sekigahara. One army (about eighty thousand strong) was led by Ishida Mitsunari and the other (about seventy thousand strong) by Tokugawa Ieyasu. The battle is popularly called 'the Decisive Battle of Sekigahara'. Sekigahara is located very close to Fuwa Barrier where three roads (Nakasendo, Hokkoku-kaido and Ise-kaido) met. The battle began early in the morning, and ended in the victory of the East-army around noon. It was the beginning of Ieyasu's reign.

It can be said that Ieyasu had already laid rails to reign the whole country at the Oyama War Council before he won the Sekigahara Battle.

日光杉並木街道
Nikko Cryptomeria Avenues

　日光杉並木街道は、相模国（現、神奈川県）玉縄（甘縄とも）の城主松平正綱（1576 – 1648）とその子正信が植栽して東照宮に寄進したもので、国の特別史跡、特別天然記念物の二重指定を受けている。

　日光杉並木街道は、日光山内の山菅橋（神橋）を起点として今市（日光市今市）に至り、そこから三方に分れ、それぞれ日光領の境である山口（日光市山口）、小倉（日光市小

Giant cryptomerias that line the avenues leading to Nikko were planted by Matsudaira Masatsuna (1576-1648), feudal lord of Tamanawa Castle in Sagami Province (now, Kanagawa Prefecture), and his son Masanobu. After planting the trees, they presented them to Toshogu Shrine. The cryptomeria avenues are now doubly designated as National Special Historic Site and Special Natural Monument.

　Nikko Cryptomeria Avenue leads out of Nikko at The Sacred Bridge in

日光杉並木（例幣使街道）　Nikko Cryptomeria Avenue

倉)、大桑(日光市大桑)に至っている。一般に、山口に至る街道は日光街道、小倉に至る街道は例幣使街道、大桑に至る街道は会津西街道と言われる。日光杉並木街道の総延長は約37kmに及び、現在、約12,500本の杉の木が沿道に聳え、中には目通り直径が2m近い杉もある。

　神橋そばの起点および山口、小倉、大桑の3ヶ所の終点にはそれぞれ並木寄進碑が立てられており、その文面によると、20余年の歳月をかけて杉を植栽し、家康公の三十三回忌にあたる1648年(慶安元)4月17日に東照宮に寄進する旨が松平正綱の名前で記されている。正

並木寄進碑
Monument Commemorating the Planting of Cryptomeria

San'nai and reaches Imaichi where it diverges into three directions. One goes straight to Yamaguchi, the second turns right and reaches Kogura, and the third turns left for Okuwa. They continue until they come to the end of Nikko domain. The avenue leading to Yamaguchi is called Nikko Avenue, the one leading to Kogura is called Reiheishi Avenue, and the last one leading to Okuwa is called Aizu Nishi Avenue. The total length of avenues added is about 37 km and about 12,500 giant cryptomeria are planted along these avenues. Some of them are 2m in diameter at the height of eye-level.

　We can see Namiki Kishin no Hi (a monument that commemorates the planting of cryptomeria trees) near Sacred Bridge and at three other places: Yamaguchi, Kogura and Okuwa. The monument says that it took Masatsuna about 20 years to plant the trees and that they were presented to the Toshogu Shrine on April 17 on the 32nd anniversary of Tokugawa Ieyasu. Masatsuna died on June 22 soon after he returned to Edo after the memorial service of Ieyasu's death. This implies that the monuments were built by Masanobu, his son.

　By the way, there is an interesting episode. Ieyasu and Matsudaira Masatsuna were very good friends. Ieyasu gave permission to Masatsuna to marry O-Kaji, Ieyasu's former concubine, but one month after they got married, Ieyasu

綱は日光での家康の三十三回忌の法要をすませ江戸に帰った直後の6月22日に他界しており、寄進碑は息子の正信が父の遺志を継いで建てたものである。

蛇足ながら、杉を植栽した松平正綱は将軍家康と親密な間柄であったらしく、正綱は家康の側室であったお梶を一時正室としたが、わずか一ヶ月後に、家康にお梶を取り上げられてしまったというエピソードもある。

日光杉並木街道は、1868年（慶応4）の戊辰戦争の折、新政府軍と旧幕府軍との間で激しい戦闘が繰り広げられた所でもあり、その時に打ち込まれた砲弾の痕が残る「砲弾打込杉」とよばれる杉もある。その他、街道の杉には色々と面白い名前がつけられた杉がある。

例幣使街道

今市から三つに分岐する街道のうち南西方向に延びる街道は例幣使街道と呼ばれ、毎年、朝廷から派遣される例幣使が通った道である。例幣使は、毎年、東照宮に幣帛を奉納する為に春の大祭に合わせて派遣された。第1回目の日光例幣使は1647年（正保4）に派遣され、以後、

砲弾打込杉　a tree with a bullet mark

took away O-Kaji from Masatsuna.

During the Boshin Civil War, there was a fierce battle between the Pro-imperial Forces and the Pro-Tokugawa Forces near and along Nikko Cryptomeria Avenue. There is a cryptomeria tree with a bullet mark of that time.

The tree is called "Cryptomeria with a bullet mark." There are some other trees with interesting nicknames.

Reiheishi Avenue

Reiheishi Avenue is the avenue that goes south-west from the crossroads at Imaichi. It was used by Imperial Envoys on their annual visit to Toshogu Shrine. They were sent from the Imperial Court to dedicate offerings to Toshogu Shrine at the time of Spring Festival. The first Envoys were sent in 1647 and they were sent every year for 221 years until the Restoration of the Imperial Rule in

1867年（慶応3）の大政奉還まで221年間、1回も途絶えることなく継続された。

例幣使の一行は約50人で構成され、4月1日に京都を出発して4月15日に日光に至り、4月16日の東照宮の大祭に奉幣して、帰りは江戸を経て4月30日に京都に戻るのが慣例であった。例幣使の一日の行程は、日によって異なるが長い時には一日に14里（約54km）、短い時には七里五丁（約29km）であった。

追分地蔵尊

日光杉並木街道の分岐点である今市には追分地蔵尊がある。一説によると、この地蔵尊は弘法大師が刻んだもので、以前、日光の憾満（かんまん）が渕に安置されていたが、大谷川の洪水でここ今市まで押し流されて来たものという。地蔵尊は、一時、近くの如来寺に安置されていたが、1625年（寛永2）に現在地に移されたという。また、別の説によると、多数の平家残党が平ヶ崎で自害したことを聞いた源頼朝が彼等を憐れんで、供養のためにと地元住民に与えた金をもとに建てられたという。赤い頭巾とよだれ掛けを着けたこの地蔵尊は、重量約8t、頭回りが1.6m、顔の長さが0.6mある。

1867.

Imperial Envoys usually consisted of about 50 members. They left Kyoto on the 1st day of April and arrived at Nikko on the 15th of April. And next day they dedicated offerings to Toshogu Shrine at the Spring Festival. It was their custom to go back by way of Edo and return to Kyoto on April 30th. The distance covered by Imperial Envoys in a day was, depending on the day, about 54 km at the longest and 29 km at the shortest.

Oiwake Jizo

At the Crossroads of Cryptomeria Avenues at Imaichi, there is a jizo statue named Oiwake Jizo. According to legend, this jizo statue was carved by Kobo Daishi. It was once near Kanman-ga-fuchi Rapids in Nikko, but it was washed down to Imaichi by a flood. People dug it out of stones and sands and placed it at the Nyorai-ji Temple nearby. It was later moved to the present place in 1625. Another legend says that the statue was built with funds granted by Minamoto no Yoritomo to appease the spirits of Heike people who killed themselves at Hiragasaki. The Statue, which wears a red hood and a bib, weighs about 8,000 kg, 160 cm around its head, and its face is 60 cm long.

測量基準点：観象台跡
Nasu Ground Datum Line
那須塩原市千本松

観象台（北点）跡 Site of Nasu Ground Datum Line

　那須塩原市千本松にある畜産草地研究所の正門近くの国道400号線沿いには、お椀を伏せたような形をした高さ約1m、直径約2mの小さな塚がある。「観象台跡」と呼ばれる塚である。
　近代国家を目指した明治政府は

There is a small mound near the main gate to Nasu National Institute of Livestock and Grassland Science in Senbonmatsu, Nasu-Shiobara City. It looks like a bowl about 1m in height and 2m in diameter. The mound is called 'Observatory' site.

　The Meiji Government, aiming at

日本全国の正確な地図を作成するにあたり、三角測量をする際の基準の長さとなるものとして、1873年（明治6）に勇払基線（北海道開拓使）、1878年（明治11）に那須基線（内務省地理局）、1882年（明治15）に相模野基線（陸軍省）などの基線を設けた。理論的には、基線は一つ設定すれば十分なのだが、明治政府は正確を期すために全国で13カ所の基線測量を行なっている。基線は、平地の二つの地点を直線で結び、その長さを精密に測量して設定された。

やがて、地図の作成は陸軍省の

the modernization of Japan, decided to draw a precise map of the whole nation. First of all, they established ground datum lines, which served as a base in triangular surveying, at 3 places in Japan: Yufutsu Line in Hokkaido in 1873, Nasu Line in Tochigi in 1878 and Sagamino Line in Kanagawa in 1882. Theoretically, only one line was sufficient, but the Meiji Government appointed 13 places in the country to make the work more precise. The lines were established by measuring the exact length between two points on level ground.

Some years later, the Ministry of Army assumed jurisdiction over the business of making the map and the Sagamino Line (which the Ministry had

たて道　Tate-michi Line

管轄するところとなり、これらいくつかの基線のうち最終的には陸軍省が測量した相模野基線が全国を網羅する大三角点網の基準とされ、残念ながら、那須基線は全国測量の基線とはならなかった。

那須基線は、西那須野町千本松から大田原市実取（みどり）に至る約10.6km（正確には、10,628m 31cm 5.89mm）の基線で、当初、千本松の観象台と実取の観象台には木のやぐらが組んであり、直線道路の先にお互いのやぐらを目視確認できたという。この基線は、通称、「たて道」と呼ばれ、現在でも公式名称は「たて道」という表記になっている。

現在、那須基線は畜産草地研究所の正門から南東方向に延び、東北自動車道の下を通って、国道4号線と交差し、更に、まっすぐに南東に延びて東北新幹線の下をくぐって大田原市実取（みどり）に至る10km余に及ぶ直線道路である。

北点と南点を結ぶ「たて道」に沿って車を走らせていると、明治時代の日本国家の意気込みがひしひしと伝わってくる感じを覚える。

been engaged in) was finally adopted as the base line for the national triangular surveying. Regrettably, the Nasu Line was not adopted.

The Nasu Line ran from Senbonmatsu, Nasu-shiobara, to Midori, Otawara, for about 10.6 km (exactly, 10.628m 31cm 5.89mm). There were wooden stages built at both ends, and people on one end could see the stage on the other end with the naked eye. People called this line 'Tate-michi,' and it has become its official name today.

Today, we can see that the Line running about 10km south-east straight from the gate of Nasu National Institute of Livestock and Grassland Science, goes under the Tohoku Highway, crosses National Route 4, goes further southeast, goes under the Tohoku Shinkansen Line and to Midori.

When we drive along Tatemichi between the north and south points, we can feel the enthusiasm of the Meiji people.

消えた県都の近代化産業遺産
Vanished Industrial Modernization Heritage of Utsunomiya

宇都宮市石井町

2014年（平成26）6月、富岡製糸場と絹産業遺産群がユネスコ世界遺産に登録された。

それを遡ること7年、2007年（平成19）11月、経済産業省は、歴史を軸として先人に学ぶべく、地域活性化の有益な「種」と成り得るものとして「近代化産業遺産群」33を選定している。全国に約450ヵ所の幕末から戦前の近代化産業遺産群を含む33のストーリー（近代化産業遺産が紡ぎ出す先人達の物語）の中に栃木県の近代化産業遺産が4か所含まれ、現存している。しかし、栃木県、特に県都が移る前の宇都宮の産業近代化に大きな足跡を残しながら歴史上、まさに忽然と姿を現し、忽然と跡形もなく消え去ったのが大嶋商舎である。日本の産業革命を先駆として牽引した明治初期の模範工場であった。

大嶋商舎は1871年（明治4）創業、そして、1915年（大正4）廃業となっている。その間、1876年、アメリカ、フィラデルフィアの万国博覧会に出品した生糸製品が高く評価

In June, 2014 "Tomioka Silk Mill and Related Silk Industry Heritage" was inscribed on the UNESCO World Heritage List.

Seven years prior to that, in November, 2007, Ministry of Economy and Industry selected 33 heritages of industrial modernization in order that new "seeds" can be discovered to vitalize the regional industries, learning from forerunners' history. There are 33 stories of the forerunners including about 450 sites throughout the country. Among them are 4 sites presently existing in Tochigi prefecture. However, it was a silk mill named Oshima-shosha that historically left a huge footprint to Utsunomiya's industrial modernization before it became the capital of Tochigi prefecture, and disappeared almost all of sudden without leaving much trace. It was a modern factory of early Meiji period that foreran the Japan's industrial revolution.

Oshima-shosha was founded in 1871 and closed in1915. Their silk products were highly valued at the 1876 Philadelphia Expo. In return they invited General Ulysses Grant to their plant, who was president of the US from 1869 to 1877 (2 full terms of office). To their

大嶹商舎器械製糸場作業風景（「栃木県史」史料編近現代6より）Working scene of Oshima-shosha

され、そのお礼として、1869年から1877年にかけて大統領を二期務めたユリシーズ・グラント将軍を招待したところ、あろうことか、1879年その訪問が実現した。国賓としての日本訪問のついでではあるが、まだ鉄道も開通していない時に、周りに見るべきものは何もない（ついでに見せた物はアユ漁のみ）田舎の寒村、石井村にグラント将軍は日光からの帰途、馬車で訪問した。その前後には国是としての殖産興業、外貨獲得

surprise, General Grant accepted their invitation and visited Oshima-shosha during his visit to Japan as a state guest in 1879. As there had not been a railway available yet, on his way back to Tokyo from Nikko by horse-drawn carriage, he visited the deserted village, Ishii-mura where there was nothing to see other than sweet fish fishing. Around that time, under the slogan, "Encouragement of New Industry and Acquisition of Foreign Currency" as the state policy, some people of importance such as Inoue Kaoru, Arisugawanomiya, Okuma

の号令の下、当時の要人、井上馨、有栖川宮、大隈重信、岩倉具視らが富岡製糸工場設立に先立つこと一年創業の、その日本初の近代イタリア式私営器械製糸工場設備を見学に訪れている。

　江戸日本橋に住む豪商（材木商）、川村迂叟（1822-1885）が大嶋商舎の生みの親である。彼は江戸勘定奉行御用達十人衆の一人であった。最後の宇都宮藩主、戸田家は、そのおかげで修営奉行を命ぜられた事業、山稜修補、への多額の資金提供をはじめ、戸田家の肥前島原から宇都宮藩への復帰資金など、長年の川村家からの積借未払の返礼として川村家に碌500石を贈り、船生村、石井村、桑島村、汗村、塩原村一円を迂叟の所管とした。

　後に大嶋商舎を購入した原富太郎（三渓）は、「原三渓翁伝」の中で川村迂叟を出色の篤志家と評しているが、その新しい社会への意欲的な挑戦は、まさに不毛の地を開墾し、桑畑を拓くことから始め、川の氾濫に備えて土手を築き、工場設置、海外輸出まで、宇都宮における農業、工業、商業の総合分野で殖産興業・外貨獲得を具現したと言える。迂叟が晩年受賞した藍綬褒章の下賜の文には、以下のように記さ

Shigenobu, Iwakura Tomomi, and so on also visited Oshima-shosha in order to see the most modernized equipment brought to Japan from Italy for the first time, which was a year prior to the establishment of Tomioka Silk Mill.

Kawamura Uso (1822-1885), a wealthy merchant (lumber dealer) as well as one of the ten purveyors to the Commissioner of Finance, who lived in Nihonbashi, Tokyo (Edo), founded Oshima-shosha. The last feudal lord of Utsunomiya Han, Todas was appointed Commissioner of Repair Work as a reward for his repair work of imperial mausoleums. Kawamura provided Todas with the finance for this repair work and the travel expenses for their return from Shimabara, Nagasaki to Utsunomiya Han on top of their long term debts they owed Kawamura. In return, Todas gave Kawamura 500 koku stipend and the right to control Funyu, Ishii, Kuwajima, Fuzakashi and Shiobara village.

Hara Tomitaro (Sankei), who later bought Oshima-shosha, described in his biography that Kawamura was an outstanding philanthropist. It was Kawamura's strongly motivated challenge to the society that he brought the barren land under cultivation to grow mulberry trees to begin with, built banks in case of river flooding, and established mills, including exporting the silk products, in which "Encouragement of New Industry" and "Acquisi-

れている。「夙に志を公益に励まし、慶応年間より下野国絹川（鬼怒川）沿岸に於いて榛莽を開墾して桑樹を栽培し工場を設置して子女を教え専ら力を絲繭の改良に用い、且桑苗を頒布して広く養蚕の道を開く。尚拮据経営二十余年、遂に其志を達し之を海外に輸出するに至る。」

驚くべきことに、戸田氏の開墾要請があったにせよ、私財を投じた開墾、土木事業、工場建設であった上に当時の宇都宮藩士族の子女を多く採用し、教育し、労働規則、等級制賃金を設置、製品管理を徹底したという。

また、工場内に医療設備を設置、医師を常駐させた。蒸気を使う仕事のため、特にやけどの治療、薬（軟膏）の開発が進み、その評判が評判を呼び、患者は全国からやけどの治療にわざわざ大嶹商舎を訪れたという。（石井河岸菊池記念歴史館、菊池芳夫館長談）

茶を愛した川村迂叟は、また、工場内に神社を建造、待春軒（自邸）を近傍より移し、そして、寒月庵と呼ばれた茶室を江戸本邸から移築した。いずれも原三渓が工場を富岡製糸所に移した時に、その価値を認め、横浜三渓園に移転したが、神社は戦災で失われ、待春軒は戦後に

tion of Foreign Currency" were embodied over all sorts of field in Utsunomiya such as agriculture, industry, commerce, and so forth. Kawamura Uso in his later years won a Blue Ribbon Medal whose certificate says, "he promoted the public work for the common good, cultivating the land along the Kinu (silk) River, growing mulberry trees, building mills, and training girls to improve silk thread cocoons and broadened the sericulture since Keio period. Over his management of the mills for more than 20 years, it finally came to export the products to foreign countries."

To our surprise, although there might have been a request from Toda family, he gave his whole fortune to the land cultivation, public works, and mill building. Besides, he employed and trained a number of daughters of samurai class in Utsunomiya Han and did thorough product control with proper labor rules and wages.

Also a medical clinic with a doctor was stationed within the mill site. As steam was frequently used for silk reeling, new special ointment was developed to cure scald from the steam. It became widely well- spoken of and patients visited the clinic from all over the country to receive treatment for their scald. It was reported by Mr. Kikuchi Yoshio of Ishii-Kashi Kikuchi Memorial History Museum.

Kawamura loved tea ceremony and had a tea ceremony house named Kan-

焼失、寒月庵は熱海市伊豆山の老舗旅館、桃李境に移築された。

　志賀直哉は晩年、伊豆山に居を構え、週末には東京から編集者らを呼んで麻雀に興じていたが、近所の桃李境に移築された寒月庵が気に入り、武者小路実篤、川端康成、鈴木大拙らと、よく茶談したという。残念ながら、2011年、桃李境は廃業し、寒月庵は解体されたと考えられている。

　国道123号線を宇都宮から水戸へ向かい鬼怒川を渡ってすぐ右手あたりに大嶋商舎は位置していた（現、宇都宮市石井町・鎧山町）。工場敷地は約3.4ha（約3万坪）、はじめは鬼怒川から水路を引いての水力であったが、1887年（明治10）には蒸気機関を設置、工女は200名を超えた。

　当時は下野の領主的商品経済の盛んな水運の要地とされたものの、周りには何もない不毛の僻地、石井村に遠く海外にも伝わる模範工場が出現したのは、奇跡という他はない。想像を超えて、江戸の豪商は巨大な財力を蓄えていたのだが、1900年（明治33）、川村家が経営していた宇都宮の第三十三国立銀行が一千万円の政府融資の突然に中止を期に経営悪化、大嶋商舎は

getsu-An brought over from Edo (Tokyo) and reassembled together with his house called Taishun-Kan from nearby and a shrine newly built, all within the mill site. When Hara Sankei bought, relocated and reconstructed Oshimashosha at the Tomioka Silk Mill site, he highly valued the three buildings and kept them for himself at Yokohama Sankei En. The shrine was destroyed by fire after the war, and Kangetsu-An was relocated and reconstructed at an old established ryokan, Torikyo in Izusan, Atami city.

Shiga Naoya lived in Izusan in his late years and enjoyed playing mahjong with editors from Tokyo there. He liked Kangetsu-An very much and often enjoyed talking and having tea with people such as Mushanokoji Saneatsu, Kawabata Yasunari, and Suzuki Daisetsu. Unfortunately, Torikyo closed down in 2011 and Kangetsu-An seemed to be removed at the same time.

If you go along Route 123 from Utsunomiya down town toward Mito, you will see huge rice fields on your right immediately after crossing the Kinugawa river, where Oshima-shosha used to exist (presently Ishii-machi or Koteyama-cho, Utsunomiya shi). The area of the silk mill site was approximately 3.4 ha (30,000 tsubo). Water power had been used through water courses from the Kinugawa river until steam engines were installed in 1887 employing over 200 factory girls.

三井高良（三井銀行）に譲渡され、その二年後、原三渓（富太郎）に買い取られた。1915年（大正4）には廃業し、工場は原富岡製糸所に移転された。

大嶹商舎は、明治期の40年余りの短い命であったが、宇都宮家およびその家臣団はさておき、その後、郷土に愛着を持たないように見える歴代の藩主の下、近代化をどうしていいかわからず、蒲生君平らが唱えた、なんとなく商人を蔑み、帰農を良とする気分の中に、私営ながら颯爽と近代化産業の「種」を落として消えた様に思えるが如何だろうか。

もしかすると、民間企業群で、現在、宇都宮清原工業団地が内陸型工業団地として、国内最大級の出荷額・規模を誇っているのは、川村家が播いた「種」が変遷を経て、芽を出した証かもしれない。

It was almost a miracle that a modern model silk mill known to overseas appeared in Ishii village, barren land in the middle of nowhere though it was just an important place for water transportation especially of seigneur's trade. Wealthy merchants of Edo accumulated huge assets beyond our imagination, however in 1990, Utsunomiya's Number 33 State Bank, which Kawamura family ran went bankrupt due to the sudden suspension of ten million yen finance from the government and Oshima-shosha was sold to Mitsui Bank. Two years later, it was purchased by Hara Sankei. In 1915, it discontinued its business and the plant was moved to the Tomioka Silk Mill site.

In a mood where merchants were looked down upon under the back-to-the-land movement Gamo Kunpei put forward and where the past feudal lords except for Utsunomiya clan and their vassals seemed to feel no attachment to their land and did not know what to do to modernize the region, Oshima-shosha existed in Utsunomiya only for a little more than 40 years in Meiji period and swiftly disappeared, which seems to have left "seeds" for the modernized industry to come in the future.

Perhaps, the fact that Utsunomiya Kiyohara Industrial Park presently enjoys the top shipment value of all the inland industrial parks in Japan may be the proof of what the Kawamuras started in Utsunomiya in Meiji period.

「桜並木ここにありき」
There Once was a Cherry-tree Avenue Here

宇都宮市戸祭、桜

1904年（明治37）から1905年（明治38）にかけて、日本は満州（中国の東北地域）、朝鮮の覇権をかけて帝政ロシアと戦った。いわゆる「日

Japan fought the war with Czarist Russia from 1904 to 1905 for supremacy in Manchuria (now, north-east part of China) and Korea. It was called Russo-Japanese War. The war ended

桜通り（軍道）

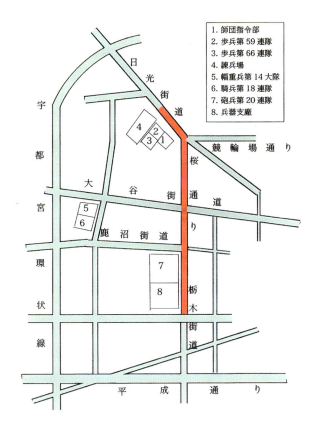

露戦争」である。この戦争は日本の勝利に終わったが、この戦争の反省から様々な問題が提起され、とりわけ、わが国の兵力の増強の必要性が痛感された。そして、1905年（明治38）4月には、陸軍を従来の12師団＊から18師団に増強することが決定され、まず、13,14,15,16の4個師団が増設されることになった。

＊師団→旅団→連隊→大隊→中隊→小隊

　宇都宮では、この決定に呼応して、増設される師団の一つを宇都宮に誘致しようという運動が展開され、1907年（明治40）9月、第14師団が宇都宮にくることが決定した。

　これに伴って、宇都宮では兵営の建設や道路の整備が始まり1908年（明治41）には宇都宮材木町から西へ大谷街道が開通した。同年3月末には、早速、歩兵第66連隊が到着し、11月には師団長陸軍中将鮫島重雄率いる第14師団が宇都宮に移駐してきた。

　師団司令部は国本村（現、国立病院機構栃木医療センター）に置かれた。現在、病院入口そばにあるしだれ桜は、当時、司令部衛兵所前にあったものである。城山村（現、作新学院高校附近）には騎兵第18連隊と輜重兵第14大隊が、そし

in the victory of Japan, but it presented various problems to Japan. Especially, Japan felt it absolutely necessary to build up its army. In April, 1905, it was decided that the number of divisions＊ should be increased from 12 to 18. It was also decided that, first of all, 4 divisions (Divisions 13,14,15 and 16) should be increased.

＊ division → brigade → regiment → battalion → company → platoon

　In accordance with this decision, Utsunomiya City began a drive to invite one of the 4 divisions to Utsunomiya. In September, 1907, it was decided that the 14th Division would be stationed in Utsunomiya.

「桜並木ここにありき」
"There once was a Cherry-tree Avenue Here"

て、姿川村（現、宇都宮短期大学附属高校附近）には野砲兵第20連隊が駐屯した。これより少し遅れて1909年（明治42）5月には国本村（現、とちぎ福祉プラザ附近）に歩兵第59連隊が駐屯した。かくして、宇都宮は「軍都」の姿を整えていったのである。14師団が直接宇都宮市内に落とす金額は、当時の宇都宮市の一般会計の5倍にもなったと言われる。

　師団司令部と野砲兵第20連隊（兵器廠^{へいきしょう}）とを結ぶ約2kmには幅10間（約20m）の道路が造られ「軍道」とよばれた。

軍道桜植樹記念碑
Monument commemorating the planting of cherry trees

In Utsunomiya, construction works of barracks and roads started in 1908. A road running west from Zaimoku-cho to Oya was newly built. At the end of March of the same year, the 66 Infantry Regiment arrived, and in November the 14th Division led by Lt. Gen. Samejima Shigeo came to Utsunomiya.

The Headquarters of the 14th Division was established in Kunimoto (now, where National Hospital Organization Tochigi Medical Center is). A weeping cherry tree that stood near the guardhouse of the headquarters can still be seen near the entrance to the hospital. The 18th cavalry regiment and the 14th transport battalion were stationed in Shiroyama (now, where Sakushin High School is), the 20th artillery regiment in Sugatagawa (now, where High School Attached to Utsunomiya Junior College is), and, a little later, the 59th infantry regiment was stationed in Kunimoto (now, where Tochigi Welfare Plaza is) in May, 1909. In this way, Utsunomiya gradually became a 'military city.' It was said that the money the 14th Division spent in Utsunomiya was five times the general account of Utsunomiya City.

A new road, 20m wide, running for some 2 kilometers, was built between the headquarters and the 20th artillery regiment. It was called 'Gundo' (a military road).

And, at the suggestion of Lt. Gen. Samejima Shigeo, the road was bordered on both sides with more than

軍道の両側には鮫島重雄師団長の発案で桜の苗千本余が植えられた。その植樹の由来を記した記念碑が、かつて、師団長官舎（現、宇都宮地方合同庁舎）前に建てられていた。高さ2m、幅1.2mの仙台石でできた記念碑で、碑面には鮫島師団長の篆額、額下段には時の県知事中山己代蔵が漢文で書いた「軍道と桜植樹の由来」が刻まれていた。現在は、この記念碑は撤去され、宇都宮市茂原の陸上自衛隊宇都宮駐屯地にある防衛資料館に保管されている。

「軍道」は第二次大戦後には「桜通り」と名が変えられ、春の桜の季節には市民の憩いの場となっていたが、車の交通量の激増に伴う道路拡張計画により1963年に伐採された。今では、足利銀行本店北の道路際に「桜並木ここにありき」（横川知事筆）の碑が残るのみである。

1,000 cherry trees.

Near the office of the divisional commander (now, where Utsunomiya Gov. Office Building is located), there once was a monument commemorating the planting of cherry trees. It was 2m tall, and 1.2m wide and was made of Sendai Stone. On the upper part of the monument were inscribed letters written by the commander in the 'ten' style of writing, and under them were inscribed sentences in classical Chinese by Nakayama Miyozo, Governor of Tochigi Prefecture, explaining the origin and the purpose of planting cherry trees along gundo. The monument was removed from its orginal place and is now kept at the museum of Utsunomiya Base of the Japan Ground Self-Defense Force.

After World War II, the name of the road was changed from 'Gundo' to 'Sakuradori' (sakura road). In spring, a lot of citizens went to see cherry blossoms there, but, with the increase of traffic, the road had to be widened and cherry trees on both sides of the road were cut down in 1963. Today, only the monument near Ashikaga Bank tells us that "There once was a Cherry tree Aveue here."

清流戻る渡良瀬川
Watarase River

　2006 年（平成 18）6 月から 2007年 9 月までの、1 年 4 カ月にわたり、読売新聞宇都宮支局は栃木版で「渡良瀬 100 年」を連載した。渡良瀬遊水地を中心に、その自然、歴史、文化をきめ細かく紹介するヒット企画であった。この連載が終了した 2007 年は、1906 年の谷中村廃村からちょうど 100 年、それに合わせるように足尾銅山は世界文化遺産候補として文化庁に申請された。さらに、その 5 年後の 2012 年（平成 24）7 月 3 日、渡良瀬遊水地がラムサール条約湿地に登録された。

　渡良瀬川は日本百名山の一つ皇海山（標高 2144m）に源を発し、渡良瀬遊水地において巴波川及び思川と合流し、更に下流で利根川と合流する総延長 106km の川である。利根川から枝分かれする江戸川は、埼玉県と千葉県の県境を流れて江戸と結ばれていたため、往時は、渡良瀬川、巴波川、思川は、鬼怒川と共に、江戸へ物資を運ぶ河川として大いに利用され、足尾の銅、足利の織物、宇都宮の大谷石、野木の煉瓦などはこの水運を利用して江戸に

Over a year and four months since June, 2006 till September, 2007, Utsunomiya branch of Yomiuri Shinbun ran a serial, "Watarase 100 years" on their Tochigi edition. It was a hit that meticulously reported and depicted the nature, history and culture of Watarase Retarding Basin and its surroundings. In 2007 when the serial ended, 100 years had passed since the abandonment of Yanaka village in 1906, and Ashio Copper Mine was recommended to Cultural Affair Agency as a candidate for UNESCO World Cultural Heritage. After 5 years, on July 3rd, 2012, Watarase Retarding Basin was registered as a wetland under the Ramsar Convention.

Watarase River, totally 106km long, runs all the way from Mt. Sukai, one of Japan's Famous 100 Mountains, to Tonegawa River. It joins Uzumagawa River, which flows through Tochigi City, and Omoigawa River, which flows through Oyama City, and then joins Tonegawa River at the southwest of Koga City, Ibaraki Prefecture. As Tonegawa River branches into Edogawa River, Watarase River, Uzumagawa River, and Omoigawa River together with Kinugawa River were used as water transport since Edo period. Copper in Ashio, textile in Ashikaga (via Tochigi

運ばれた。

足尾銅山

　足尾銅山は、秋田県の小坂銅山、愛媛県新居浜市の別子銅山と共に日本三大銅山といわれた。大正時代の最盛期には国内銅産出量の4割を超える国内随一の銅山であった。

　江戸時代初期には、幕府直営で「寛永通宝」を鋳造し、「足尾千軒」と言われるほど町は栄えたが、幕末には生産量が落ち一度閉山した。

　しかし、1877年（明治10）に古河市兵衛（1832-1903）が再興し、大正時代には最盛期を迎えたが、それと同時に公害問題が深刻化していった。そして、足尾銅山は1973年に閉山となった。

　足尾銅山の公害問題に敢然と立ち向かった人物が田中正造（1841－1913）であった。クリスチャンであった正造は、小中村（現、佐野市）に生まれ、1913年、佐野市の支援者宅で客死するまでの全生涯を足尾の公害問題解決のために捧げた。正造は1901年に足尾鉱毒問題解決を求めて明治天皇に直訴をしている。正造が訴えたことは、単に、公

City), Oya-ishi stone in Utsunomiya, bircks in Nogi, and so on all enjoyed the benefit of closeness to this water transport.

Ashio Copper Mine

The three major copper mines in Japan used to be Kosaka Copper Mine in Akita Prefecture, Ashio Copper Mine in Tochigi Prefecture, and Besshi Copper Mine in Niihama City, Ehime Prefecture. Among them, Ashio produced copper over 40% of the copper produced in Japan at the peak, being the top copper mine in Japan.

At the beginning of the Edo period, "Kan'ei-Tsuho" currency was minted by the government in Ashio and the town enjoyed prosperity as people said, "(there are) A thousand houses in Ashio." However, toward the end of the Edo period, the mine was closed as the production of copper declined.

In 1877, however Furukawa Ichibe'e revived the mine and its golden age of production came in the Taisho Period, and after that, the pollution became so serious that the mine was closed in 1973.

As recorded and introduced by many researchers through publications and films, Tanaka Shozo has been known to have made a direct appeal to Meiji Emperor in order to solve the Ashio mining pollution problems. However, not many people are aware that he was born in Konaka Village (presently Sano

害をなくせ、ということだけではなく、環境、農業、人権、平和などに及びその先見性が高く評価されている。

渡良瀬遊水地

渡良瀬遊水地は足尾鉱毒問題解決を目指した明治政府が有害な銅化合物やカドミウムを沈澱させることを目的に計画された。1906年（明治39）の谷中村廃村を経て1922年（大正11）に完成、栃木、群馬、茨城、埼玉の4県にまたがり、現在は国土交通省が管理する。総面積は約3,300ha（山手線内側の半分）であるが、1947年（昭和22）のカスリーン台風後は、水害防止機能が重視され、上空から見るとハート型に見える広さ450haの渡良瀬貯水池（谷中湖）も1990年（平成2）に完成し、水害の恐れは遠のいた。今では、自然の宝庫に生まれ変わり、ラムサール条約の通り、「利用しながら保護する」という理念の下、多くの人が野鳥を観察しに首都圏から訪れるようになった。

春の訪れを告げる風物詩となったヨシ焼きは害虫駆除とヨシの新芽の成長を促すために必要であるが、

City), that he was a Christian, that he died in the house of one of his supporters in Sano City, that he appealed people not only for antipollution but for environment, agriculture, human right, and peace, and that his foreseeability was highly valued by the society.

Watarase Retarding Basin

In order to settle the Ashio mining pollution problems, the Meiji government completed the construction work for Watarase Retarding Basin in 1922 after Yanaka Village was abolished in 1906, precipitating cadmium and noxious copper compounds. It covers parts of 4 prefectures, Tochigi, Gunma, Ibaraki, and Saitama and is taken charge of by the Ministry of Land, Infrastructure, and Transport. Having total area of 3,300 hectare (half the area within JR Yamanote Line), Watarase Retarding Basin was expected more of its flood control function after experiencing Typhoon Kathleen in 1947. In 1990, Watarase Reservoir (Lake Yanaka), which looks heart-shaped from the sky, was completed and fear for flood was gone. Watarase Retarding Basin has been born again to be a rich repository of nature and has enjoyed having a number of people who come to watch wild birds from the metropolitan area under the principle of Ramsar Convention, "Preserve and utilize it at the same time."

Yoshiyaki (reed burning) in Wata-

刈り残しが無かった昔は、不要であった。2013年現在、中国産の台頭で、よしず職人が600人から6人にまで減り、刈り残しのヨシが増えたからである。半夏生の自生地としても有名で、スカイスポーツ（熱気球、スカイダイビングなど）、カヌー、ウインドサーフィンなどとともに人々を惹きつける魅力になっている。

rase Retarding Basin has become a reminder that sring has come nowadays and become necessary to kill harmful insects and promote reeds to sprout, however it was not needed in the past when there were no reeds left to burn. There are much more reeds left not reaped nowadays than before since the number of reed screen craftsmen has decreased from 600 (before) to 6 (2013) due to the popular imported cheap China-made reed screens. It is well-known as a natural habitat of Hangesho (Lizard's Tail) and attracts people who love sky sports, such as hot-air balloons and sky diving as well as canoeing and wind surfing.

野木町ホフマン煉瓦窯　Nogi Town Brick Kiln

野木町煉瓦窯

　渡良瀬遊水地を見下ろす南東の高台（野木町の西端）に、不思議な形をした建造物がある。平面正16角形、外周100m、煙突高34m強のホフマン式輪窯で、1979年（昭和54）、国の重要文化財に指定された。ホフマン式輪窯は、埼玉県深谷市、京都府舞鶴市、滋賀県近江八幡市にも部分的に残っているが、いずれも楕円形や長方形で、国内で完全な形で残っているのは、この野木町煉瓦窯だけである。

　1888年（明治21）、旧下野煉化製造会社が設立され、当時の近代化建造物に必要な赤煉瓦の建築材料としての需要に応え、1890年（明治23）にこの輪窯は完成した。赤煉瓦の原料となる粘土、砂を旧谷中村（現谷中湖）から採取し、「手抜き」と呼ばれる方法で製造した素地を円形環状トンネルの16室で24時間、順次、絶え間なく、乾燥、焼成するもので、上部には400個の投炭孔を配し、一基での年間最大焼成数250〜300万個を誇る、当時としては画期的な窯であった。思川の水運を利用して、1895年には、日清戦争後の戦後景気に加え、日本鉄道株式会社からの大量注文を受けるなど、日本の近代化に大きく

Nogi Town Brick Kiln

　In addition, there is a strange shaped building on a hill that looks down Watarase Retarding Basin from south-east (on the west side of Nogi Town). It is a Hoffman-style ring kiln that has a regular polygon (16) shape on plan, 100m outer periphery, and 34m high chimney, which was designated as an important cultural property of the country in 1979. Hoffman-style kilns are remaining partially in Fukaya City, Saitama Prefecture, Maizuru City, Kyoto Prefecture and Omihachiman City, Shiga Prefecture, and all of them are either of oval or rectangular shape, while the only whole ring kiln that is preserved in perfect condition is Nogi Town brick kiln.

　In 1888, Shimotsuke Renga Manufacturing Company (Shimo-Ren) was established to meet with the increasing demand for red bricks as one of the building materials required for the modern architectures at that time, and the kiln was completed in 1890. The raw materials for red bricks, clay and sand were gathered in Yanaka Village (presently Lake Yanaka). After the materials are molded and removed from the molds by hands, they are incessantly (24 hours a day) dried and fired in sequence in 16 tunnel chambers laid in circle with 400 holes above the chambers to throw in coal through. It was a revolutionary kiln at the time that could possibly produce as many as 2.5 to 3 million bricks a year. In addition to the post war boom

貢献した。

　1972年には、煉瓦需要の減少に伴い製造が中止されたが、創立後80年間にわたり、大煙突から黒煙が立ち上り、野木町の風物詩となった。その後、貴重な近代化産業遺産として保存されている。

　足尾銅山、野木町煉瓦窯、いずれも、日本の殖産興業のトップランナーとして、国策産業を牽引した。日本近代を代表する思想家、田中正造の足跡を経て、産業遺産として保存され、渡良瀬遊水地という自然資産へと生まれ変わりつつある。この渡良瀬100年が示す、殖産興業から環境重視へのシフトの象徴である渡良瀬遊水地は、その自然資産としての魅力から、これからさらに知名度を増し、多くの人々を惹きつけて止まないに違いない。

after the Sino-Japanese War, there was an extensive order from the Japan Railway Company in 1895. Utilizing Omoigawa River as water transport, the kiln contributed greatly to modernization of Japan.

In 1972, the production of bricks was discontinued due to their decreasing demand, however over 80 years since the establishment of the kiln, it gave poetic charm to Nogi Town, giving off black smoke from the huge chimney. At the moment, it is being preserved as an important heritage of industrial modernization.

As forerunners of Japan's Encouragement of New Industry policy, both Ashio Copper Mine and Nogi Brick Kiln were the driving force behind the industries fostered by the government. With the footmarks of Tanaka Shozo, one of the thinkers representing modern Japan, they have been preserved as industrial heritages and in the process of being reborn to be a nature asset, "Watarase Retarding Basin." As shown in these Watarase 100 years, Watarase Retarding Basin symbolizes the switchover from Encouragement of New Industry to Environmental Protection policy, and it will be known more widely and visited by more people because of its attractiveness.

御用邸と御料牧場
Imperial Villas and Imperial Stock Farm

　栃木県には、かつて、日光と塩原に御用邸があり、現在では那須に御用邸、そして、高根沢・芳賀に御料牧場があるなど皇室との係わりが深い県である。

　現在、全国には御用邸が葉山（神奈川県1894〜）、那須（栃木県1926〜）、須崎（静岡県1971〜）の3カ所のみであるが、明治期には葉山を含めて12カ所あった。古い

　Tochigi Prefecture has many facilities related with Imperial House. Before the war, there used to be imperial villas in Nikko and Shiobara. And today there is an imperial villa in Nasu and Imperial Stock Farm in Takanezawa.

　Today, there are only 3 imperial villas in Japan: in Hayama (est. 1894), Nasu (est. 1926), and Suzaki (est. 1971). There used to be 12 villas during the Meiji Period. They were in the order of establishment: Kobe, Ata-

旧田母沢御用邸　Former Nikko Tamozawa Imperial Villa

順に挙げてみると、神戸、熱海、伊香保、山内（日光）、沼津、葉山、宮の下（箱根）、田母沢（日光）、鎌倉、静岡、小田原、塩原である。

栃木県内にあったものは山内、田母沢、塩原の3カ所であった。12の御用邸の大半は戦災や廃止によって無くなってしまったが、日光市の旧田母沢御用邸は「日光田母沢御用邸記念公園」として、また、塩原の旧塩原御用邸は「天皇の間記念公園」としてかつての姿を留めている。

旧日光田母沢御用邸

旧日光田母沢御用邸は栃木県日光市にある。1898年（明治31）、日光出身の銀行家小林年保が所有していた別邸に赤坂離宮から旧紀州徳川家江戸中屋敷を移築して造営を開始、1899年に完成、1900年から大正天皇の皇太子時代の夏の静養所となった。

1912年（大正元）皇太子、嘉仁殿下の大正天皇即位後、1918年から1920年にかけて大正天皇の御用邸として大規模な増改築が行われ、結果、総面積は1360坪となり、数ある御用邸の中でも最大級の規模と格式となった。現在の姿はほぼ100年前のものである。

mi, Ikaho, Sannai (Nikko), Numazu, Hayama,Miyanoshita (Hakone), Tamozawa (Nikko), Kamakura, Shizuoka, Odawara, and Shiobara.

3 of them were in Tochigi Prefecture. Most of the 12 villas were abolished after World War II. But Tamozawa Imperial Villa in Nikko still exists under the name of "Nikko Tamozawa Imperial Villa Memorial Park," and Shiobara Imperial Villa under the name of "Emperor's Room Memorial Park."

Former Nikko Tamozawa Imperial Villa

Nikko Tamozawa Imperial Villa Memorial Park (the Former Tamozawa Imperial Villa) is in Nikko. The Villa was built in 1898 in the premises which belonged to Kobayashi Nempo, a banker and a native of Nikko. Building materials of the former sub-residence of the Kishu Tokugawa Family were carried from Akasaka Detached Villa to Nikko to build the villa. The construction work completed in 1899. Since 1900, the villa was used as summer residence for Crown Prince Yoshihito.

After Crown Prince Yoshihito became Emperor in 1912, a large-scale renovation of the villa was made from 1918 to 1920. The villa was now 1360 tsubo (about 4.5㎢) in area, and was

田母沢御用邸は大正天皇の病状悪化のため葉山御用邸で療養を始めた1925年（大正14）まで、毎夏の静養所として機能し、そのほか、昭和天皇の避暑地、および東京大空襲に備え、当時、学習院初等科5年生であられた皇太子（今上天皇）の疎開先としても利用されたが、1947年（昭和22）に廃邸になった。

その後、2000年（平成12）に修復工事が完了し、江戸、明治、大正の各時代の建築が調和する「日光田母沢御用邸記念公園」として復元され、2003年、国の重要文化財に指定された。

旧塩原御用邸

県令三島通庸（1835-1888）は塩原の渓谷美と湯量豊富な温泉に感嘆し、1884年（明治17）塩原に大きな別荘を構えた。通庸の死後、1903年（明治36）になって、長男の三島弥太郎（1867-1919）＊はこの別荘を当時病弱であった皇太子明宮（後の大正天皇）の養生のためにと皇室に献上し、塩原御用邸となった。

＊徳富蘆花作「不如帰」の川島武男のモデルとされる。

now the greatest villa in Japan in grandeur and in scale. Today we can see the villa as it was about 100 years ago.

Tamozawa Imperial Villa was used by Emperor Taisho as summer resort until 1925 when His Majesty started to get medical treatment at Hayama Imperial Villa because His Majesty's condition took a turn for the worse. The villa was also used as a summer resort by Emperor Showa and as a refuge from the Tokyo air raid by Akihito, the then Crown Prince. Akihito was in the 5th grade of Gakushuin Primary School at that time. The Villa was closed in 1947.

The restoration work of the villa was completed in 2000. The villa was now named Tamozawa Imperial Villa Memorial Park and had beauties of the residence of Edo, Meiji and Taisho combined. It was registered National Important Cultural Property in 2003.

Former Shiobara Imperial Villa

Mishima Michitsune (1835-1888), governor of Tochigi Prefecture during the Meiji period, was very much attracted by the beautiful ravines of Shiobara and by the abundance of hot-spring water there, built a house in a large area of land in Shiobara in 1884. After his death, his son, Yataro (1867-1919)*, presented the land to the Imperial Family in 1903 to be used by Crown Prince Haru-no-miya (later, Emperor Taisho) who was suffering from ill health then.

1905年（明治38）には御用邸内に新御座所が造営された。新御座所は木造平屋の本格的な数寄屋造りで、明治の日本建築史上貴重な存在である。御座所は第二次世界大戦中には三笠宮殿下、更には孝宮（鷹司平通氏夫人）、順宮（池田隆政氏夫人）、清宮（島津久永氏夫人）の三内親王の疎開中の御殿ともなった。

　戦後になり、塩原御用邸は失明者社会復帰施設として厚生省に払い下げられ、1954年（昭和29）には国立塩原視力障害センターと改称され、近代的施設に改築されること

* Yataro is generally thought to be the model of "Takeo" in the novel *Hototogisu* by Tokutomi Roka.

In 1905, a new Imperial Residence was constructed there. It was a single-story wooden house with a Sukiya-zukuri style* and is a precious building in the history of construction of Japan. During World War II, the residence was used as a place of refuge by Prince Mikasa-no-miya as well as by the three Imperial Princessses, Takanomiya, Yorinomiya, and Suganomiya,

* a style of residential architecture incorporating features characteristics of a building where the tea ceremony is performed

After the war, the Imperial Residence Area was disposed of to the Ministry of

天皇の間記念公園　Emperor's Room Memorial Park

になった。1981年（昭和56）に、御座所は旧御用邸敷地から原型のまま那須塩原市下塩原の現在の場所に移築され、「天皇の間記念公園」として一般に開放されている。

那須御用邸

　那須町にある那須御用邸は、1926年（昭和元）以来、昭和天皇、今上天皇が主に夏に、御静養の場として利用されている。特に、昭和天皇は那須をこよなく愛され、那須での植物研究の成果を「那須の植物誌」として出版されている。昭和天皇は那須で「ナスヒオウギアヤメ」（p.74）などの新種を発見されている。

　2011年5月22日、那須御用邸敷地の約半分の560ヘクタールが今上天皇のご意向により在位20年の節目に宮内庁から環境省に移管された。現在、「平成の森」として一般に開放されている。

高根沢御料牧場

　1966年、千葉県成田に新空港が建設されることが決まり、それに伴って85年の歴史をもつ下総御料牧場が閉鎖されることになった。そ

Welfare to be used as a halfway-house for the blind. It was named as "National Shiobara Visual Disabilities Institution" and the building of Imperial Residence was relocated to Shimo-Shiobara, Nasushiobara City. The relocated building retains its original form and is now open to the public as "Emperor's Room Memorial Park".

Nasu Imperial Villa

Nasu Imperial Villa has been used as a summer resort by Emperor Showa and the reigning Emperor since 1926. Emperor Showa loved Nasu very much and studied the flora of Nasu and published the result in a book titled Nasu no Shokubutsushi. There Emperor Showa found new varieties like Nasu Hiougi Ayame ('Iris setosa var. nasuensis')(p.74).

In accordance with the wishes of the Emperor, the administration of about half of the premises (560ha) of Nasu Imperial Villa was transferred to the Environment Agency on May 22, 2011. It was the 20th year since the Emperor acceded to the throne. Today, the transferred land is open to public as "Heisei Forest."

Takanezawa Imperial Stock Farm

When it became evident that a new airport was scheduled to be built in Narita, Imperial Stock Farm in Shimousa (Chiba Prefecture), which had a history

の代替地として栃木県の高根沢町と芳賀町にまたがる地域が決定した。

総面積は、耕地及び放牧地134ha、樹林地66.4haを含む252.2ha、そこに事務所、貴賓館、宿舎、畜産製酪所・肉加工所等を含め100棟が建設された。以後、皇室の用に供する家畜の飼育管理、飼料作物の生産調整、畜産物の処理加工、蔬菜の栽培、さらに皇室の接伴場として在日外交官等の接待に使用されている。

1926年〜1946年の20年間、同時期に三か所(日光、塩原、那須)の御用邸が存在し、御静養の地として皇族の方々が頻繁に利用され、さらに御料牧場をも有する栃木県の果たす役割は、天皇や皇族にとって重要なものとなっている。

of 85 years, had to be closed down. Part of Takanezawa and Haga Towns was chosen as its substitute.

The site has its arable and pasture land of 134 ha and woodland of 66.4 ha, all together 252.2 ha 100 buildings including the office, guest house, lodging house, livestock dairy products plant, and meat processing plant buildings were constructed there. Since then, the livestock and forage crop farming, meat and dairy product processing, and vegetable growing have been done there for the Imperial House. Moreover, it has been used by the Imperial House for the entertainment of the foreign diplomats living in Japan.

Having viewed the Imperial Villas and Imperial Stock Farm in Tochigi Prefecture, we can say that there were 3 imperial villas (Nikko, Shiobara, and Nasu) simultaneously existing in Tochigi for 20 years from 1926 to 1946 and being often in use for the Imperial Family's relaxation. Together with the fact that Tochigi has Imperial Stock Farm in operation, the role Tochigi Prefecture plays for the Emperor and Imperial Family has become very significant.

中世の歴史を語る小山城（祇園城）
Oyama-jo Castle (Gion-jo Castle)
小山市城山町

　小山城は小山氏が守護神として崇める祇園社にちなんで祇園城とも言われる。かつて、小山城があった場所は、現在では城山公園として整備され、ソメイヨシノ、イチョウ、カエデなどの木々の合間に芝生広場、そして自然路が整い、市民憩いの公園になっている。城趾のあちこちには、空堀や土塁、そして曲輪（くるわ）の跡が残り往時を偲ばせてくれる。なお、小山城跡は、鷲城跡及び中久喜城跡と合わせて「小山氏城跡」として国の史跡に指定されている。

　The Oyama-jo Catsle is also called the Gion-jo Castle after its guardian deity, "Gion-sha." The site of the Oyama-jo Castle has been designed as Shiroyama Koen Park, having lawn open space among Someiyoshino cherry trees, Gingko trees, maple trees, and so forth, as well as natural footpaths to be a relaxing place for citizens. There still are remains of the dry moats, mounds, and compounds, which reflects what they looked like in the past. Together with the sites of "the Washi-jo Catsle" and "the Nakakuki-jo Catsle," the site of Oyama-jo Castle is designated a national historic site as "the site of Oyama clan's castles."

　It is believed that the Oyam-jo Castle originates from the fact that a direct descendant of Fujiwara no Hidesato, Oyama Masamitsu built a castle at the point of great strategic importance in 1148 (Kyuan 4). Oyama Masamitsu was an active leader of a band of warriors and his wife, Samukawa no Ama had been a wet nurse of the founder of Kamakura Bakufu, Minamoto no Yoritomo. Masamitsu had three sons, Tomomasa, Munemasa, and Tomomitsu. Tomomasa inherited the head family, Munemasa became the forefather of the Naganuma

小山城趾 Ruins of Oyama Castle

小山城は、藤原秀郷の直系子孫である小山政光（?-?）が1148年（久安4）に要害の地に築城したのが始まりとされる。小山政光は武士団の棟梁として活躍し、源頼朝の乳母であった寒河尼を妻としている。政光には朝政（1158-1238）、宗政（1162-1241）、朝光（1168-1254）の三人の息子があり、朝政が本家を継ぎ、宗政は長沼氏祖、そして、朝光は結城氏祖となった。頼朝の挙兵に際し、寒河尼は元服前の朝光を連れて鎌倉に馳せ参じた。頼朝は非常に喜び、進んで朝光の烏帽子親となっている。

小山氏は代々鎌倉幕府の中枢にあって、関東の名族の地位を得た。政光の頃の本拠は、神鳥谷曲輪で、政光はそこに館を構えていたと推定される。

小山氏の支配する領地拡大に伴い、城の規模は次第に拡張されていった。南北朝末期、11代小山義政（?-1382）の時に鎮守として祇園社（現須賀神社）を祀っている。しかし、この義政が、鎌倉公方足利氏満の制止を無視して宇都宮城主基綱を討ち取ったことが原因で、「小山義政の乱」（1380～1382年）が起こった。敗れた義政は自害し、小山氏直系は応永4年（1397）

clan, and Tomomitsu became the forefather of the Yuki clan. At the Yoritomo's raising of an army, Samukawa no Ama hastened to Kamakura with Tomomitsu who was yet to have his coming of age ceremony. Yoritomo was so pleased that he was willing to be Tomomitsu's eboshioya*.

* a person who puts an eboshi hat on a young man's head on his ceremony of attaining manhood.

Oyama clan was at the center of the Kamakura Bakufu for generations and became an illustrious family of the Kanto region. The base was at the Hitotonoya compound during the Masamitsu's time, and it is presumed that Masamitsu took up his residence there.

As the territory the Oyama clan ruled grew bigger, the size of their castle became larger. At the end of the period of Northern and Southern Courts, the 11th lord, Oyama Yoshimasa(?-1382) venerated Gion-sha (presently the Suga Shrine) as their Chinju (guardian deity). However, Yoshimasa killed the lord of the Utsunomiya Castle, Mototsuna, rejecting control of Kamakura Kubo (Governor-general of the Kanto region), Ashikaga Ujimitsu, which caused the riot of Oyama Yoshimasa (1380-1382). Having been defeated, Yoshimasa killed himself and the Oyama clan's direct descent was once discontinued in 1397 (Ouei 4). Later on, a member of the clan, Yuki Yasutomo succeeded and retrieved the family, living in the Gion-jo

に一旦滅んでしまう。後に一族の結城泰朝（ゆうきやすとも）が小山氏を継ぎ、再興させ、この祇園城に入り、以後代々の本城になった。泰朝の孫である15代持政の時に城の大改修が行われたという。

戦国時代の動乱期には、交通の要地であった小山氏の領地や居城は、越後の上杉氏や小田原の北条氏といった有力な戦国大名に狙われ、盛衰を繰り返していった。

1575年（天正3）、北条氏照によって祇園城は攻め落とされ、20代小山秀綱は追放されてしまう。氏照は大規模に城を拡張整備して、北条氏の支城にした。その後、名族小山氏の復活が図られていく。北条氏の当主北条氏政の養女が小山氏21代政種に嫁ぎ、北条氏の傘下に入るというなか、小山氏は再び祇園城に戻ることになった。しかし、小山氏は1590年（天正18）の秀吉による小田原征伐に際し、北条氏とともに豊臣秀吉に対抗したため、祇園城は秀吉側についた結城氏によって攻略され、ついに小山氏は4世紀半の幕を閉じたのである。なお、小山家の墓所は小山城跡の北、天翁院にある。

1600年（慶長5）、「関が原の戦い」の2か月前、徳川家康による「小

Castle. Since then, it became their main castle from generation to generation. It is said that the castle was renovated on a large scale when Yasutomo's grandson, Mochimasa was the 15th lord.

During the upheavals of the Sengoku Period (the Warring States Period), Oyama clan's territories and castles were targeted by powerful daimyo (feudal lords) of the Sengoku Period such as Uesugi clan of Echigo or Hojo clan of Odawara because they were key areas for transportation, and repeatedly went through rise and fall.

In 1575 (Tensho 3), the Gion-jo Castle was attacked by Hojo Ujiteru and the 20th lord, Oyama Hidetsuna was banished from the castle. Ujiteru worked on the maintenance and expansion of the castle to make it the branch castle of Hojo clan. After that, the revival of the illustrious family, Oyama clan was planned. The daughter of Hojo Ujimasa, the head of the Hojo family, married Masatane, the 21st lord of Oyama clan. However, together with the Hojo clan, the Oyama clan opposed Toyotomi Hideyoshi, and because of that, at the conquest and siege of Odawara in 1590 (Tensho 18), the Gion-jo Castle was attacked by the Yuki clan who was on the Hideyoshi's side and the history of Oyama clan for four and a half centuries came to an end.

The grave site of the Oyama clan is at the Tennouin Temple, north of the Oyama-jo Castle site.

山評定」が小山城域の南・須賀神社で行われ、家康の天下支配が確定した。

　江戸時代に入ると、家康の腹心である本多正純（1565 -1637）が小山3万3千石の城主となり、1608年（慶長13）、東西790m、南北1336mという広大な平山城が出来上がったのである。正純は領地の検地も行っている。その後、正純は1619年（元和5）、宇都宮城主に国替えとなり、小山城は廃城となった。

　また伝説によると、小山城が落城した時、姫が井戸に身を投げ、家臣が供養のためイチョウの小枝をさしたところ、そのイチョウは根付いたが実を付けることがなかったことから「実なし」イチョウと呼ばれ、今でも奥の曲輪に樹齢数百年という大木（樹高15m、目通り直径6m、枝張り12m）が枝を広げている。江戸後期の旅行記「日光駅程見聞雑記」に「高さ3丈もある古木あり」と記されている。

Two months before the Battle of Sekigahara in 1600, "Oyama War Council" was held by Tokugawa Ieyasu at the Suga Shrine, south of the castle site and Ieyasu's rule of the whole country became certain. In 1608 (Keicho 13), a trusted advisor of Ieyasu, Honda Masazumi (1565-1637) was given 33,000 koku of rice as the lord of the Oyama-jo Castle under the Edo Shogunate and built a huge Hirayama-jo castle of 790 m from east to west and 1336 m from north to south. Masazumi also conducted the land survey (Kenchi) of his fief. After that in 1619 he was transferred to Utsunomiya and the Oyam-jo Castle was closed.

There is a legend."The princess threw herself into the well. One of her retainers put in a twig of a gingko tree for the repose of her soul there. It took root, but never bear fruit. It is called "Minashi" (bear no fruit) gingko tree."- As a matter of fact, there presently is a huge gingko tree (15 m high, 6 m eye-level diameter, and 12 m wide branches) in the back compound. The record of personal travel experience of the late Edo period, *Nikko Ekitei Kenmon Zakki* says that there is an old tree, about 9m high.

歴史に名を残す景勝「太平山」
Mt. Ohira: Historical Spot with Scenic Beauty

栃木市

太平山(おおひらさん)は、足尾山系最南端に位置する山で、標高は340mと低いがその展望は素晴らしい。戦国時代に北条氏と対立した上杉謙信も関東平野の広い眺めに驚嘆したと伝えられ、「謙信平」という地名が残っている。

太平山から晃石山(てるいし)一帯は、県立自然公園に指定されており、景勝に恵まれ、県内外から訪れる客が多い。なかでも、「桜のトンネル」(太平山を周遊する遊覧道路の桜並木4000本)や「アジサイ坂」(太平山神社表参道)、秋の紅葉、などが季節を彩る。

Mt. Ohira commands a fine view although it is not very high (340 m) since it is located southernmost of the Ashio mountain range. It is said that Uesugi Kenshin was surprised at its broad view of the Kanto Plain when he confronted the Hojo clan during the Warring States Period. There still is a place named "Kenshin Daira" probably to demonstrate that.

The region from Mt. Ohira to Mt. Teruishi is designated as a prefectural natural park, having many scenic areas and attracting many visitors from Tochigi and other prefectures. Among them, "Cherry Blossom Tunnel" (cherry-tree-lined path round Mt. Ohira with 4,000 cherry trees), "Hydrangea Slope" (front

山本有三の文学碑　A stone monument of Yamamoto Yuzo

たったひとりしかない自分を
たった一度しかない一生を
ほんとうに生かさなかったら
人間、うまれてきたかいが
ないじゃないか

路傍の石

なお、「謙信平」には栃木市生まれの山本有三の文学碑があり、「路傍の石」の一節「たった一人しかない自分を……」が刻まれている。

この太平山一帯は、自然景観の美しさばかりでなく、歴史的な余韻・余情に満ちている。

東側の太平山山麓には円仁によって開かれたという太山寺(たいさんじ)がある。この寺はシダレザクラの老木で有名であるが、徳川3代将軍家光の側室、お楽の方(4代将軍家綱の生母)が病気静養していた所としても有名である。

表参道二の鳥居脇には連祥院(れんしょう)六角堂がある。この六角堂は、太平

approach to the Ohira-san Shrine), and tinted autumnal leaves color each season.

In addition, at "Kenshin Daira," there is a stone monument engraved with a passage from "*Robo no Ishi*" (The Wayside Pebble) written by Yamamoto Yuzo, who was born in Tochigi City.

The region around Mt. Ohira is full not only of the beauty of natural scenery but also of allusive and suggested feeling of history.

At the eastside foot of Mt. Ohira is the Taisan-ji Temple which is believed to have been founded by En'nin. While this temple is famous for the old weeping cherry tree, it is well known as the place where Oraku no Kata (mother of the 4th shogun, Ietsuna), a concubine of

太平山　Mt. Ohira

山神社の境内地にあった連祥院般若寺が明治初年の廃仏毀釈ですべて破壊されて、その後1904年（明治37）にこの地に再建されたものである。1509年（永正6）、連歌師宗長（そうちょう）は、当地を訪れ、「東路（あづまじ）の津登（つと）」に「太平とて山寺あり、般若寺といふ」と記し、連歌の会を開いている。

山頂近くに鎮座する太平山神社の祭神は、天照大神（あまてらすおおみかみ）の孫瓊杵尊（ににぎのみこと）で、天照大神・豊受姫命（とようけひめのみこと）を配祀している。神社の創建は明らかではないが社伝によると、大和国大神神社（おおみわ）（現奈良県桜井市三輪）の分霊を勧請（かんじょう）したものとか、円仁が太平山に登った際に創建したものと伝えている。

神社に登る階段の途中にある随神門の下に「水戸天狗党太平山本陣跡」の木碑があり、さらに謙信平には「勤皇義士旗揚碑」がある。いずれも水戸天狗党が太平山に滞在したことを示す記念碑である。

この天狗党は水戸藩における過激な尊王攘夷思想を持つ一派で、1864年（元治元）藤田小四郎を中心に筑波山に挙兵し、下野で同志を募り、徳川幕府の聖地「日光東照宮」占拠を目指したものである。しかし幕府側の警護が厳しいことから

the 3rd shogun, Iemitsu was recuperating from her illness.

The Rensho-in Rokkakudo is at Ni no Torii (the second archway) of the front approach. This Rokkakudo (hexagonal building) was rebuilt there in 1904 after the buildings of the Rensho-in Han'nya-ji Temple, which used be in the precincts of the Ohira-san Shrine, were all destroyed due to Haibutsu-Kishaku (a movement to abolish Buddhism) in the 1st year of the Meiji Period. A Renga poet (linked-verse poet), Socho visited there to hold a Renga party in 1509 and wrote in his "*Souvenir of the Eastland*" that there was a temple called the Han'nya-ji Temple in Mt. Ohira-san.

Near the peak is the Ohira-san Shrine whose deity is the grandchild of Amaterasu Omikami, and it jointly enshrines Amaterasu Omikami and Toyoukehime no Kami. Although it is unknown when the shrine was founded, the shrine biography says either that the divided deity of Yamato no kuni Omiwa-jinja Shrine (presently Miwa, Sakurai City, Nara Prefecture) was transferred there or that it was founded by En'nin when he visited there.

There is a wooden monument at the shrine gate along the stairs to the shrine, which says "the site of Mito Tengto's Mt. Ohira Headquarters" and another monument saying "Monument of Pro-Imperial Warriors' Raising of an Army" at Kenshin Daira. Both monuments

謙信平　Kenshin Daira

日光行きを断念して、太平山に滞陣し、この地で天下に向けて尊王攘夷の檄(げき)を飛ばし、資金集めや勢力拡大を図った。一か月半の太平山滞在中、下野の各地からも天狗党に加盟した者が90名余、天狗党は総勢400名の部隊になったという。

この後、天狗党の一隊が栃木町において金銭強奪、町家放火を行い（「愿蔵(げんぞう)火事」という）、民衆は天狗党から離反し、破滅の道を突き進んでいく。

show that Mito Tenguto stayed at Mt. Ohira.

Tenguto is a group of extreme Son'no Joi (revere the emperor, expel the barbarians) doctrine in the Mito Domain. Fujita Koshiro and his group raised an army at Mt. Tsukuba in 1864 (Genji 1), rallied like-minded people in Shimotsuke , and attempted to occupy the Tokugawa shogunate's sacred place, Nikko Tosho-gu Shrine. However, they abandoned their attempt to go to Nikko due to its severe guard. Instead, they stayed in Mt. Ohira in order to circulate

これらの歴史的内容は、歴史小説家吉村昭の「天狗争乱」(1994年作) に詳しく述べられている。

太平山の西、晃石山の南斜面の中腹には、10万 ha という広大な境内をもつ「太平山大中寺」がある。境内は常に森閑として人気なく、いかにも禅寺らしい静寂が漂う。上田秋成作の「雨月物語」の中に、稚児への愛執から鬼となった僧が登場する「青頭巾」という物語があるが、これは当寺の開山縁起を題材としたものである。そして、この寺には、「青頭巾」の話にまつわる「根無し藤」はじめ、「七不思議伝説*」が伝わっている。

＊根無し藤、油坂、不断釜、馬首の井戸、不開の雪隠、東山の二つ拍子木、枕返しの間

their manifesto, raise fund, and expand their power. During their stay there, over 90 people joined Tenguto from various areas of Shimotsuke and Tenguto became a troop of 400 in all.

After that, a gang of Tenguto robbed the people in Tochigi Town of money with violence and set fire to the houses (called "Genzo Fire"), which made them lose the support from the public and fall into ruin.

The stories of those historical incidents are told in detail in *"Tengu Soran"* (Tengu Disturbance) (1994) written by a writer of historical novels, Yoshiomura Akira.

On the southern slope, halfway up Mt. Teruishi in the west of Mt. Ohira is "Ohira-san Daichu-ji Temple," which has huge precincts of 100,000 square meters. In the precincts, it is very quiet with no sign of life and stillness of a Zen temple reigns over the area. In *"Ugetsu Monogatari"* written by Ueda Akinari is a story, "Aozukin" (The Blue Hood) which tells about a priest who became an ogre because of his strong attachment to his page who died of illness. This story is based on the history of the temple's foundation. This temple has "Legends of Seven Wonders*" such as "Nenashi Fuji" (Rootless Wisteria) regarding "Aozukin."

＊"Rootless Wisteria," "Oil Slope," "Ceaseless Cooking Stove," "Horse Head Well," "The Bathroom whose door never opens," "Clapping Twice in Higashiyama," and "Room of Makuragaeshi Ghost."

シモツケコウホネ（下野河骨）
スイレン科コウホネ属

世界中で栃木県の4か所
（日光市、那須烏山市、さくら市、真岡市）にだけ生育する。
平成18年に、環境省の絶滅危惧IA類に指定されている。

第4章 祈りと救い
Prayers and Salvation

大慈寺（円仁修行の場）　Daiji-ji Temple (where Ennin practiced asceticism)

栃木の神社のいろいろ
Shrines in Tochigi

栃木県内には、一体、どの位の数の神社があるのであろうか。少し古い資料であるが、「栃木県神社誌」（昭和39年発行）によると、1903年（明治36）頃には約1,200、そして、1940年（昭和15）頃には約3,300の神社があったという。

同書によると、これら約3,300の神社のうち、創立年代が判っているものは718社で、古いものでは、5世紀前半の仁徳天皇の時代に創建された那須神社（大田原市金丸）、舒明天皇（593-641）の時代に創建された那須温泉神社（那須町湯本）等がある。

延喜式神名帳

平安時代の927年（延長5）に撰進された「延喜式」巻9、巻10の神名帳に記載されている栃木県内の神社、いわゆる、式内社は次の11社である。

大神神社（栃木市惣社町）
大前神社（栃木市藤岡町）
村檜神社（栃木市岩舟町小野寺）
二荒山神社（宇都宮市馬場町）
大前神社（真岡市東郷）

How many shrines are there in Tochigi Prefecture? According to *Shrines in Tochigi* (publ. in 1964), there were about 1,200 shrines in 1903, and about 3,300 in 1940.

According to the book, the origins of 718 shrines out of 3,300 are known. Among the oldest shrines are Nasu Shrine established during the era of Emperor Nintoku (the former half of the 5th century) and Nasu Yuzen Shrine established during the era of Emperor Jomei (593-641).

Engi-shiki Jinmyocho

11 Shrines in the province of Shimotsuke listed in the 9th and 10th fascicles of *Engi Shiki** are as follows:

Omiwa Shrine (Tochigi City)
Omae Shrine (Tochigi City)
Murahi Shrine (Tochigi City)
Futaarayama Shrine (Utsunomiya City)
Osaki Shrine (Moka City)
Arakashi Shrine (Motegi Town)
Takemuyama Shrine (Nakagawa Town)
Yuzen Shrine (Nasu Town)
Miwa Shrine (Nakagawa Town)
Awa Shrine (Oyama City)
Munakata Shrine (Oyama City)
One more shrine, Takahashi Shrine

荒榿神社（茂木町小井戸）
健武山神社（那珂川町和見）
温泉神社（那須町湯本）
三和神社（那珂川町三輪）
安房神社（小山市粟宮）
胸形神社（小山市寒川）

　これら11社に高椅神社（小山市高椅）を加えて12社とすることがあるが、これは高椅神社が以前は下総国（現、茨城県の一部）に属していて後に下野国に編入された関係である。

　日本全国にある神社は、1871年（明治4）に出された太政官布告により官幣社と国幣社に分けられた。官幣社とは、宮内省から幣帛を頂いた神社を言い、国幣社とは国庫から幣帛を頂いた神社を言った。

　官幣社は、大社、中社、小社及び別格官幣社に分けられ、国幣社も大社、中社、小社の三つに分けられた。官幣社と国幣社以外の神社は府県社、郷社、村社、無格社に分けられた。栃木県内の神社では、日光東照宮と唐沢山神社が別格官幣社、日光二荒山神社と宇都宮二荒山神社は国幣中社とされた。

栃木県内の神社とご祭神

　栃木県内にある神社名で数の多いのは、星宮神社、稲荷神社、八幡

in Oyama City, can be added to the list. This shrine once belonged to the province of Shimousa (now, part of Ibaraki Prefecture) and was later incorporated into the province of Shimotsuke.

＊a collection of 50 fascicles of governmental regulations in the early 10th century

The Dajokan Fukoku (the Decree by the Grand Council of State) issued in 1871 classified shrines in Japan into two categories: Kanpeisha (imperial shrines) and Kokuheisha (national shrines). Kanpeisha were shrines that received offerings from the Imperial Household Department, while Kokuheisha received offerings from the national treasury.

Kanpeisha was divided into 4 categories : major imperial shrines, middle imperial shrines, minor imperial shrines and imperial shrines of special status. Kokuheisha was divided into 3 catgories: major national shrines, middle national shrines and minor national shrines. Other small shrines were classified into either prefectural, provincial, village or no-status shrines. In Tochigi Prefecture, Nikko Toshogu Shrine and Karasawasan Shrines were classified as imperial shrines of special status, and Nikko Futarasan Shrine and Utsunomiya Futaarayama Shrines were classified as middle national shrines.

Deities in Tochigi Shrines

Shrines in Tochigi Prefecture can be grouped by their names: Hoshinomi-

神社、温泉神社、高龗神社などで、愛宕神社、天満宮、八坂神社などがこれに続く。

星宮神社は県下全体に存在している。この神社の御祭神は、磐裂神・根裂神で、時に、瓊瓊杵尊であることもある。

稲荷神社も県下全体に見られる神社で、御祭神は倉稲魂命で五穀・食物を司る神様とされる。

八幡神社は八幡宮とか八幡社ともよばれ、県下全体に分布している。御祭神は誉田別命、即ち、応神天皇で、弓矢・武道の神様として広く信仰されている。これら八幡神社の本社は大分県の宇佐八幡宮である。

温泉神社という名のつく神社は栃木県下に約80社あり、その殆どが県の北部に集中している。温泉神社の御祭神は大己貴命で、別名、大国主命とか大黒様という名前で広く親しまれている神様である。福の神、医薬の神、温泉の神とされる。

高龗神社は高尾神社とか高男神社などの字を当てることもある。御祭神は高龗神で、この神は闇淤神と共に祈雨、止雨の神とされる。

ya shrines, Inari shrines, Hachiman shrines, Onsen shrines, Takao shrines. There are still other shrines called Atago shrines, Tenmangu shrines, and Yasaka shrines.

Hoshinomiya shrines are found all over in Tochigi Prefecture. They are dedicated to deities of Iwasaku and Nesaku.

Inari shrines are also found all over in Tochigi Prefecture and are dedicated to Uganomitama-no-mikoto, the deity of harvest and food.

Hachiman shrines (also called Hachiman-gu or Hachiman-sha) are found in many places in Tochigi. They are dedicated to Homutawake-no-mikoto (Emperor Ojin) who is regarded as a deity of archery and marshal arts. The Usa Hachimangu in Oita Prefecture is the central shrine for many Hachiman shrines scattered all over Japan.

There are about 80 Onsen shrines, mostly, in the northern part of Tochigi Prefecture. Onsen shrines are dedicated to Onamuchi-no-mikoto (also known by the name of Okuninushi-no-mikoto or Daikoku-sama), who is depicted as a deity of benevolence, medicine, and hot springs.

Takao shrines (sometimes written in different Chinese characters) are dedicated to two deities, Takao and Kurao, who have the power of bringing or stopping rain.

宇都宮二荒山神社
Utsunomiya Futa'arayama Shrine
宇都宮市馬場通り

　現在、宇都宮二荒山神社が鎮座する辺りには、かつて、北に臼が峰（現、二荒山神社）、南に荒尾崎（現、パルコ辺り）という二つの小高い丘があり、この二つを結んで南北に稜線が続いていたという。

　二荒山神社のご祭神は崇神天皇の第一皇子豊城入彦命である。最初、二荒山神社は荒尾崎に祀られたが、838年（承和5）に、荒尾崎から現在の臼が峰に移された。この遷座の神事を今に伝えるのが毎年1月と12月に行われる春渡祭（冬渡祭）である。

There used to be two low hills around the place where we see the Futa'ara-yama Shrine today. One hill in the north was called Usugamine, and the other hill in the south was called Araosaki. The two hills were connected with a mountain path.

The Futa'ara-yama Shrine is dedicated to Toyokiirihiko-no-mikoto, first son of Emperor Sujin. In the beginning, the shrine was located on Araosaki, but it was later transferred to Usugamine in 838. The Otariya Festival held in January and December at the shrine every year retains some vestige of the transfer.

二荒山神社 Futa'arayama Shrine

県社に格下げ？

　二荒山神社の歴史は古く、927年（延長5）に撰進された「延喜式神名帳」に「下野国河内郡一座^大二荒山神社^{大明神}」と書かれている。すなわち、下野国河内郡には大社が一座あり、それは二荒山神社大明神である、というのである。

　時代は下り、宇都宮二荒山神社は1871年（明治4）の明治政府による太政官布告によって国幣中社に列せられた。

　しかしながら、1873年（明治6）2月、二荒山神社は国幣中社から県社に降格となった。二荒山神社が延喜式神名帳に記された神社である確証がないというのがその理由であった。幸い、かつて、宇都宮藩の家老であった縣六石（1823-1881）らによる社格回復運動の努力が実り二荒山神社は1883年（明治16）に国幣中社の栄誉を回復することができた。

招魂社とおよりの鐘

　二荒山神社が最初に祀られた荒尾崎の地は、838年（承和5）に神社が現在の臼が峰に遷座すると下之宮と呼ばれた。

　1872年（明治5）11月、下之宮の小高い丘の上に招魂社が建て

Lowered in Rank to a Prefectural Shrine?

The Futa'arayama Shrine is a very old shrine. Its name is found in the old governmental regulations *Engi Shiki Jinmyocho* issued in the early 10th century, which says "There is a great shrine called Futa'arayama Shrine in the province of Shimotsuke."

In 1871, the shrine was listed among kokuhei-chusha by Dajokan Fukoku.

In February, 1873, however, the Futa'arayama Shrine was lowered in rank from kokuhei-chusha to a prefectural shrine for the reason that there was no evidence to prove that the shrine was really the shrine listed in *Engi Shiki Jinmyocho*. Fortunately, thanks to the efforts of Agata Rikuseki (1823-1881), former chief retainer of Utsunomiya Domain, Futa'arayama Shrine regained the honor of its former status as kokuhei-chusha in 1883.

Shokonsha and Oyori-no-kane

Araosaki where the Futa'arayama Shrine once was until 838 came to be called Shimo-no-miya after the shrine was transfered to Usugamine.

In November, 1872, a small shrine named Shokonsha was built by Toda Tadatomo (1847-1924), the last lord of

られた。宇都宮城最後の藩主戸田忠友 (1847-1924) が、戊辰戦争 (1868-9) で戦死した旧藩主戸田忠恕(ただゆき) (1847-1868) と藩兵 96 名の霊を祀るためであった。

招魂社には「およりの鐘」があった。この鐘はかつては東勝寺（廃寺）にあったもので、宇都宮第八代当主宇都宮貞綱 (1265-1316) が奉納した鐘といわれ、宇都宮氏の「三ツ巴(みつどもえ)」の家紋がほどこされている。この鐘は、昭和の初期まで時を告げ続けていた。太平洋戦争中、金属回収令により供出の危機に見舞われたが、由緒ある梵鐘であったため供出を免れた。

その後、招魂社は 1939 年（昭和14）4 月、現在の宇都宮市陽西町に移され栃木県護国神社と改称され、「およりの鐘」は宇都宮駅近くの宝蔵寺に移された。そして、招魂社のあった高台はいつの間にか姿を消してしまった。

「およりの鐘」のある宝蔵寺鐘楼
Bell Tower of Hozo-ji Temple

Utsunomiya Castle, on the low hill of Shimo-no-miya. It was for the repose of the souls of the former lord Toda Tadayuki (1847-1868) and 96 warriors who died in the Boshin Civil War (1868-9).

In Shokonsha, there was a bell named Oyori-no-kane which once belonged to the Toshoji Temple (now, extinct). The bell was dedicated to the temple by Utsunomiya Sadatsuna (1265-1316), the 8th lord of Utsunomiya Family, and it bears the crest of 'Mitsu-domoe' of Utsunomiya Family. The bell told the time to people until the beginning of Showa period (1925-1940). During World War II, the bell was almost taken away in response to the Metal Recovery Act, but it was not taken away because it was a bell which has a long history.

Shokonsha was transferred to Yosai-machi in western Utsunomiya in April, 1939, and changed its name to Go-koku-jinja Shrine. Oyori-no-kane was taken to the Hozo-ji Temple near JR Utsunomiya Station. And the low hill where Shokonsha once stood cannot be seen any more.

三ツ巴の家紋　Utsunomiya Family Crest

木幡神社
Kibata Shrine
矢板市木幡

矢板市木幡にある木幡神社は、延暦年間 (782-805) に征夷大将軍坂上田村麻呂 (758-811) が山城国 (現、京都府南部) 宇治郡の許波多神社を勧請して建てられた神社であると言われる。坂上田村麻呂は、791年 (延暦10) 蝦夷の反乱を抑えるよう命じられ、出発に先立ち、宇治の許波多神社に参詣して戦勝を祈願し、蝦夷をうまく征伐できた暁には神社を一社建立することを誓った。田村麻呂一行は下野国塩谷郡峯村 (現在、木幡神社が建つ地) まで軍を進めて宿陣、更に、軍を進め、4年の年月をかけてやっと蝦夷を服従させた。田村麻呂は戦勝の帰路、再び、この地に立ち寄り約束通り神社を建立した。これが木幡神社である。

時代は下って、940年 (天慶3) 藤原秀郷 (？ - ？) (別名、俵藤太) は「平将門の乱」に際し木幡神社に戦勝を祈願している。また、1051年 (永承6) には、源頼義 (988-1075)、義家 (1039-1106) 父子が安倍貞任を追討するに当り (「前九年の役」)、

The Kibata Shrine at Kibata, Yaita City, was founded during the Enryaku period (782-805) by a Barbarian-subduing Generalissimo, Sakanoueno Tamura-maro (758-811). When he was ordered to subdue Ezo* in 791, Tamura-maro visited the Kohata Shrine in the province of Yamashiro (now, part of Kyoto) and prayed for the victory in the coming battle with Ezo and pledged that he would build a shrine when he could successfully subdue Ezo. Tamura-maro and his men came all the way to Mine village in the province of Shimotsuke and from there they farther advanced to the north and successfully subdued the Ezo people. On his way back, he visited Mine village again and built a shrine there as he had pledged. He prayed for the transfer of the spirit of the Kohata Shrine in Yamashiro to the new shrine. The new shrine is the Kibata Shrine that we see today.

*Ezo: the aboriginal inhabitants of northern Japan

Years later, in 940, Fujiwara-no-Hidesato (?-?) visited the Kibata Shrine to pray for the victory in the coming battle with Taira-no-Masakado. In 1051, Minamoto-no-Yoriyoshi (988-1075) and his son Yoshiie (1039-1106) also visited here. They spent a week to pu-

この地で一週間の散齋致齋*をして戦勝を祈願したと言われる。

*散齋致齋：酒や肉食を謹んで心身を清めること

　木幡神社の本殿と楼門は国の重要文化財に指定されている。また、境内には、日光東照宮から移された「南蛮鉄灯籠」（松平土佐守忠義寄進）がある。

rify themselves by abstaining from alcohol and refraining from eating meat and prayed for the victory.

　Honden (the main building) and Romon (the two-storied gate) of this shrine have been designated as National Important Cultural Property. In the precincts of this shrine, there is a lantern called "Nanban-tetsu-toro" (a lantern made of iron imported from a western country) which was moved from the Nikko Toshogu Shrine.

木幡神社　Kibata Shrine

伝説:ふり面てり面

　木幡神社には「赤鶴面」と呼ばれる赤い天狗の面がある。この面は「ふり面」とも言われる。言い伝えによると、この面は坂上田村麻呂が赤松の木を使って彫り、そこに討ち取った蝦夷の首領であった大多鬼丸の血を塗り固めて仕上げたものという。人間の顔より二回りも大きい形相のすさまじい面である。この面には雨を降らす不思議な力があると信じられていて、旱魃で困った時、村人たちがこの面を神社近くの内川の水に浸すと、西の山に急に雲が現れ、雨が降りだしたとの言い伝えがある。

　しかし、雨が降り続いて田畑が水に浸り困ることがあったので、いつの頃からか、「てり面」が作られたという。

Legend: Furi-men and Teri-men

The Kibata Shrine treasures a red mask of Tengu* (Akatsuru-men) which is popularly called Furi-men (a mask that brings rain). A legend says that the mask was carved by Sakanoueno Tamuramaro. He carved the mask on a Japanese red pine tree, and plastered it with the blood of Otaki-maru, leader of the Ezo tribes, whom he captured and slain. The mask is twice as large as a real human face and has a terribly furious look. It is popularly believed that the mask has a strange power of bringing rain. When villagers suffered from a long spell of dry weather, they would soak the mask in River Uchikawa nearby. This caused dark clouds to rise in the western sky and bring rain. Once the rain continued to fall for a long time and caused flood, and people had to make another mask Teri-men (a mask that brings fine weather).

＊ tengu: half-man, half-bird creature with a long nose of Japanese folklore

羽黒山神社
Haguro-san Shrine
宇都宮市今里町

羽黒山は、宇都宮市北部の今里町にある標高458mの山で、以前は、河内山とも呼ばれていた。栃木百名山の1つに選ばれている。この山の周辺は比較的平坦な土地であるため、そのお椀を伏せたような美しい姿は東北本線を走る列車や東北自動車道を行く車の車窓から容易に望まれる。

Mt. Haguro (458 meters high) is located in Imazato in the northern part of Utsunomiya City. The mountain was once called by another name Mt. Kawachi. It is among the 100 Famous Mountains in Tochigi Prefecture. It has a beautiful shape of an upside-down wooden bowl and can be seen from the trains running on the Tohoku Line and from car windows running along Tohoku Expressway.

羽黒山の梵天祭り　the Brahma Festival of Mt. Haguro

山頂に至る登山道はよく整備されており、十国が一望に眺められることから名付けられたという十国平からは360度の景観を楽しむことができ、よく晴れた日には富士山や東京スカイツリーが見えるという。羽黒山は「蝋梅の里」とも言われ、早春にはあたり一面がうすい黄色味をおびた蝋梅の花で埋めつくされる。

山頂には羽黒山神社が祀られている。神社の主祭神は宇迦之魂大神という農耕を司る神様である。羽黒山神社の創建は康平年間（1058－1064）とされ、宇都宮氏初代当主藤原宗円が活躍していた時代である。羽黒山神社の創建は宗円の宇都宮城築城となんらかの関連があると考えられている。

近世になると、羽黒山神社は宇都宮城主奥平氏の崇敬を受けている。そして、江戸時代の慶安年間（1648-1652）には、奥平光重が出羽の国から宇都宮に移封になった折、出羽の羽黒山の分霊をこの羽黒山神社に合祀している。

1830年（文政13）に建てられた神社本殿の基壇部には「力持ち」が彫り込まれている。境内には、かつての、神仏習合の名残りが見られ1702年（元禄14）に建てられた鐘楼堂や石仏が見られる。

The road to the top of the mountain is in good condition and you can enjoy a 360-degree panoramic view at Jikkoku-daira Flat Land. The flat land is so called because you can command a view of 'Jikkoku' (10 provinces). On a fine day, you can see Mt. Fuji and Tokyo Sky-tree from the flat land. Mt. Haguro is sometimes called "the Village of Robai (Winter Sweet)." The mountain is covered with buff yellow flowers of 'robai' in early spring.

On the top of the mountain is Haguro-san Shrine. It is dedicated to Uga-no-Mitamano-mikoto, the god of agriculture. The origin of this shrine goes back to the Kohei period (1058-1064), when Fujiwara Soen, the first lord of Utsunomiya Castle, was playing an active role. It is generally believed that the founding of Haguro-san Shrine is somehow related with the building of Utsunomiya Castle by Soen.

During the Early Modern period, the Haguro-san Shrine enjoyed the deep respect of the Okudairas, lord of Utsunomiya Castle. And, when Okudaira Mitsushige was transferred from Dewa to Utsunomiya during the Keian period (1648-1652), he prayed for the transfer of the spirit of the Haguro-san Shrine in the province of Dewa to the Haguro-san Shrine.

At the base of Honden (Main Shrine) building built in 1830, there are carvings of 'Chikara-mochi' (figures of men with great strength). There are some

梵天祭り

　毎年、11月23日、24日の2日間羽黒山神社で「梵天祭り」が催される。この祭りは今からおよそ300年前の江戸時代の中頃に始められた伝統ある祭りである。

　秋の収穫を祝い感謝をこめて、神社に「梵天」を奉納する祭りである。「梵天」とは、長さ15m以上もある孟宗竹の先端に幣束を結んだ長い竿のことである。揃いの半てんをまとい、鉢巻き、白足袋姿の若衆が羽黒山神社までの約3kmを、「ホイサ、ホイサ」の掛け声勇ましく「梵天」を空高く投げ上げる動作をくり返しながらかつぎあげて神社に奉納する姿は壮観である。

伝説:ダイダラボウ

　羽黒山には「ダイダラボウ」という雲をつくような大男の伝説が伝えられている。ダイダラボウの伝説は日本各地にあり、古くは、「常陸国風土記」「播磨国風土記」などにも記載が見える。地方により伝説の内容は様々であるが、大男が大量の土を

---

vestiges of the mixture of Shintoism and Buddhism in the precincts like Shorodo built in 1702 and stone Buddhist images.

Bonten Festival

　The Bonten Festival is held on Nov. 23 and 24 every year to thank the deity of the Haguro-san Shrine for good harvest. This famous festival has a long history. It originated about 300 years ago during the mid-Edo period.

　In the festival, people carry up several bamboo poles (Bonten) of about 15m long which are attached at the top with paper streamers called heisoku. Young people wearing hanten* and white socks, with towels around their heads, carry up the poles to the Haguro-san Shrine, frequently lifting the poles high up, shouting "Hoisa, hoisa" all the way. The poles are carried about 3km to the shrine and are dedicated there. This festival is very spectacular.

* a kind of short coat worn at festivals with the name of the shrine on the back and lapels

Legend: Daidarabo

　Related with Mt. Haguro is a legend about a giant named Daidarabo. The legend of Daidarabo is found in many places of Japan and its name is found in *Hitachi Fudoki* and *Harima Fudoki*. There are some variations about its story, but there are a lot in common about its great scales. For example, Daidarabo brought a lot of soil on a rope basket

モッコで運んできて山を造ったり、大男が歩いた足跡や手をついた跡が沼になった、といったスケールの大きい話は共通している。

ここ羽黒山のダイダラボウの伝説は次のようなものである。昔、出羽国の羽黒山にダイダラボウという大男が住んでいた。ある日、ダイダラボウは羽黒山の土をモッコに乗せて歩き出し、下野国河内郡にやってきた。下野国に着いたとき、ダイダラボウは一休みしようとモッコを降ろし、ひどく喉が乾いていたので鬼怒川の水を飲んだところ川の水がまたたく間に干上がってしまった。大男は、休憩した後、モッコをそのまま置き忘れて行ってしまった。この土が現在の羽黒山で、大男が肘をついたところが現在の「肘内」という地名、足跡が残って沼となったのが「芦沼」になったと言う。

and created a mountain; the prints he made with his hands and feet later became marshes.

The story of Daidarabo in Mt. Haguro is as follows. There once was a giant called Daidarabo. He lived on Mt. Haguro in the province of Dewa. One day the giant left the mountain with the soil of the mountain on a rope basket and came to Kawachi in the province of Shimotsuke. He placed the basket on the ground and took a rest there. He was so thirsty that he started drinking the water of the Kinu River, and soon dried it up. He went away leaving the basket there. The soil he placed is now Mt. Haguro. The place where he made a print with his hiji (an elbow) is now called Hijiuchi. And the footprint he made later became a numa (a marsh) named Ashinuma.

ダイダラボウの石　Daidarabo Rock

古峰神社
Furumine Shrine

鹿沼市草久(くさぎゅう)

　古峰神社の御祭神は日本武尊(やまとたけるのみこと)である。この神社の奥社と呼ばれる深山巴ノ宿(じんぜんともえのしゅく)は日光開山の祖勝道上人が修行をした所と言われる。

　神社内には御祭神の使者である天狗の大きな面が二つある。一つは

The Furumine Shrine is dedicated to Prince Yamatotakeru. It is said that the Inner Shrine of this shrine, Jinzentomoe no shuku is where Priest Shodo, founder of Nikko mountains, once practiced asceticism.

　The shrine treasures two huge masks

勝道上人像　Statue of Shodo Shonin

「大天狗」の面で顔の長さ176cm、重さ134kg、鼻の高さが91cmある。もう一つは「烏天狗」の面で、顔の長さ158cm、重さが156kg、鼻の高さが91cmある。

山伏の碁

古峯神社には、次のような話が伝わっている。

ある時、古峰神社にお参りに来た人たちが夕食の後のつれづれに身の上話や故郷の話をはじめた。その中の一人が「自分は碁が大好きで、碁打ち仲間では本因坊と言われ、あまりに強いので碁の相手をしてくれる人がいないのです。誰か一局お手合わせ下さい。」と言って、周りを見回した。本因坊と言われては誰も名乗り出る人はいない。

その時、突然、部屋の隅で一部始終をだまって聞いていた山伏が「わしが相手になって進ぜよう。」と突然名乗り出た。山伏は一人の小僧をそばに呼びよせて何かを耳打ちした。やがて、小僧は碁盤と碁石の入った2つの碁笥（容器）を持って入ってきた。

「さあ、打つぞ。」と言うなり、山

of 'tengu' (a half-man and half-bird creature in Japanese folklore with long nose and wings), messenger of the prince. One mask is called O-tengu, and the other is called Karasu-tengu. The O-tengu mask is 176cm in length and weighs 134kg. Its nose is 91cm long. The mask of Karasu-tengu is 158cm in length and weighs 156kg. It has a nose of 91cm in length.

Game of 'Go' by a yamabushi

The following story is told about the Furumine Shrine.

People who were staying at Furumine Shrine gathered one evening in a room after supper and began to talk about themselves and about their native places. One of the visitors began to talk about himself, " I am very fond of the game of Go. I am so good at the game that my fellow Go-players call me hon'inbo (the grand master of Go) and nobody won't play with me. Will anyone of you play a game with me?" So saying, he looked around. But, nobody dared to play with the hon'inbo.

Then, suddenly, a yamabushi (a Buddhist priest practicing asceticism in the mountains), who had been in the corner of the room listening silently to what was going on , suddenly said, "I will play with you." The yamabushi called a boy to him and whispered something to him. After a while the boy brought in a wooden Go board and two bowls of Go stones.

伏はいきなり白石を天元（盤の中央）に打った。碁を打つ場合には黒石を持った者が先に打つものであるが、山伏はそんなことにはお構いなしに白石を先に打ったのである。本因坊は、この山伏は何も碁のことを知らないなと思いながら、自分の碁石入れを開けて見てびっくりした。中には山伏と同じく白石が入っていたのである。「白どうしでは碁は打てません。」と本因坊がいうと、山伏は「いや、いっこうに構わぬ。早く打て。」とせき立てる。その時、本因坊は、ふと、顔を上げて驚いた。山伏の目はらんらんと輝き、本因坊を睨みつける顔はまるで天狗のようだった。そのするどい目つきにうろたえていると、山伏は「白石と黒石がなければ碁が打てないとは笑止千万。勝負ごとはすべて心で争うもの。道具や小手先で争うのは素人のすること。貴殿は、まだまだ、修行が足りない。」と言った。それを聞いて本因坊はこそこそと部屋を出ていってしまった。

Now, let's play." So saying, the yamabushi placed a white stone on the center point of the board. It is a rule of Go that the player who has black stones is the first to play. The yamabushi ignored the rule and placed a white stone first. The hon'inbo, thinking that the yamabushi knew nothing about the game of Go, opened the lid of his bowl and was astonished because his stones were also white. He said to the yamabushi, "We cannot play Go if we both have white stones." The yamabushi urged, "It does not matter at all. Place your stone." The hon'inbo was at a loss. Then, he looked up and saw that the eyes of the yamabushi were glaring at him. It was a face of a tengu. While the hon'inbo sat stunned at the glaring eyes, the yamabushi added: "How absurd it is to think that you cannot play Go if you don't have white and black stones. Any kind of game should be played with heart. It is nonsense if you try to win a game with tools or techniques. You still lack self-training." The hon'inbo sneaked out of the room.

古峰神社前の天狗面
Mask of Tengu in front of Furumine Shrine

時代でつづる栃木の仏教
Buddhism in Tochigi

栃木県内の寺院数は、1980年に出版された「栃木県大百科事典」によると976で、この数を平成26年版の文化庁編「宗教年鑑」の991と比べてみると、過去約30年間に15増加している

なお、1868年の「神仏判然令」に伴って県内で廃寺となった寺院は344であったという。

栃木県内の寺院を「栃木県大百科事典」に拠って宗派別にみてみると、次のようである。

天台宗	130
真言宗	379
浄土宗	85
曹洞宗	195
臨済宗	51
時宗	37
浄土真宗	54
日蓮宗	44
その他	1

以下、県内の仏教の流れを時代をおってみてみる。

奈良時代

奈良時代において、まず挙げねばならないのは下野薬師寺の存在

According to Tochigi-ken Dai-Hyakka Jiten (Encyclopedia of Tochigi Prefecture) published in 1980, there were 976 temples in Tochigi Prefecture. Compared with 991 temples given in Shukyo Nenkan (Religious Yearbook) published in 2014, there was an increase of 15 temples in the past 30 years.

Incidentally, 344 temples were abolished after the Law of Separating Shintoism and Buddhism was enforced in 1868.

The number of temples classified by sects are as follows:

Tendai Sect	130
Shingon Sect	379
Jodo Sect	85
Soto Sect	195
Rinzai Sect	51
Ji Sect	37
Jodo Shin Sect	54
Nichiren Sect	44
Others	1

A brief history of Buddhism in Tochigi Prefecture will be given below.

Nara Period

The temple that deserves to be mentioned first is the Shimotsuke Yakushi-ji Temple. It is believed that this temple

がある。下野薬師寺は7世紀末に下毛野古麻呂（?-709）によって建てられたと考えられている寺で、奈良の東大寺、太宰府の観世音寺と並んで戒壇＊の設置を許された全国で三つの寺院の一つであった。

＊戒壇：僧や尼に戒律を授けるための壇

下野薬師寺は、その後、1338年（暦応元）に足利尊氏（1305-1358）が夢窓疎石（1275-1351）の勧めによって全国六十余州に安国寺を設けた際に、安国寺と改称している。

安国寺の少し南方には、安国寺の別院とされる龍興寺がある。ここには弓削道鏡（?-772）の墓と伝えられる道鏡塚がある。道鏡は称徳天皇（718-770）の信頼を受け、太政大臣禅師、ついで、法王にまで登りつめ、ついには皇位につくことを企てた僧であるが、称徳天皇の崩御後、下野国薬師寺別当に左遷された。

平安時代

平安時代に入ると、慈覚大師円仁（794-864）が活躍した。円仁は若い時、県南の岩舟町にある大慈寺で修行をした。伝教大師最澄（766-822）を師と仰ぎ、全国に天台宗の寺院を凡そ700寺建立した。

was founded by Shimotsuke no Komaro (?-709) toward the end of the 7th Century. It was one of the 3 temples in all Japan that were allowed to have an Ordination Hall＊. The other two temples were the Todai-ji Temple in Nara and the Kanzeon-ji Temple in Dazaifu, Kyushu.

＊Ordination Hall: A platform erected for giving Buddhist commandments to priests

The Shimotsuke Yakushi-ji Temple was renamed Ankoku-ji Temple in 1338 when Ashikaga Takauji (1305-1358) followed the recommendation by a priest Muso Soseki (1275-1351) and ordered that temples named Ankoku-ji should be built in each province throughout Japan.

In the south of the Ankoku-ji Temple is its branch temple called Ryuko-ji Temple. In the grounds of this temple, there is a small mound called Dokyo Tumulus, which is said to be the grave of Yuge no Dokyo (?-772). Dokyo was a priest who was trusted by Empress Shotoku (718-770). He became Prime Minister Zen Monk, and then Pope. And at last he attempted to ascend to the Imperial Throne. However, he was relegated to a steward of Shimotsuke Yakushi-ji Temple after the Empress died,

Heian Period

Ennin (794-864), known as Jikaku Daishi, played an active part in the Buddhist world during the Heian Period. When Ennin was young, he practiced

円仁より少し前には、勝道上人
(735-817) が下野国の南高岡 (現、
真岡市) に生を受けている。現在、
高岡には勝道上人の開創になる
仏生寺がある。

勝道上人は山岳崇拝の先駆的な
修行者で、おのれの道を求めて幾多
の辛苦を乗り越え782年 (天応2)
日光二荒山 (男体山) の登頂に成功
した。

784年には、勝道上人は中禅寺
湖東岸の歌ケ浜に立木観音を刻み
中禅寺 (天台宗) を開基している。

栃木市出流町にある満願寺も
765年に勝道上人が開いた寺であ
る。修験道の行者たちは本堂の右
手の大悲の滝で37日間滝に打た
れ結願のあと日光山に入ったと伝え
られている。

栃木県内には平安時代に、
法相宗から真言宗に改宗した古刹
がいくつかある。矢板市の観音寺、
益子町の西明寺、そして、足利市の
鶏足寺などである。

宇都宮市大谷にある大谷寺境内
の洞穴壁面には千手観音、釈迦三
尊などの諸像が造像されていて、こ
れらの磨崖仏は、国指定特別史跡
と重要文化財の二重の指定を受け
ている。

洞穴の奥壁近くからは側臥屈葬位

asceticism at the Daiji-ji Temple in
Iwafune in the southern part of Tochigi Prefecture. He looked up to Saicho
(766-817), known as Dengyo Daishi, as
his mentor, and built about 700 temples
of the Tendai Sect across the country.

A little before Ennin, Saint Shodo was
born in Takaoka (now, part of Moka
City) in the province of Shimotsuke. At
present, in Takaoka, there is a temple
named Bussho-ji which was founded by
Saint Shodo.

He was a pioneer ascetic of mountain worship. In order to attain spiritual
salvation, he went through many hard-
ships and finally succeeded in reaching
the summit of Mt. Nikko (Mt. Nantai)
in 782.

In 784, Saint Shodo carved a statue
of Kannon and established a temple
named Chuzen-ji. The temple belongs
to the Tendai Sect of Buddhism.

The Mangan-ji Temple in Izuru,
Tochigi City, was also founded by Saint
Shodo in 765. It is said that the ascetics
of Shugendo (Japanese mountain ascen-
ticism) stood under the falling water of
the Daihi Falls on the right side of the
temple for 37 days until the expiration
of the term of vow. After this, they went
up to Mt. Nikko.

During Heian Period, some old temples in Tochigi Prefecture converted
from Hosso Sect of Buddhism to Shingon Sect. The Kannon-ji Temple in
Yaita City, Saimyo-ji Temple in Mashiko Town, and Keisoku-ji Temple in

大谷寺　Oya-ji Temple

の人骨が出土しており、約9千年前の男性のものと推定されている。

鎌倉・室町時代

　鎌倉・室町時代に入ると、栃木県内に禅宗系と浄土宗系の寺院が多く創建された。

　鎌倉時代の禅宗建築の特徴をよく伝える寺院に足利市の鑁阿寺（真言宗）がある。鑁阿寺は、1196年（建久7）に足利義兼が邸内に持仏堂を建てたのが始まりとされ、本堂が2013年（平成25）に国宝の指定を受けている。鐘楼と経堂は重要文化財。

　浄土宗では、宇都宮市大通りの清巌寺や益子町大沢の円通寺がある。清巌寺は1215年（建保3）宇都宮頼綱（蓮生）の開基になる古刹

Ashikaga City are among them.

　In the precincts of Oya-ji Temple in Oya, Utsunomiya City, figures of thousand-armed Kannon, Shaka Sanzon, etc. are carved on a rock face in the cave. They are designated both as a special historic site and as an important cultural property.

　Human bones were found near the inner wall in the cave. The body was buried with its body bent and lying on its side. It is presumed that they are of a male about 9000 years ago.

Kamakura and Muromachi Periods

　During the Kamakura and Muromachi periods, many temples of Zen and Jodo Sects of Buddhism were established.

　The Banna-ji Temple in Ashikaga City (Shingon sect) well preserves a traditional Zen-style architecture of the Kamakura period. The origin of this temple goes back to the year 1196 when Ashikaga Yoshikane (1154-1199) built a small hall where he kept his private Buddha statue. The Main Building of the temple was designated as national treasure in 2013, and Shoro (bell tower) and Kyodo (hall where holy scriptures are kept) were designated as national important cultural property.

　The Seigan-ji Temple in Utsunomiya and the Entsu-ji Temple in Mashiko belong to the Jodo Sect. The Seigan-ji Temple is an old temple built by Ut-

で、円通寺は1402年（応永9）良栄（1347-1428）による開基である。円通寺はかつては508寺を有する浄土宗名越派本山で、武家の藩校などとは一線を画した学問所・図書館、大沢文庫があった。

県内の浄土真宗の寺院の中で、特筆すべきは、親鸞（1173-1262）が1225年（嘉禄元）自ら開基となった唯一の寺である専修寺（真岡市高田）である。

専修寺は関東における初期浄土真宗教団活動の中心地であった。御影堂、如来堂、楼門、総門は国の重要文化財に指定されている。

これらの他に、浄土宗の流れを汲む時宗の寺院として宇都宮市の一向寺がある。遊行上人、捨聖と呼ばれた一遍（1239-1289）が確立した寺院で、1276年（建治2）、宇都宮景綱による開基である。国家非常時に汗をかくといわれる「汗かき阿弥陀」は国の重要文化財に指定されている。

この時期に創建された禅宗系の寺院として、大田原市雲巌寺の雲巌寺（臨済宗、1283年、仏国国師による開山）、宇都宮市今泉の興禅寺（臨済宗、1314年、宇都宮貞綱による開基）、そして、大田原市黒羽町の大雄寺（曹洞宗、

sunomiya Yoritsuna (Rensho) in 1215, and the Entu-ji Temple was built by Ryoei (1347-1428) in 1402. The Entsu-ji temple used to be the head temple of the Nagoe School of Jodo Sect and once had 508 branch temples. Unlike 'han' schools owned by samurai families, this temple had a library named Osawa Library.

Of all the temples of Jodo Shin Sect, particular mention must be made here of the Senju-ji Temple in Moka City. It is the one and only temple that was established by Shinran (1173-1262) himself in 1225.

The Senju-ji Temple played a central role in the initial stage of mission work of Jodo Shin Sect in Kanto Region. Mieido, Nyoraido, Romon Gate, and Somon Gate are all designated as national important cultural properties.

The Ikko-ji Temple in Utsunomiya City belongs to Ji-shu School of the Jodo Sect. It was established by Ippen (1239-1289), an itinerant priest, who is popularly called Sutehijiri. Utsunomiya Kagetsuna founded it in 1276. In this temple, there is a statue called 'Aseka-ki Amida' (the statue of Amitabha that sweats) . It is believed that this statue begins to sweat at the time of national emergency. It is designated as an national important cultural property.

The temples of Zen Sects line, established at this time of period are Ungan-ji Temple in Ungan-ji, Otawara City (Rinzai Sect, founded by Bukkoku

1404年、大関増次による開基）がある。雲巌寺を開山した仏国国師の「国師」とは朝廷から高僧に贈られた称号である。雲巌寺は禅宗の寺院の中で、聖福寺（福岡県）、永平寺（福井県）、興国寺（和歌山県）とともに禅の四大道場となっている。

宇都宮市今泉にある臨済宗妙心寺派の寺院興禅寺は、1314年（正和3）宇都宮貞綱（弘安の役の現地の最高司令官）による開基である。日本三大仇討ちの一つ「赤穂四十七士の仇討ち」に影響を与えた「浄瑠璃坂の仇討ち」の発端となった寺院でもある。

黒羽町（現、大田原市黒羽）にある曹洞宗の大雄寺は黒羽城主、大関家の菩提寺である。本堂、庫裡、御霊屋、座禅堂など室町時代の伽藍配置をよく示している。

Kokushi in 1283), Kozen-ji Temple in Imaizumi, Utsunomiya City (Rinzai Sect, founded by Utsunomiya Sadatsuna in 1314), and Daio-ji Temple in Kurobane, Otawara City (Soto Sect, founded by Ozeki Masutsugu in 1404). "Kokushi" in Bukkoku Kokushi, who established Ungan-ji Temple is a title for a high priest given by the Imperial Court. Ungan-ji Temple was one of the four largest training halls (Dojo) among all the temples of Zen Sect over the country. The other three were Shofuku-ji Temple in Fukuoka Prefecture, Eihei-ji Temple in Fukui Prefecture, and Kokoku-ji Temple in Wakayama Prefecture.

The Kozen-ji Temple in Imaizumi, Utsunomiya City, is a temple of Myoshin School of Rinzai Sect. It was founded by Utsunomiya Sadatsuna, the front-line supreme commander at the Koan War (the second Mongol invasion) in 1281. "The Joruri-zaka Revenge Incident" which was triggered by a happening in this temple worked as a model for "the Ako Forty-Seven Ronin (masterless samurai) Incident," one of the three major revenge incidents in Japan.

Daio-ji Temple of Soto Sect in Kurobane Town (presently Kurobane, Otawara City) is a family temple of Ozeki Family, the lord of Kurobane Castle. Its main hall, monk's living quarters, mausoleum, Zen meditation hall, and so forth show the typical arrangement of the temple buildings of Muromachi Period.

大雄寺 Daio-ji Temple

下野薬師寺跡
the Site of Shimotsuke Yakushi-ji Temple
下野市薬師寺

下野薬師寺跡　Site of Shimotsuke Yakushiji Temple

　下野薬師寺は、かつては、現在の地名「下野市薬師寺」一帯にまたがる広大な地域を占めた大寺院であった。その寺跡は1921年（大正10）に国史跡の指定を受けた。

　1966年（昭和41）から栃木県教育委員会が発掘調査を行い、東西約250m、南北約350mの壮大な伽藍を持つ寺院であったことが確認された。

　県教委の調査の後、南河内町（現、下野市）が発掘調査を行い、金堂跡、講堂跡、中門跡、西回廊跡等

　The Shimotsuke Yakushi-ji Temple used to cover a large area in the present Yakushi-ji, Shimotsuke City. The temple site was designated as a National historic Site in 1921.

　Tochigi Prefectural Board of Education conducted the excavation and research starting in 1966 and it was validated that it had a large temple hall 250 m from east to west and 350 m from north to south.

　After that, another excavation and research was done by Minamikawachi Town (now, Shimotsuke City), remains of Kondo (main hall), Kodo (lecture hall), Chumon Gate (inner gate), and West Corridor were found, and the unearthed roofing tiles made it possible to presume when the temple was founded and how the temple building were laid out.

　The Shimotsuke Yakushi-ji Temple was founded at the end of 7th century, and it is estimated that it was renovated as a Kanji (state sponsored temple) in the early 8th century. Along with the Horyu-ji Temple and the Shiten'no-ji Temple, it was permitted to own 500 hectares of new rice field owing to "Konden Einen Shizai Ho" (the law permitting permanent ownership of newly

が確認され、多量に出土した瓦など
から創建年代や伽藍配置等が推定
できるようになった。

　下野薬師寺が創建されたのは7
世紀末で、8世紀前半に官寺とし
て改修されたと推定される。743年
（天平17）の「墾田永年私財法」
によって、下野薬師寺は法隆寺、四
天王寺などと並んで500町の墾田
所有が許されている。これは同寺が
中央の大寺と同格に扱われた証左
である。

　聖武天皇(701-756)の時代には、
下野薬師寺は、東大寺、観世音寺
と並んで日本三戒壇の一つとして、
東国における仏教文化の中心にあ
り、東山道の碓氷峠以東、東海道
の足柄峠以東の授戒を受け持つ大
寺院であった。戒律を受けることは、
僧侶と俗人とを区別し、寺院と世俗
社会とを区画する印でもあり、古代
社会にあっては極めて重視された
儀式であった。この重要事が下野薬
師寺で行われ、東国の僧侶が必ず
訪れる寺院であったのである。現在、
下野市の安国寺の六角堂が建つあ
たりにかつての戒壇があったと考え
られている。

　下野薬師寺がなぜこの地に造営さ
れたのかについては、下毛野古麻呂
という人物が大きく関わっていたと

cultivated land) in 743. This proves that
the Shimotsuke Yakushi-ji Temple was
regarded as equivalent as the other central large temples.

　During the reign of Emperor Shomu
(701-756), the Shimotsuke Yakushi-
ji Temple was the main temple for the
Buddhist culture in the eastern part of
Japan as one of the 3 temples that were
permitted to establish an Ordination
Hall, along with the Todai-ji Temple
in Nara and the Kanzeon-ji Temple in
Dazaifu. It was a large temple which
is responsible for the ordination in the
east of Usui-toge Pass in the Tosando
Region as well as in the east of Ashigara-
toge Pass in Tokaido Region. Receiving
the commandments of Buddhism clearly separates priests from secular persons
and at the same time it is a sign to divide
temples from secular world, being an ex-
tremely important event in the ancient
society. This important event was held
at the Shimotsuke Yakushi-ji Temple
where every priest in the eastern part of
Japan visited. At present, it is believed
that the ordination platform used to be
where the Rokkaku-do (hexagonal hall)
stands at the Ankoku-ji Temple in Shimotsuke City.

　It is surmised that Shimotsike no Komaro was very much involved with why
the Shimotsuke Yakushi-ji Temple was
founded there. Shimotsuke no Komaro
was born in the Shimotsuke clan. He
played an active role in the central political world being involved in the estab-

考えられる。下毛野古麻呂は下毛野氏を出自とし、中央政界で活躍し、大宝律令の制定にかかわり、兵部卿等に就いた人である。一族の中に下毛野朝臣岩代という人物がおり、古麻呂の影響で、下毛野川内朝臣岩代に改名している。「川内」は「河内」であると想定され、薬師寺を建立する場所を決めるにあたって、下毛野氏が本拠地とする河内郡に定めたものと思われる。

9世紀には、「あたかも七大寺*のごとく資材また巨多なり」（「続日本後紀」）と記されたこの下野薬師寺は、10世紀以降、衰退の一途をたどり、11世紀末には全盛期の勢いを維持することができなかった。1092年（寛治6）には、下野薬師寺から東大寺別当に対し、寺の荒廃の様子を述べ、復興についての援助を求める書状が出されている。

＊七大寺とは、奈良の東大寺、興福寺、元興寺、大安寺、薬師寺、西大寺、法隆寺の総称。

鎌倉時代に入ってからは、幕府の手厚い保護を受け、一時、下野薬師寺は復興する。中興の祖として名前が残っているのが慈猛上人で、上人はこの寺を拠点に真言密教の教学に努める傍ら授戒の僧を務め、地方武士をはじめ俗人にも戒を授けた

lishment of Taiho Code, and became the Hyobukyo (Minister of Military Affairs) etc. In the same clan was a person named Shimotsuke no Ason Iwashiro, who changed his name into Shimotsuke no Kawachi Ason Iwashiro due to the influence of Shimotsuke no Komaro. 川内 is assumed to be 河内, and it is believed that Kawachi District was chosen since it was the base of the Shimotsuke clan when it came to the decision of where to build the Yakushi-ji Temple.

In the 9th century, the Shimotsuke Yakushi-ji Temple was described in *Shoku Nihon Koki* (Later Chronicles of Japan Continued), "It is as if it were one of the seven great temples of Nara*, having a large indefinite number of properties." However, after the 10th century, it continued to decline and could not maintain its property toward the end of the 11th century. In 1092, a letter that describes how devastated the temple was and requests assistance for restoration was sent from the Shimotsuke Yakushi-ji Temple to the chief priest of the To-dai-ji Temple.

＊ The seven great temples of Nara are Todai-ji Temple, Kofuku-ji Temple, Ganko-ji Temple, Daian-ji Temple, Yakushi-ji Temple, Saidai-ji Temple, and Horyu-ji Temple.

During the Kamakura period, the Shimotsuke Yukushi-ji Temple was once restored, deriving considerable support from the Kamakura Bakufu. Jimyo Shonin (Saint Jimyo) is remembered as the restorer of the temple. It is

ことが記されている。

　室町時代に入り、足利尊氏の政策（「天下泰平・武運長久を祈らしむ」薬師寺縁起）により全国に安国寺を建立することとなり、下野国では、下野薬師寺を安国寺と改称したという。

　近世の下野薬師寺は、1688年に編集された「下野風土記」によると、大寺の大伽藍とはかけ離れ、わずかに本堂と戒壇堂が建つ荒廃した寺であったという。

　現在、下野薬師寺跡の保存整備事業が着々と進められており、2001年（平成13）春には「下野薬師寺歴史館」がオープンした。

recorded that Jimyo Shonin as an ordained priest gave the precepts of Buddhism to local samurai as well as laymen while he was engaged in education and learning of the Shingon Esoteric Buddhism, being based at this temple.

During the Muromachi period, according to Ashikaga Takauji's policy, "Pray for peace to reign over the country and good fortune to be brought in battles" (*Yakushi-ji Engi*) (the Origin and History of the Yakushi-ji Temple), Ankoku-ji Temples were to be built over the country and the Shimotsuke Yakushi-ji Temple was renamed the Ankoku-ji Temple.

The Shimotsuke Yakushi-ji Temple in early modern period was a desolate temple having a main and ordination platform hall only, which was completely different from the large temple with a large temple hall. (*Shimotsuke Fudoki*)

The preservation and maintenance project has been progressing steadily at the site of the Shimotsuke Yakushi-ji Temple at present and "Shimotsuke Yakushi-ji History Museum was opened in spring, 2001.

安国寺の六角堂　Rokkaku-do at the Ankoku-ji Temple

下野国分寺・国分尼寺
Shimotsuke Kokubun-ji and Kokubun-niji

下野市国分寺

　聖武天皇（在位724〜749）の勅願によって、全国に国分寺、国分尼寺が造られたのは、741年（天平13）のことである。当時の社会不安を取り除くため国家安泰を願って、全国68か国に国分寺と国分尼寺を建立したのであった。これはま

It was in 741 (Tempyo 13) that Kokubun-ji Temples and Kokubun-niji Temples were built throughout the country by the order of Emperor Shomu. In order to overcome the social unrest at the time and pray for well-being of the nation, they were founded at 68 locations over the country. It was a

下野国分尼寺跡　Site of Shimotsuke Kokubunniji

さに国家の命運をかけた一大プロジェクトであった。当時、国分寺を建てるには、災害がなく、末永く繁栄できるような「よき場所」を選ぶ必要があった。下野国分寺跡は全国の国分寺跡の史跡中でも、屈指の良保存状態で残されている。

ところで、下野国国分寺の地としてなぜ国分寺（現、下野市）が選ばれたのであろうか。その理由としては次のようなことが考えられる。一つには、この地の西方約2.5kmには下野の「国府」があったこと。2つには、東山道に近く交通の便に恵まれ、久しく安穏の地で、国華として仰ぎ見るのによい地形であったこと。3つには、この地に大型古墳が現存していることから分かるように、当時、地方豪族が支配した土地で、ある種の神聖視がなされていたこと、などである。

国分寺の正式名称は「金光明四天王護国之寺」、そして、国分尼寺は「法華滅罪之寺」という。全国の国分寺・尼寺は国の予算で運営される官営の寺で、国分寺には20人の僧、尼寺には10人の尼を置くことが決められていた。僧尼たちは、国の安全・安心のために経典を学び、修行に励み、法会を開いた。

big project to decide the nation's destiny. For building Kokubun-ji Temples in those days, such "good locations" have to be selected that there would be no natural calamities there and they would have everlasting prosperity. The site of the Shimotsuke Kokubun-ji Temple is well-preserved in the outstanding condition in comparison with the other historic remains of the Kokubun-ji Temples in the country.

Incidentally, why was the site, Kokubun-ji, chosen as the location for building the Shimotsuke Kokubun-ji Temple? The possible reasons are as follows. First, there was "Kokufu" (provincial office) 2.5 km west of the site. Second, the site was the place of easy access being close to Tosando Road as well as the place of peace for a long time having such good geographical features that it could be looked up as national pride. Third, the site was regarded as a sort of sacred place since it was once ruled by a powerful local clan as you can tell from the large tumulus still presently existing there.

The official name of the Kokubun-ji Temples is "Konkomyo shiten'no gokoku no tera" (temples for the protection of the country by the four guardian deities of the golden light) and of the Kokubun-niji Temples "Hokke metsuzai no tera" (nunneries for eliminating sin by means of the Lotus Sutra). The Kokubun-ji and Kokubun-niji Temples over the country are nationalized tem-

下野国分寺の規模は次の通り。

塔：「七重の塔」と推定。基壇 18m
四方、高さ推定 60m
金堂：基壇 東西 33.6m、 南北
21m 礎石 1.5m 四方（約 1 トン）
を 36 個使用
回廊：北面 69.6m、西面 51.9m、
梁行き幅 4.8m
南門：柱間の間隔 4.8m
南大門：基壇 東西 21m、南北 9.6m
講堂：基壇 北面 69.6m、西面
51.9m
僧坊：東西に各 5 部屋 基壇東西
74.1m、南北 16.8m
鐘楼：基壇 東西 9m、南北 12m
経蔵：基壇 鐘楼とほぼ同じ

　この史跡地一帯は、「天平が丘
公園」という四季折々の花の名所
になっており、特に春の桜（薄墨桜
をはじめ枝垂れ桜、八重桜など約
500 本の桜）が有名で、1 年間に訪
れる人は十数万人になるという。
　第 1 回「全国国分寺サミット」が
2000 年（平成 12）に東京都国分
寺市（武蔵国国分寺跡）で開かれ
た。その趣旨は全国で「国分寺を持
つ市町村が一堂に会して親善友好・
情報交換を進め、文化財の保存活
用を図る」ことである。

ples being run by the government, and
it was determined that 20 monks should
be posted to the respective Kokubun-ji
Temples and 10 nuns to Kokubun-niji
Temples. Those monks and nuns were
to study the Buddhist Scripture, devote
themselves to ascetic training for the
national safety and security, and hold
Buddhist Services.

　The size of the Shimotsuke Kokubun-
ji Temple is as follows:

Tower : Presumed to be seven storey Pagoda 60 m high, with podium, 18 m
square
Main Hall : Podium, 33.6 m from east
to west and 21 m from north to south,
withfoundation stones, 1.5 m square
(about 1ton) each
Corridor: North side, 69.6 m long, and
West side,51.9 m long, both 4.8 m wide
(crossbeam length)
South Gate:Distance between pillars,
4.8 m
Nandaimon Gtae: Podium, 21 m from
east to west and 9.6m from north to
south
Lecture Hall : Podium, 69.6 m north
side and 51.9 m west side
Sobo (priests' temple quarters): Five
rooms each at east and west side with
podium, 74.1 m from east to west and
16.8 m from north to south
Bell Tower : Podium, 9 m from east to
west and 12 m from north to south
Scripture House : Podium, the same size
as Bell Tower

続く第2回サミットは栃木県の国分寺町（現、下野市）で2001年（平成13）に開催された。以後、このサミットは引き続き開催され、2013年（平成25）には第9回サミットが津山市（美作国分寺）で、2015年（平成27）には第10回が壱岐市（長崎県）で開かれた。

下野市は、2006年（平成18）からこの国指定史跡を保存・活用していくため、国分寺跡一帯の遺構整備を進め、2014年に完成している。

This whole historic site has become a notable place of seasonal flowers, named "Tempyogaoka Park," and the cherry blossoms in spring are especially famous having Usuzumi Zakura (light-ink colored cherry blossoms), Weeping cherry trees, Double-flowered cherry trees, and so on to make about 500 cherry trees in total. It is said that hundreds of thousands of people annually visit here

The first "National Kokubun-ji Temple Summit" was held in Kokubun-ji City, Tokyo (at the site of the Musashi no kuni Kokubun-ji Temple) in 2000 (Heisei 12). Its purpose was that the cities where a Kokubun-ji Temple is built get together to promote friendly relations with one another and attempt preservation and utilization activities of the cultural properties.

The second summit was held in Kokubun-ji Town, Tochigi Prefecture (presently Shimotsuke City) in 2001. After that, the summit continued being held and in 2013, the ninth summit was held in Tsuyama City (Mimasaka Kokubun-ji Temple) and the tenth in Iki City(Nagasaki Prefecture) in 2015.

In 2006, Shimotsuke City refurbished the entire remains of the Kokubun-ji Temple in order to preserve, maintain, and make good use of this National Historic Site. It was completed in 2014.

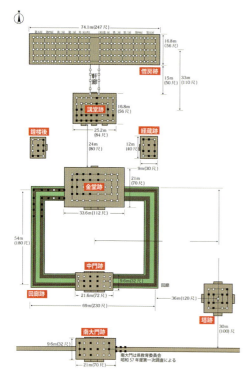

下野国分寺の伽藍配置図
Shimotsuke Kokubun-ji Temple Layout

高田山専修寺
Takada-san Senju-ji Temple

真岡市高田

浄土真宗の開祖親鸞上人（1173-1262）の750回大遠忌が2011年に催された。これと前後して、それまで明らかにされていなかった親鸞の東国布教に関する研究が注目を浴びている。筑波大学名誉教授今井雅晴氏は、2010年4月3日から、1年半にわたり下野新聞に「下野と親鸞」を連載した。

親鸞は人生の最も充実した時期42歳〜61歳を東国、つまり、常陸国と下野国にまたがる一帯で過ごし、そこで、唯円らを育て「教行信証」を書き上げた。

親鸞と宇都宮一族

法然の弟子達が開いた会合に後鳥羽上皇が寵愛する女官2人が出席した。このことがきっかけとなって、法然一派に対する後鳥羽上皇の態度が硬化し、旧仏教による法然一派に対する嫌がらせが顕著になった。そして、1207年、法然は讃岐へ、弟子親鸞は越後へ流罪となった。

法然、親鸞は共に4年後の1211

The 750th anniversary of the death of Shinran (1173-1262) , founder of Jodo Shinshu sect of Buddhism, was held in 2011. Some research works on Shinran's missionary activities in Kanto region, which had been unknown so far, have attracted people's attention. The Shimotsuke carried a series of articles "Shimotsuke and Shinran" by Imai Masaharu, professor emeritus of Tsukuba University, starting April 3, 2010. It lasted over a year and a half.

Shinran spent his flowering period of life between 42 and 61 in the Kanto region, especially in the provinces of Hitachi and Shimotsuke. There he trained his disciples such as Yuien and wrote *Kyogyoshinsho* (Teaching, Practice, Faith, and Enlightenment).

Shinran and Utsunomiya Family

Two court ladies who were favorite with Ex-Emperor Gotoba attended a meeting held by disciples of Honen. This triggered the anger of His Majesty and the anti-feeling movement against the Honen school became very active among priests of existing sects of Budhism. In 1207, Honen was forced into exile to Sanuki and Shinran to Echigo.

年に赦免されたが、法然は翌1212年に入寂している。法然の死後、延暦寺の衆徒達は浄土宗の弾圧にかかり、東山の法然の墓を破壊し、更に、遺骸を鴨川に流そうとしたのである。これを伝え知った法然の弟子達は、機先を制して、法然の遺骸を掘り起こし、嵯峨の二尊院に運ぶことにした。その際、遺骸の移送の護衛に当たったのが、浄土宗の信徒であった蓮生（前、宇都宮城主宇都宮頼綱）と信生（前、川崎城主塩谷朝業）の兄弟や六波羅探題＊の武士団1,000人であった。

＊六波羅探題：京都六波羅に置かれた鎌倉幕府の機関またはその長。

Four years later, Honen and Shinran were excused, but Honen died in the following year. After his death, a large scale suppression against disciples of Honen by the monks of the Enryaku-ji Temple began. They desecrated Honen's grave at Higashiyama and planned to throw his body into the Kamo River. Honen's disciples learned about this plan beforehand. They dug out the body and carried it to the Nison-in Temple in Saga guarded by Rensho (former lord of Utsunomiy Castle) and Shinsho (former lord of Kawasaki Castle) who were believers in Jodo-shin Shu sect of Buddhism. 1,000 warriors from Rokuharatandai＊also guarded the transfer.

＊Rokuharatandai: office of shogunal deputies stationed at Rokuhara in Kyoto

専修寺　御影堂　Mieido, Senju-ji Temple

親鸞が越後での流罪を赦免された後、妻や子供*を連れて下野を経由して常陸へ向かったのも蓮生と蓮生の末弟稲田九郎頼重を頼ってのことと考えられ、親鸞と宇都宮一族との密接な関係が推測される。親鸞は常陸国と下野国で20年間を過ごし、その間、唯円などの弟子を育て、「教行信証」を書き上げている。

＊親鸞は越後に滞在していた4年の間に結婚している。親鸞は公に結婚をした最初の僧侶である。

高田山専修寺

1225年（嘉禄元）、53歳の時、親鸞はそれまで過ごした稲田（現、笠間市）を離れ、高田（現、栃木県真岡市）に入り、三谷草庵を結び、下野での本格的な布教を開始した。その拠点となったのが高田山専修寺である。この寺は親鸞自身が創立した唯一の寺院とされ、浄土真宗高田派では別格の存在で、本寺と呼ばれている。

高田派においては、専修とは「専修念仏」（ひたすら念仏を唱えて阿弥陀仏の救いを求める）という意味を持つが、これは浄土真宗の別の派が考える意味とは異なるという。

After he was released from exile in Echigo, Shinran headed for the province of Hitachi via the province of Shimotsuke with his wife and children. It may be safe to imagine that he chose Hitachi because Inada Kuro Yorishige, youngest brother of Shinsho and Rensho, was living there. This implies close relationships between Shinran and the Utsunomiya clan. Shinran spent about 20 years in the provinces of Hitachi and Shimotsuke, and during that time, he trained Yuien and other disciples and wrote *Kyogyoshinsho*.

＊ Shinran got married during the 4 years in Echigo. He was the first Buddhist priest who openly got married.

Takada-san Senju-ji Temple

In 1225, when Shinran was 53 years old, he left Inada (now, in Kasama City) for Takada (now, in Moka City). He built a thatched hut "Miya Soan" and started his genuine missionary work in the province of Shimotsuke. His base was at the Senju-ji Temple. The Senju-ji is the only temple that Shinran established himself, and it is given a special status among the temples of the Takada school of Jodo-shin Sect. It is called 'Honji' (main temple).

People who belong to the Takada school of Jodo-shin Sect believe that "Senju" means "to seek salvation by reciting nembutsu (Buddhist prayers) earnestly." People who belong to other schools of Jodo-shin Sect, however, believe that

15世紀に蓮如が登場して浄土真宗が村落共同体と結びついて大教団になって以来、真宗十派のうち末寺数第一位が本願寺派（11,000寺）、第二位が大谷派（9,000寺）、第三位が高田派（600寺）となっている。

親鸞没後、蓮如が登場するまでの200年間、高田門徒は東国布教の中心的役割を果たしており、その中心に、高田山専修寺があった。

現在、高田山専修寺の境内は国指定史跡で、総門、楼門、御影堂、そして如来堂はいずれも国の重要文化財に指定されている。

総門を出て200mのところには、親鸞が明星天子から夢告を受けた聖跡「般舟石」がある。

また、境内から約2km程離れた山中の竹林には専修寺の飛び地境内があり、そこに専修寺建立中親鸞が仮住居として利用していたという三谷草庵があり、これも国指定史跡となっている。

"Senju" has a different meaning.

With the appearance of Rennyo in the 15th century, Jodo-shin Sect became linked with village communities and became a huge religious organization. The approximate number of branch temples by schools were as follows.

Hongan-ji School	11,000
Otani School	9,000
Takada School	600

For about 200 years after Shinran died until Rennyo came onto the religious stage, the followers of the Takada school performed central roles in the missionary work in the Kanto region. Its center of activities was the Senju-ji Temple.

Today, the precincts of the Senju-ji Temple are designated as a National Historic Site, and buildings such as Somon (main gate), Romon (2-storeyed gate), Mieido and Nyoraido are all designated as National Important Cultural Properties.

About 200 m from the main gate of the temple, there is a rock named Hanjuseki. This is a holy place where Shinran received a revelation in his dream from Myojo Tenshi (Venus Emperor, one of the three sons of Heaven).

In a piece of land about 2 km away from the Senju-ji Temple, there is a thatched hut named Miya Soan among bamboo grove. This is where Shinran lived while the Senju-ji Temple was being built. This hut is also designated as a National Historic Site.

円通寺大沢文庫
Entsu-ji Temple and Osawa Bunko (Library)
益子町大沢

　益子町北西部に円通寺という古刹がある。近くには大羽川(おおば)が流れ、角海武氏著の「続ましこ雑話」によれば、かつて、この川には寺に通じる能化橋(のうけばし)と所化橋(しょけばし)と呼ばれる二つの橋があり、能化橋は位の高い僧が、所化橋は勉強中の僧が渡る橋とされていた、という。

　円通寺は、浄土宗名越派(なごえ)の派祖良弁上人(りょうべん)から数えて五代目に当た

The Entsu-ji is a noted temple with a long history in the north-western part of Mashiko Town. A river named Oba-gawa is flowing near the temple. According to "*A Sequel to the Mashiko Zatsuwa* (Mashiko Miscellany)" written by Kakumi Takeshi, there used to be two bridges, Noke and Shoke, across the river. Nouke was for the use by priests of high rank and Shoke for apprentices still under training.

　The Entsu-ji Temple was founded

円通寺表門　Front Gate of Entsu-ji Temple

一切経堂 Issaikyo-do

る良栄上人が1402年（応永9）に開いた寺で、学問所として大沢文庫を設け多くの名僧を輩出した。残念ながら、円通寺は1541年（天文10）の火災で伽藍の大部分を焼失したが、幸い、室町時代に建造された表門（国指定重要文化財）は焼失をまぬがれた。

　1559年、良迦上人が寺を再興し、1574年には正親町天皇の勅願所となって栄えた。円通寺十一世道残は正親町天皇より天皇の学問指南の綸旨を賜り、正親町、後陽成両天皇の精神的学問的支柱となった。時あたかも（1582年）信長

in 1402 by Ryoei, the 5th descendant of Priest Ryoben, founder of Nagoe School of Jodo sect of Buddhism. Ryoei established Osawa Bunko in the temple which helped to produce many great priests. To our great regret, however, most part of the Entsu-ji Temple was burned down in a fire in 1541. Only the Omote-mon Gate (National Important Cultural Property) built during the Muromachi period was left unburned.

　In 1559, a priest named Ryoga restored the temple. And in 1574, the Entsu-ji Temple was appointed 'chokugansho' (a temple where the emperor prayed) and Dozan, the 11th chief priest of the temple, received an imperial order to lecture in front of Emperor

が本能寺に倒れた後で、武士社会の動乱の時世に皇室を安泰に置いた業績は大きい。

道残が示した実践哲学を根本とした大沢流思想（独裁否定）は、全国統一、朝鮮出兵という野望に燃える豊臣秀吉の意図にそぐわず、道残は秀吉の圧迫を受けて、その地位を退いたという。

最盛期には、円通寺大沢文庫の8万坪の敷地には38の学棟があり、数百人の学僧が学んでいたと言われる。

現在では、本堂奥の一段高い所に、1809年（文化6）に再建された一切経堂（県の重要文化財）があり、わずかに中世の大沢文庫の面影を伝えている。

円通寺大沢文庫は、同じく中世の学問所として重要な存在である足利学校や金沢文庫と比較すると、足利学校や金沢文庫が武士の教育のためであったのに対し、大沢文庫は僧侶の純粋な学究の場であり続けた。大沢文庫は明治維新の廃仏毀釈の嵐に遭うまで、約500年の間、純粋に祈りと学問の灯を守り続けてきたのである。

円通寺の長い歴史は、すぐれた僧侶を多く輩出しているが、名僧の中の一人第十八世良無について、次

Ogimachi. He gave strong mental and scholarly support to Emperors Ogimachi and Go-Yozei and contributed greatly to the peace and security of the Imperial Household during the social and political unrest in the warrior society after Nobunaga was killed at the Honno-ji Temple in 1582.

The fundamental teaching principle of Osawa School (denial of dictatorship) which was based on practical philosphy, however, did not go well with Hideyoshi's intention to dominate all Japan and to send soldiers to Korea, and Dozan was forced to resign the post of the chief priest.

At its peak, there were 38 school houses in the site of 80,000 tsubo (26.5 hectares) of the Entsu-ji Temple and several hundreds of learned priests were studying there.

At present, the only building that tells us the splendor of the temple during the Middle Ages is Issaikyo-Do (rebuilt in 1809) in the back of the Main Hall.

When we compare Osawa Bunko with Ashikaga Gakko and Kanazawa Bunko which also functioned as learning centers during the Middle Ages, we find that both Ashikaga Gakko and Kanazawa Bunko started as institutions for training samurai warriors. Osawa Bunko, on the other hand, continued from its start to be an institution for training highly educated priests and had been the place of fervent prayer and learning for about 500 years until it was caught in a

のようなエピソードが伝えられている。

　円通寺に学ぶ学僧の中に、村の娘たちを魅了する良無という好男子がいた。ある日、良無は先輩の僧のお供をして農家を回っているうちに、ある長者の娘から恋文を受け取り、その後二人は時々人目を忍んで相会う深い仲になった。いつしかその娘は身ごもった。このことを知って、良無は非常に驚き食事ものどを通らぬ程の心の痛みを覚えた。この様子を不審に思う寮長から事情を聞かれた良無はすべてを告白する。「これからは女と会わずに勉強に打ち込め。」と説得され禁足の身となる。

　このことを知って思い悩んだ娘は所化橋から身を投げて死んでしまった。良無は慟哭し思い悩んだが、やがて、一大奮起して学問に精進し、優れた学僧となり学頭の座に就いた。そして円通寺十八世（1661-1672）に迎えられたという。

storm of the anti-Buddhist movement at the beginning of Meiji Restoration.

Many great priests were born during the long history of the Entsu-ji Temple. Here is a story about Ryomu, the 18th Chief Priest of the Temple.

Among the priests who were studying at the Entsu-ji Temple was a young, good looking man named Ryomu who attracted many girls in the village. One day, Ryomu received a love letter from a rich man's daughter while he was visiting houses in a village with a senior priest. The girl and Ryomu soon became very close friends and found every chance to meet in secret. Soon the girl became pregnant. When Ryomu was told about it, he was greatly shocked and could eat nothing. The dorm leader noticed about it and asked him what was wrong with him. Ryomu told everything to him. After listening to the whole story, the dorm leader said, "Don't meet the girl any more. Devote yourself to studying." And Ryomu was placed under confinement.

When the girl learned all about this, she was greatly distressed and killed herself by jumping from the Shoke Bridge into the river. Ryomu wailed over the girl's death. But after a while, he began to devote himself to the study of Buddhism and soon became a scholar priest with profound learning. He later became schoolmaster and was finally invited to be the 18th Chief Priest of the Entsu-ji Temple (1661-1672).

岩船山高勝寺と地蔵尊
Iwafune-san Kosho-ji Temple and Jizo Bosatsu

栃木市岩舟町静

　岩船山は足尾山系の最南東端にある標高173mの奇岩怪石からなる山で、山全体が船の形をしているところから岩船山と言われる。江戸時代に始まった岩船石の採掘で現在では山容が大きく変化している。

　岩の露出するこの山は、昔から、死者の霊魂が集まる霊山として信仰されてきた。岩船山は、青森県の恐山、鳥取県の大山などと並ぶ霊山として名が知られ、また、関東の高野山とも呼ばれ、宗派を問わず死霊のあつまる聖地として関東一円

Mt. Iwafune (173m in height) is located at south-easternmost part of the Ashio mountain range. It consists of oddly formed stones and weirdly shaped rocks. Its name Iwafune ('rock-ship') came from its shape like a ship. Its original shape, however, has changed greatly because too much stone has been quarried out.

The surface of Mt. Iwafune is mostly covered with bare rock and the mountain has been believed to be the sacred gathering place of the souls of the deceased. It is well known as one of the sacred mountains in Japan together with Mt. Osorezan in Aomori Prefecture and Mt. Dais-

岩船山　Mt. Iwafune

に崇敬され栄えてきた。

　600段の石段を登りつめた山頂には高勝寺がある。この寺は岩船山蓮華院と号する天台宗の寺院で、地蔵菩薩が本尊として祀られている。この地蔵尊は、越後（新潟県村上市岩船町）、上総（千葉県大原町岩船）の地蔵尊と共に日本三大地蔵尊の一つと言われる。

弘誓坊明願と地蔵尊

　かつて、伯耆の国（現、鳥取県西部）に地蔵尊を深く信じる弘誓坊明願という修行僧がいた。彼は地蔵尊を深く信じ、常々、一度でいいから生き身の地蔵尊を拝みたいものだと考えていた。

　ある夜のこと、明願の夢の中にお地蔵様が現れて「生き身の地蔵菩薩を拝せんと思わば、下野国岩船山に登るべし。必ず生き身の地蔵尊を拝すべし。」と告げた。

　明願は早速下野の国に向けて出発し、やっとの思いで岩船山にたどり着いた。すでに日はとっぷりと暮れていた。明願はどこか今晩泊めて

en in Tottori Prefecture. It is sometimes called Koyasan* in Kanto region, and has been revered by people of every sect of Buddhism as a sacred place where the souls of the deceased get together.

* Koyasan: the Buddhist monastic complex of the Shingon sect on Mt. Koya in Wakayama Prefecture.

If you go up 600 stone-steps, you will come to the Kosho-ji Temple. The temple belongs to the Tendai Sect of Buddhism and is dedicated to Bodhisattva Jizo. The statue of Jizo of this temple is called one of the three most famous jizo in Japan. The other two jizo are in Murakami City, Niigata Prefecture and in Ohara, Chiba Prefecture.

Guzebo Myogan and Jizo

There once lived an ascetic named Guzebo Myogan in the Province of Hoki (now, part of Tottori Prefecture). He firmly believed in Jizo, one of the most popular bodhisattvas in Japanese Buddhism, and it was his dream to see Living Jizo some day.

One night, Jizo appeared in his dream and told him. "If you want to see Living Jizo, go to Mt. Iwafune in the province of Shimotsuke. You are sure to see Living Jizo there."

Myogan left for the province of Shimotsuke at once, and finally arrived there. It was quite dark when he arrived. He looked for some lodging, but there was no house around. He felt helpless and kept on walking along a dark

くれる家はないものかとあたりを探したが一軒の家もない。困り果てて、あてもなく暗い山道をとぼとぼと歩いて行くと遠くに一つの灯りが見えてきた。喜んでその灯りを目指して暗い山道を歩いていくと、一軒のみすぼらしい小屋にやってきた。小屋の中では顔中髭だらけの一人のお坊さんが机に向って何か書き物をしていた。明願が一夜の宿を頼むと、お坊さんは明願を快く中に招き入れてくれた。

しばらくして、お坊さんは尋ねた。「ところでこんな山奥に何をしに来られた？」明願は自分がお地蔵様を深く信仰していることや夢の知らせのことを話すと、お坊さんは「そうですか。では、明日の朝、私が山の上に案内して進ぜよう。生きたお地蔵様に会えるかもしれない。」と言ってくれた。

次の朝、明願はお坊さんに案内されて岩船山の頂上に登り、一所懸命にお経を唱えはじめた。すると、突然、目の前の岩の上に光り輝くお地蔵様が姿を現したのである。しかし、これはほんの一瞬のことでお地蔵様の姿はすぐに見えなくなってしまった。しばらくして明願は我にかえり、自分のことを案内してきてくれたお坊さんはどこにいるのだろうと

mountain pass. Then, he saw a dim light in the distance. He hurried toward the light. The light came from a humble cottage. In the cottage, there was a heavily-bearded old priest writing something at the desk. Myogan asked him for a night lodging. The priest invited him in.

After a while, the priest asked Myogan, "What has brought you here to this deserted, lonely place?" Myogan told him that he was a firm believer in Jizo and told him about the dream he had the other night. When Myogan finished his story, the priest said. "Is that so? I will take you to the top of the mountain tomorrow morning. You may have a chance to see a living Jizo."

The next morning, Myogan went up to the top of Mt. Iwafune led by the priest and started reciting a sutra there. Suddenly, there appeared Jizo, brilliant and solemn, on a rock just in front of him. It disappeared in a moment. Myogan came to himself after a while, and looked for the priest who took him to the mountain. He was nowhere to be seen. The priest was none other than Jizo itself.

Myogan went back to Hoki Province once and came to Mt. Iwafune again in 775. He built a small temple on the rock where Jizo appeared. It is called Sakanaka Jizoson. We can see the temple today halfway up Omote-sando. Jizo on Mt. Iwafune is popular among people as a deity of matchmaking.

辺りを探したがどこにも姿が見えなかった。このお坊さんこそがお地蔵様だったのである。

　明願は一度伯耆の国に戻ってから775年（宝亀6）に再び岩船山を訪れ、お地蔵様が現れた岩の上に小さなお堂を作りお地蔵様をお祀りした。これが表参道の中腹にある坂中地蔵尊で、地蔵と明願の出会いの地である。こんなことから、岩船山の地蔵尊は出会い、つまり、縁結びの地蔵尊として人々の信仰を受けている。

お楽の方

　なお、岩船山には、陰陽二体の地蔵尊が祀られている。一つは岩船山の奥の院に祀られている「陰」の地蔵で、女性を象徴しており、もう一つは孫太郎地蔵尊と呼ばれる「陽」の地蔵で、男性を象徴しているといわれる。春秋の彼岸に護摩焚きを終えた後、この両地蔵尊を参拝すれば子宝に恵まれるという。

　徳川三代将軍家光の側室、お楽の方は岩船地蔵尊を信仰していて、江戸城に入る時、岩船山のお地蔵様に子孫繁栄と武運長久を祈ったという。その御利益を得て生まれたのが四代将軍家綱といわれている。

坂中地蔵尊　Sakanaka Jizoson

O-Raku

There are two other Jizo statues on Mt. Iwafune. One is a statue in Oku-no-in ('inner sanctuary') representing 'a female' and the other is a statue called Magotaro Jizo representing 'a male'. If you visit these two statues after the ceremony of goma ('the holy fire for invocation') during the equinoctial week in spring or autumn, you are sure to be blessed with a child.

O-Raku, one of the concubines of the third shogun Iemitsu, was a devout believer of Jizo on Mt. Iwafune. It is said that she prayed the Jizo for family prosperity and good luck before she was called into Edo Castle. Fortunately, her prayer was answered and she was blessed with a baby boy, who later became the 4th Shogun of the Tokugawa Shogunate, Ietsuna.

佐貫石仏
Stone Image of the Buddha at Sanuki

塩谷町佐貫

　塩谷町佐貫の鬼怒川に架かる観音橋近くには高さ約64mの大きな岩があり、その岩面には大日如来坐像が彫られている。坐像の線刻はよく目を凝らして見ないと分らない程である。この坐像は「佐貫観音」と呼ばれ、弘法大師一夜の作と伝えられる磨崖仏である。

　岩の右上部には奥の院大悲窟があり、中に貴重な宝物が納められている。その中の一つ「銅板阿弥陀曼荼羅」には「建保五年」(1217年)と記されており、この磨崖仏は鎌倉時代の初期に彫られたものと考えら

　In Sanuki, Shioya Town, there is a bridge called Kannon Bridge over the Kinu River. Near the bridge, we can see a carving of sitting statue of Dainichi Nyorai on the surface of a huge rock. The rock is about 64m high. This statue is popularly called Sanuki Kannon. Many people spend a long time trying to find the carving lines of the statue on the rock. A legend goes that Priest Kukai carved this statue overnight.

　On the upper-right part of the rock, there is a cave called Inner Temple in which important articles are stored. On one of the articles, Doban Amida Mandara, is inscribed the year '1217',

佐貫観音　Sanuki Kannon

れている。「奥の院」は62年に一度開帳される。

　1926年（大正15）2月24日に「佐貫石仏」として国の重要文化財に指定された。

　観音像の近くには「亀の子岩」と呼ばれる亀の形をした珍しい岩がある。

尚仁沢
<small>しょうじんざわ</small>

　佐貫観音の近くには、尚仁沢という湧水群があり、そこから流れ出る水は原生林の間を流れている。一日約65,000t.の豊かな湧水量を誇り、全国名水百選の一つに選ばれている。湧水の温度は四季を通じて摂氏11度前後と一定している。なお、尚仁沢上流部のイヌブナ自然林は国の天然記念物に指定されている。

which tells us that the Dainichi Nyorai was carved during the early days of the Kamakura period. The Inner Shrine is opened to public once in 62 years.

　Sanuki Kannon was designated as National Important Cultural Asset on Feb. 24, 1926.

　Near the carving of the Dainichi Nyorai, there is an interesting rock formation called Kamenoko-Iwa (Tortoise Rock).

Shojin-zawa

　Near Sanuki Kannon, there are a group of springs called Shojin-zawa where water comes up naturally from the ground and flows through virgin forest. More than 65,000 tons of water flows out of the ground everyday. Shojinzawa is among the 100 Best Springs in Japan. The temperature of the water is about 11℃ all year round. The natural forest of "inubuna"(Japanese beaches) is designated as a nation's natural monument.

尚仁沢　Shojin-zawa

寺山観音寺
Terayama-Kannon-ji Temple
矢板市長井

矢板市長井にある寺山観音寺は、かつては、法相宗法楽寺といい、724年(神亀元)に、高僧行基が聖武天皇の勅命を受けて高原山の一峰、剣が峰(1540m)の頂上近くに建立したと伝えられる。

803年(延暦22)、法楽寺は落雷による火災で千手観音堂のみを残して伽藍のほとんどが灰燼に帰し

The Terayama-Kannon-ji Temple at Nagai, Yaita City, was once called the Horaku-ji Temple. It belonged to the Hosso sect of Buddhism. It is believed that Priest Gyoki (668-749) founded the temple in 724 at the order of Emperor Shomu (701-756) near the top of Mt. Ken-ga-mine (height: 1,540m) in the Takahara mountains.

The temple was struck by lightning in 803 and most of the temple buildings,

寺山観音寺　Terayama Kannon-ji Temple

たが、3年後の806年（大同元）徳一上人の時に、寺は山の麓にうつされ寺山観音寺として再建された。

この寺に伝わる木造千手観音座像は弘仁時代（810-824）の作と考えられ、脇侍の木造不動明王立像、木造毘沙門天立像と共に国の重要文化財に指定されていて、60年に一度甲子の年に開帳される。

この寺には徳一上人が植えたと言われる銀杏の古木がある。かつて、この寺は女人禁制の戒律が厳しく、境内の銀杏の木でさえ一本たりとも雌木がないという。

伝説:牛石

法楽寺が火災により焼失して、数年後、それまでより人里に近いところに寺が再建された。引越に際して、千手観音の像を牛の背中に積んで運ぶことになった。牛はゆっくり山道を降りて来て、新しいお寺に到着した。

except the Senju-Kannon-Do, were reduced to ashes. In 806, a new temple was built by Priest Tokuitsu at the foot of the mountain and it was renamed Terayama-Kannon-ji.

The Terayama-Kannon-ji Temple treasures 'Mokuzo Senju-Kannon Zazo' (Wooden Sitting Statue of Thousand-armed Kannon) which was made during the Konin period (810-824) . Together with two flanking attendants 'Mokuzo Fudo-Myo'o Ritsuzo' (Wooden Standing Statue of Fudo-Myo'o) and 'Mokuzo Bishamon-ten Ritsuzo' (Wooden Standing Statue of Bishamon-ten), the Senju-Kannon Zazo is designated as a national important asset. It is opened to public once in 60 years, in the year of 'kinoe-ne' (the first year of the sexagenary cycle).

There is an old ginkgo tree in the precincts of this temple. It said that Priest Tokuitsu planted it. Once women were strictly prohibited to visit this temple, and even a 'female' ginkgo tree (which is polygamous) was prohibited to be planted in the precincts.

Legend: Bull Stone

When the Horaku-ji Temple was moved to the foot of the mountain after it was burned to ashes, the Thousand-armed Statue of the temple was tied to the back of a bull and was carried down to a new temple. The bull slowly came down a narrow mountain path, and reached the new temple.

牛石　Bull Stone

　慈悲深い観音様は牛をねぎらい戻るように言ったが、牛は観音様の側をはなれようとしなかった。そこで、観音様は牛がいつまでの自分の側に居られるようにと牛を石の姿に変えてやったという。

　その石は「牛石」と呼ばれ、今でも寺山観音寺への山道の脇に横たわっている。牛石の白と黒のまだら色は、この時の牛のまだら模様が残っているものだと言う。

The merciful Kan'non appreciated the service of the bull and told it to go back. The bull, however, would not leave the side of Kan'non. So, Kan'non transformed the bull into a stone so that it could stay by his side and serve him forever.

The stone called "Bull Stone" still lies by the roadside near the Terayama-Kannon-ji Temple. They say the black and white spots on the stone are reminders of the spots the bull had on its back.

シラネアオイ（白根葵）
キンポウゲ科シラネアオイ属

日光の白根山周辺に多く見られる。
最近はシカの食害や盗採により
殆ど絶滅状態になってしまったため、
現在は様々な保護対策が進められている。

第5章
伝統の祭
Festivals and Celebrations

日光弥生祭　Nikko Yayoi Festival

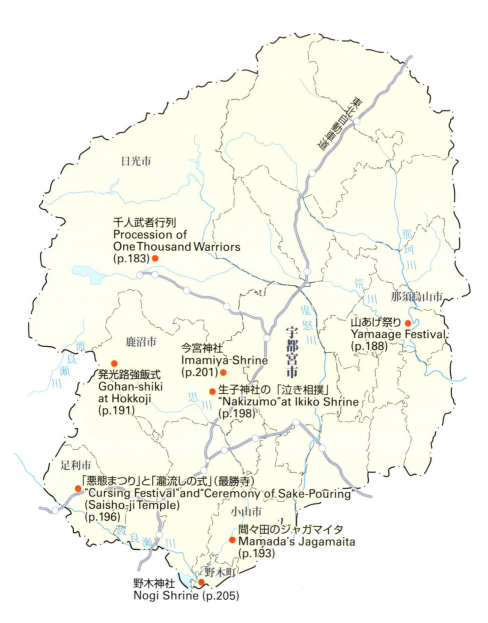

日光東照宮の「千人武者行列」
Procession of One Thousand Warriors
日光市山内

日光東照宮

日光東照宮は、神格化されて「東照大権現」となった江戸幕府初代将軍・徳川家康（1542-1616）を祀った神社である。

東照宮は、江戸時代を通じて全国に500社ほど建てられたが、明治維新（1868）以後の神仏分離により、廃社や合社が相次ぎ、現存する

Nikko Toshogu

Nikko Toshogu is the shrine where Tokugawa Ieyasu (1542-1616), the first Shogun of the Edo shogunate, is enshrined.

Once there were about 500 Toshogu shrines all over Japan, but after the movement to separate Shinto and Buddhism in the early Meiji period, some of them were abolished or combined

千人武者行列 Procession of One-thousand Warriors

のは約130社である。その中で、日光東照宮は久能山東照宮と並んで特別な存在である。

　徳川家康は1616年（元和2）4月17日に駿府城（静岡市）で没した。遺言に従い、家康の遺骸は初め久能山（静岡市）に葬られ、一年後に日光の東照社（東照宮の前身）に遷座した。

　徳川二代将軍徳川秀忠（1579-1632）のとき、家康鎮座の儀式が行なわれ、日光に東照社が建てられた。

　その後、三代将軍・家光（1604-1651）の時には巨額の費用（現在の金額で約400億円）が投ぜられ、より絢爛豪華な東照社への造り替えが行われた。「寛永の大造替」と言われるものである。

　朝廷から東照社に宮号が与えられ、日光東照社が日光東照宮となったのは1645年（正保2）のことである。以後、朝廷は、毎年4月日光東照宮に「奉幣使*」を派遣することが恒例となった。この「奉幣使」は「日光例幣使」と呼ばれ、1867年（慶応3）まで続いた。

＊勅令によって幣帛（御幣や金幣などのことで供物以外の総称）を神社に奉献する使い

　日光は、江戸の真北に位置し、「東照大権現」となった家康は、江戸幕

and, today, there are about 130 Toshogu shrines. Among them, the Nikko Toshogu Shrine and the Kunozan Toshogu Shrine are the most prestigious.

Ieyasu passed away on April 17th, 1616, in the Sunpu Castle (Shizuoka City). In accordance with his last will, he was at first buried in Mt. Kuno (Shizuoka City), and after a year, he was buried at Nikko Toshosha (now, called Toshogu).

When Tokugawa Hidetada was the 2nd Shogun of the Tokugawa shogunate, the Toshosha Shrine was built in Nikko and the ceremony of transferring the soul of Ieyasu was held.

The third shogun, Tokugawa Iemitsu (1604-1651), reconstructed the Toshosha into a gorgeous, splendid building. He spent a great amout of money (approximately 40 billion yen) on it. The reconstruction work is called "the Great Reconstrution Work of Kan'ei Era."

In 1645, the Imperial Court granted the title of 'Gu' to the shrine, and the Toshosha came to be called Toshogu. After this, the Imperial Court dispatched an envoy called Hoheishi* to the Toshogu Shrine in April every year. The envoy was called 'Nikko Reiheishi' and this lasted until 1867.

＊Hoheishi (or Hobeishi): Messenger to present offerings by order of the emperor

Nikko is located due north of Edo. The late Ieyasu, who is now buried in Nikko as "Tosho Daigongen," is watch-

府の安泰、さらには日本の平和を不動の北辰（北極星）の位置から見守り続けている。

　東照宮をいただく日光は幕府の「聖地」とされ、将軍によるたびたびの「日光社参」や、春秋の祭礼時には将軍の名代や各大名の参詣が盛んに行われた。また、朝鮮との国交が回復すると「通信使」の日光訪問がたびたび行われた。

千人武者行列

　1617年（元和3）3月15日、家康の御霊を乗せた神輿は、久能山を出発し、19日かけて日光山に到着した。このときの行列は、鎧、冑に身を包んだ騎馬武者や槍を抱えた兵ら総勢一千人に及ぶ大行列であったとされる。家康の御霊は儀式を経て正式に日光山に鎮座した。

　千人武者行列は正式には「神輿渡御祭」と呼ばれ、徳川家康の神霊を久能山（現在の静岡市）から日光に遷した際の行列を再現したもので、毎年、日光東照宮の春季例大祭（5月17・18日）のとき、盛大に行われる行事である。

　東照宮の千人武者行列は、日光山に古くから伝わる神事と合わさったものといわれている。

　行列が行われる前日の夕には、徳

ing over Edo for its welfare and, moreover, for the peace of the whole country from the high place of the polestar.

　Nikko where the Toshogu Shrine is located was regarded as a sacred place for the Tokugawa shogunate, and not only shoguns but shoguns' deputies and daimyos often visited Nikko. Chosen Tsushinshi (the Korean Emissary) also came to Nikko after its diplomatic relations with Japan were resumed.

Procession of One Thousand Warriors

　On March 15th, 1617, the procession carrying the portable shrine of Ieyasu's soul left Mt. Kuno and arrived at Nikko after 19 days. The procession consisted of a thousand warriors: warriors on horseback who were clad in armors, warriors carrying lances, and so on. Ieyasu was enshrined in Nikko after formal procedures.

　The Procession of One Thousand Warriors, which is formally called "Shinyo Togyosai," is the reproduction of the procession of carrying Ieyasu's soul. It takes place annually during the Grand Spring Annual Festival of the Toshogu Shrine on May 17th and 18th.

　It is said that the Procession is a mixture of the procession of transferring Ieyasu's soul and a traditional procession that had been observed in Nikko for a long time.

　On the eve of the Procession, the

川家康、源頼朝、豊臣秀吉の霊を遷した三基の神輿が西隣の二荒山神社に渡御し、同夜、二荒山神社拝殿において祭典が執り行われ、神職たちが宿直する。この神事を「宵成」といい、家康が西方浄土に遷ったことを意味する。

18日には、行列は二荒山神社を出て、上新道・表参道を通り、神橋の近くのお旅所までの老松の並び立つ道約1kmを行く。「お旅所」は久能山に見立てられているという。

「百物揃千人武者行列」の「百物揃」の名前の通り、行列は、神馬三頭、神剣、御旗、神輿三基を守護するように、弓持ち、鉄砲持ち、槍持ち、鎧武者、鷹匠など53種類ものさまざまな役柄の人が加わり、まさに総勢1200人に及ぶものなのである。

お旅所では、三つの神輿を神殿に祭り、宮司以下神職による神事祭りが執り行われる。そこでは「三品立七十五膳*」と呼ばれる特殊な神饌を神霊に供える。一説には、この「75」という数字は日光山中に住む神々の数とも伝えられている。神々の深遠な力を東照宮の神霊に移し、活力を与えようという意味のようである。

＊「三品立七十五膳」とは山、野、海の物からなる75種類のメニュー

three portable shrines of Tokugawa Ieyasu, Minamoto Yoritomo and Toyotomi Hideyoshi are carried to the Futarasan Shrine which is located in the west of the Toshogu Shrine. A celemony is held in the Worship Hall of the shrine. Shinto priests spend the night in the shrine. This is called Yoinari, which symbolically means that Ieyasu has returned to Saiho Jodo (the Paradise in the West).

On the 18th of May, the procession leaves the Futarasan Shrine, takes the route of Uwa Shinmichi and Omote Sando which are lined with old pine trees, and arrives at O-Tabisho near Shinkyo. O-Tabisho symbolizes Mt. Kuno. The distance covered is about 1 km.

The procession of "Hyakumono- zoroi", as its name suggests, consists of three sacred horses, the sacred sword, the flag and the three sacred portable shrines which are guarded by more than 1200 people who are playing 53 different roles such as bow-holders, gun-holders, spear-holders, armor-clad warriors and falconers.

At O-Tabisho, the three portable shrines are placed in the hall, and some rituals are performed by Shinto priests. They offer to the holy spirits a special dinner named "Sanbondat'e Nanajugozen*." Some people say that the number 75 corresponds to the number of deities in Nikko mountains. This may imply that holy powers of the deities will be added to the holy spirits of the

次に、拝殿では「八乙女の舞*」が、また、御神殿と拝殿との間の石舞台では「東遊びの舞*」が奉納される。

＊八乙女の舞：二荒山神社の巫女二人が扇を持ち神楽を舞うもの
＊東遊びの舞：東照宮の神職によって行われる。

駿河国（現在の静岡県）における天女の舞を模したのが始まりといわれる。

午後には再び行列が整えられ、東照宮に向かう。東照宮に戻ることを「還御」といい、一連の行事が終了する。

この武者行列は秋の例大祭（10月17・18日）にも同じように行われるが、二荒山神社への「宵成」の儀式はなく、神輿は一基だけ、供奉の人数は春の例大祭に比して半減する。

Toshogu Shrine.

＊ Sanbondat'e means 'products of mountains, fields, and the sea,' and Nanajugozen means '75 dishes.'

After this, a dance called "Yaotome no Mai*" is performed at the worship hall, and another dance called "Azuma Asobi no Mai*" is performed on a stone stage between the inner shrine and the worship hall.

＊ Yaotom'e no Mai: a dance played to sacred music by the shrine maidens of the Futararsan Shrine.
＊ Azuma Asobi no Mai: a dance played by Shito priests of the Toshogu Shrine.

It is believed that the origin of this dance can be traced back to the dance of the Heavenly Maiden performed in the province of Suruga (now part of Shizuoka Prefecture).

In the afternoon, the procession goes back to the Toshogu Shrine. This is called "Kangyo" (the return), which signifies the end of the series of events.

The festival of the Procession of One Thousand Warriors is also held during the Autumn Grand Festival of the Toshogu Shrine on Oct. 17th and 18th. The ceremony of Yoinari, however, is omitted, and only one portable shrine takes part in it. And warriors are about half in number compared with those of the Spring Festival.

山あげ祭
Yamaage Festival
那須烏山市

山あげ祭　Yamaage Festival

　「山あげ祭」は那須烏山市の八雲神社例大祭の奉納行事で、毎年7月に6町（元町、金井町、仲町、泉町、鍛冶町、日野町）の輪番制で開催される野外歌舞伎が中心の祭りである。1979年、国の重要無形民俗文化財に指定された。
　山あげ祭りの始まりは1560年（永禄3）全国的に疫病が大流行した時までさかのぼる。烏山城主那

Yamaage Festival is the regular festival ritual dedicated to the deity at the Yakumo-jinja Shrine in Nasu Karasuyama City. It is held in July every year. The main attraction of the festival is the outdoor Kabuki performance given in rotation by citizens of 6 towns (Moto-cho, Kanai-cho, Naka-cho, Izumi-cho, Kaji-cho, and Hino-cho). In 1979, it was designated as a national important intangible folk-cultural property.

The origin of Yamaage Festival goes

須資胤は疫病が蔓延することを防ごうと、領内の八雲神社に厄除神である牛頭天王を勧請した。

当初、奉納余興として相撲や神楽獅子等が行なわれていたが、やがて「山あげ」が行なわれるようになった。

「山あげ」とは、烏山特産の程村紙と呼ばれる和紙で作った高さ10ｍ、幅７ｍ程のハリコの「山」を「あげる（たてる）」ことで、祭りでは市内の道路約100ｍにわたって大山、中山、前山、館、橋、波などが配置され、全国でも類例を見ない絢爛豪華な野外歌舞伎が繰り広げられる。木頭の拍子木の合図で一斉に山を変化させる仕掛けは見事である。

上演される演目は「将門」、「戻り橋」などがあり、最近では「蛇姫様」が加えられた。

「将門」はお家再興を図ろうとする将門の娘滝夜叉姫が遊女になり済まし、将門の残党を捜しにきた太郎光圀に忍び寄り、色仕掛けで味方にしようとするが、見破られて失敗するという話である。妖術使いの巨大蝦蟇の登場は見せ場の一つになっている。

「戻り橋」は渡辺綱が頼光の恋の使いの帰途、一条戻り橋で娘に

back to the year 1560 when a great plague raged over Japan. Nasu Suketane, lord of Karasuyama Castle, wanting to prevent the plague from raging in his domain, performed a 'kanjo' (a ceremony of inviting the spirit of a deity) to invite Tutelary Deity, Gozu Tenno, to the Yakumo Shrine.

In the beginning, sumo wrestling and kagura-shishi dance were dedicated to the shrine, but gradually yamaage came to be performed.

Yamaage means setting up 'yama' (stage set) for a drama in a moment on an open stage which stretches for about 100m on the street. 'Yama' is made of 'hodomura paper' (handmade Japanese paper) and is about 10m high and 7m wide. 'Yama' usually consists of 'oyama' (a large-sized set), 'nakayama' (a middle-sized set), 'maeyama' (a front set) a house, a bridge, waves, etc. Spectacular open-air kabuki drama is played on the stage. We cannot find the like of this performance anywhere else in Japan. It is surprising to see the instant change of 'yama' at the signal of wooden clappers by a leader.

Major programs are "Masakado" and "Modoribashi," and recently "Hebihime-sama" was added to the repertoires.

In "Masakado," a daughter of Masakado, Takiyasha-hime, wanting to restore the former glory of her family, disguises herself as a prostitute and approaches Taro Mitsukuni who came

会うが、水に映る陰で鬼と知る。綱はそれを承知で娘に舞を所望。立ち回りの末、綱は鬼の右腕を切り取り、腕を奪われた鬼は天空へ飛び去る、という話である。

2016年、この「烏山の山あげ行事」は、県内では「鹿沼今宮神社の屋台行事」とともにユネスコの無形文化遺産に登録された。

searching for the survivors of the Rebellion. She pretends to be in love with him and tries to win him over to her side. Taro, however, reads her intentions at once. Thus, her plot turns out unsuccessful. One of the highlights of this drama is when a huge toad that practices sorcery comes out on the stage.

In "Modoribashi," Watanabe no Tsuna meets a girl at the Ichijo Modori-bashi Bridge. He is on his way back from an errand as a love messenger of his master, Raiko. Tsuna sees a form of a devil in the reflection of the girl on the water. Tsuna, however, pretends that he knows nothing and asks her to dance. After the battle, Tsuna chops off the right arm of the devil and the devil flies away to the sky.

In 2016,"Yamaage Gyoji in Karasuyama" was registered as UNESCO's "World's Intangible Cultural Heritages" together with "Yatai Gyoji of Imamiya Shrine in Kanuma" in this prefecture.

発光路の強飯式
Gohan-shiki at Hokkoji
鹿沼市発光路

　栃木県内には、飯や酒を強いるいわゆる強飯習俗の儀式が各地に見られ、日光山輪王寺の強飯式や同じく日光市七里の生岡神社で行われる子供強飯式、そして、鹿沼市発光路の強飯式がよく知られている。

　発光路は足尾山地にあり、勝道上人の男体山開山以降発達した日光修験の地で、上人のたどった道筋には日光修験に関係する寺社がおかれ、山伏が修行したところが多い。

　発光路の強飯式は南北朝時代の延文年間（1356-1360）に始められたとされ、日光輪王寺の強飯式の流れを汲むといわれる。

　式は正月三日に行なわれる。妙見神社の神事の後、最前列に坐っている頂戴人と呼ばれる人の前にお膳が置かれる。膳の上には、飯椀に高く盛り上げた小豆ご飯、汁椀には豆腐汁、壺にシモツカレとコンニャク、御平椀には塩引き、昆布、大根、人参などが載せられている。

　式はまず山伏の登場から始まる。

Ceremonies of 'gohan' (forcing to eat rice) are observed in some places in Tochigi Prefecture. The Gohan-shiki held at the Nikko Rin'no-ji Temple, Gohan-shiki by Children at the Ikuoka Shrine at Shichiri, Nikko, and Gohan-shiki at Hokkoji, Kanuma, are well-known.

Hokkoji, located in Ashio mountains, has developed as a place of practicing mountain asceticism after Priest Shodo succeeded in climbing to the top of Mt. Nantai. Along the route that Shodo took when he climbed the mountain, there are shrines and temples where people used to practice mountain asceticism.

It is said that Gohan-shiki Ceremony held at Hokkoji originated during the Enbun period (1356-1360). It is related to Gohan-shiki Ceremony at the Rinno-ji Temple.

The Hokkoji Gohan-shiki is held on the 3rd of January. It goes like this. After some rituals in the Myoken Shrine, a tray is brought before each chodainin* who is sitting in the front row. On the tray are a bowl piled with red bean rice, a bowl of miso soup with tofu in it, a jar of shimotsukare* and konnyaku, and a plate of salted salmon, sea-weed, radd-

山伏は「拙僧は役行者の末裔、峰渡りの山伏云々」と身分をあかし、強力を伴って参上したことを告げる。

次いで、強力が登場し、責め棒を高く持ち上げ「男体山に三千年立て籠もりしこの強力云々」と大声を張り上げ周りを威嚇する。

次に、山伏や強力は居並ぶ頂戴人に「例年の通り酒なら三十三杯、湯が五杯、強飯七十五膳がお定まり、一粒、一菜でも許しはしない」と伝える。

儀式は、平身低頭する頂戴人の首根っこを責め棒で押さえつけながら、山伏と強力が口上を交互に述べ合い、最後にお膳の高盛り飯を一つまみ頂戴人の口に押し込む、という形をとる。

山伏と強力の掛け合い口上の中で、村人の心得や新婿（新しく村に入ってくる若者）への諭しなどが述べられ、村人の一体感が得られるのであろう。これは庶民の知恵が生み出した祭り行事である。

発光路の強飯式は、1996年（平成8）に国の重要無形民俗文化財の指定を受けている。

ish and carrot.

* chodainin: people of importance who were given the priviledge of attending the ceremony
* shimotsukare: a local food in Tochigi Prefecture

The ceremony begins with the appearance of yamabushi, who introduces himself as a descendant of En-no-gyoja and itinerant monk, and tells that he has come with a goriki.

Then, a goriki appears and tells people that he has spent many years in Mt. Nantai. His voice is very large and threatening.

The yamabushi and the goriki tell the chodainin, "Eat and drink 33 cups of sake, 5 cups of hot water, and 75 bowls of rice. It is the custom. You are not allowed to leave even a single grain of rice or a vegetable."

Using a torture stick, they press chodainin on the neck very hard, and speak alternately for a while and, finally, force a pick of rice from the bowl into the mouth of chodainin.

While the yamabushi and goriki exchange words, they deliberately give lessons to villagers and new-comers to the village, which may help give a sense of unity among villagers. Gohanshiki Ceremony is an event that was created by folk wisdom.

The Gohan-shiki Ceremony at Hokkoji was designated as an important intangible folk cultural property of Japan in 1996.

間々田のジャガマイタ
Mamada's Jagamaita

小山市　間々田八幡宮

蛇まつり　Ja-matsuri

　小山市間々田地区の伝統ある祭り行事、「ジャガマイタ（蛇祭りともいう）」が2011年（平成23）に国の「記録作成等の措置を講ずべき無形の民俗文化財」（通称、選択無形文化財）として指定された。

　この祭りは、古く江戸時代に端を発したといわれ、地区の住民によって引き継がれてきた。

"Jagamaita" is a traditional festival held in Mamada, Oyama City. It is also called "Ja-Matsuri" (Snake Festival). In 2011, this festival was designated as "an Intangible Folk Cultural Property that deserves measures for documentation" (commonly known as "Selected Intangible Folk Cultural Property").

This festival is said to have originated during the Edo period, and has been taken over by the residents of the dis-

昔は、旧暦４月８日の花祭りの日（現在は５月５日の子供の日）に、「ジャガマイタ、ジャガマイタ」と掛け声をかけ、住民が蛇体を担いで地区町内を練り歩くことから、「ジャガマイタ」と言われるようになった。

この祭りは、蛇体の作成から始まる。各地区ごとに子どもたちが共同で大人の指導のもと、頭が龍、胴体が蛇の形をした長さ 15m ほどの模型（材料は竹、稲わら、藤つる、シダなど）を、祭りの１か月くらい前から作る。

祭り当日には、完成した７体の蛇が、間々田八幡宮に勢揃いする。これを「蛇寄せ」という。

まず神主のお祓いを受け、蛇の口に御神酒が注がれる。次いで拝殿を一周したあと、境内にある池で勇壮な「水飲み」の儀式が行われる。

その後、この蛇体は、大人から子どもまで総勢 50 人あまりの男に担がれ、それぞれ自分の町内に戻っていく。八大龍王と墨書きされた大きな旗のもと「ジャガマイタ」の掛け声とともにひとしきり町内を練り歩くのである。自分の屋敷内に蛇を入れて、厄払いを行うところもある。

そして当日の夕方、各蛇体は間々田小学校校庭に集まる。ここで、地区の若集が中心になり、くんずほぐ

trict.

This festival used to be held on Buddha's birthday (April 8th on the lunar calendar), but today it is held on Children's Day (May 5th). The festival is popularly called 'Jagamaita' because people parade through the town carrying huge papier-mache dragons, shouting 'jagamaita, jagamaita.'

About one month before the parade, children of each part of the town begin to make papier-mache snakes under the guidance of adults. The snake has the head of a dragon and the body of a snake and is made of bamboos, straw, vines and ferns. It is about 15m in length.

On the festival day, 7 snakes get together at the Mamada Hachiman-gu Shrine. This is called 'hebi yose' (the getting together of snakes).

First, the Shinto priest exorcizes evil spirits from the snakes and then sacred 'sake' is poured into the mouths of the snakes. Next, the snakes go round the Hall of Worship of the shrine.

After this, a vital ceremony of 'mizunomi' (water drinking) is held at the pond in the shrine precincts. After this, the snakes are carried back to their own districts on the shoulders of about 50 adults and children. Once they reach their own districts, they parade through streets for a while, shouting "jagamaita, jagamaita"under a huge flag on which "Hachidai Ryuo" (Eight Great Dragon Kings) is written in black ink. Some res-

れつの「蛇もみ」が行われ、一連の行事が終わる。

　祭りの発祥については、二つの説が伝えられている。一つは、釈迦誕生のとき、八大龍王が雨を降らせたという故事にちなみ、旱魃が続くと人々は龍を真似た蛇体を作り雨乞いを願ったという説。もう一つは、間々田地区の竜昌寺住職が当時の大干ばつと疫病除けを願って住民に蛇祭りを行なわせたという説である。いずれにせよ、五穀豊穣、悪疫退散を願っての伝統行事に間違いない。

　なお、「ジャガマイタ」という掛け声は、「蛇が参った」すなわち、蛇体が町内や各家々に来たという意味と、蛇がとぐろを巻くという「蛇が巻いた」という意味の二つの説がある。

idents invite the snake into their houses in order to drive out evil spirits.

In the evening, all the snakes gather in the school yard of Mamada Elementary School, where they begin 'ja-momi' (jostling of snakes). Young men shake and jostle the snakes violently, bumping frequently against each other. This is the end of the whole series of events.

There are two different views about the origin of this festival. One is related with the old legend that Hachidai Ryuo brought rain on the day of Buddha's birth. People made a dragon-like papier-mache to invite rain when there was a long spell of dry weather. The other view is based on an old tale that a priest of the Ryusho-ji Temple in Mamada had the residents perform a snake festival in order to prevent drought and to protect people from plague. In either case, it must be an traditional event to pray for good harvest of the five grains and to drive out an epidemic.

Incidentally, the phrase "jagamaita" can be interpreted in two different meanings. One is 'ja-ga-maitta,' meaning 'snakes have come.' The other is 'ja-ga-maita,' meaning 'snakes have coiled up.'

「悪態まつり」と「瀧流しの式」
"Cursing Festival" and "Ceremony of Sake-Pouring"

足利市大岩町　最勝寺

悪態まつり

　「悪態まつり」は、毎年、大晦日の晩から元日の未明にかけて足利市大岩町大岩毘沙門天最勝寺で行なわれる奇祭である。最勝寺は、天平年間（729－749）に聖武天皇の勅命により僧行基（668-749）が開いたという古刹で、大和（奈良県）の信貴山の朝護孫子寺、山城（京都府）の鞍馬山の鞍馬寺とともに日本三毘沙門天の一つといわれる。

　この祭りは毘沙門天にお参りする人、お参りを済ませて帰る人が、参道ですれ違いざまに「馬鹿ヤロー」「何だと、この大馬鹿ヤロー」などと相手構わず悪口を浴びせあう変わったお祭りである。ただし、「どろぼう」「びんぼう」といった「ぼう」のつく言葉は使ってはいけないとされている。この祭りは一年間の積もり積もった不平不満を吐き出し、さっぱりとした気分で新しい年を迎えようとするもので、江戸時代末期の慶応年間（1865－1867）から続いているといわれる。

Cursing Festival

　"Akutai Matsuri" (Cursing Festival) is a strange festival that is held at the Saisho-ji Temple, Oiwa Town, Ashikaga City. It starts on New Year's Eve and lasts until the daybreak of New Year's Day. The Saisho-ji Temple is an old temple founded by a priest named Gyoki (668-749) under the Imperial Order of Emperor Shomu during the Tempyo Period (729-749). It is one of the three major Bishamontens (the Buddhist God of Wealth and Virtue) in Japan. The other two are Chogosonsiji Temple of Shigi-san in the province of Yamato (now, Nara Prefecture) and Kurama-dera Temple of Kurama-san in the province of Yamashiro (now, Kyoto Prefecture).

　In this festival, the visitors to the shrine shout curses like "Baka-yaro!" or "You big, dumb bastard!" at anyone they happen to pass on the way. They are, however, not allowed to use words with a suffix, " – bo," such as "Doro-bo" (thief), or "Binbo" (poor person). The aim of this festival is to give vent to distresses and discontents that have accumulated within us during the old year and to ring in the new year with refreshed mood. They say that this strange

瀧流しの式

　最勝寺では「悪態祭り」に続いて「瀧流しの式」が行なわれる。「瀧流しの式」では、参加者は毘沙門天の前に直径 50cm 程の大きな盃を持って正座をし、僧侶が頭上から注ぐ御神酒が鼻筋を伝って落ちて来るのを盃に受け、それを一気に飲み干すもので、「滝のように尽きることのないご利益」があるようにとの願いをこめた儀式である。

festival has been observed since the Keio era (1865-1867) in the late Edo period.

Ceremony of sake-pouring

　After "Akutai Matsuri," "Takinagashi- no Shiki" (ceremony of sake-pouring) is held at the Saisho-ji Temple. In this ceremony, participants sit on their heels in front of the Bishamonten, holding a large cup about 50 cm across. Then the priest begins to pour 'sake' over their heads. They are to receive the sake that comes flowing down along the nose with the cup and drink it up at a gulp. This is a ceremony to pray for "unceasing divine blessing to be endowed on them like a waterfall."

毘沙門天階段　Steps to Bishamon-ten

生子神社の泣き相撲
"Nakizumo" at Ikiko Shrine

鹿沼市樅山町　生子神社

生子神社の土俵 Sumo Ring at Ikiko Shrine

　「奉納相撲」の言葉があるように、神社の境内で神仏に奉納するため相撲を行うことは、古来からの伝統行事として営まれてきたが、「泣き相撲」という全国的にも珍しい行事が鹿沼市の生子(いきこ)神社で行われている。

　9月の生子神社例大祭の日(今では19日または19日直後の日曜日)

　As the word "Honozumo" (dedicatory Sumo matches) shows, Sumo wrestling has been held in the shrine's precincts as a traditional event since ancient times in order to be dedicated to deities and Buddha. There is another event called "Nakizumo" (Crying Baby Contest), which is very rare nationwide, that is held at Ikiko Shrine in Kanuma City.

　This Shinto ritual is held on the day of Annual Festival in September (nowa-

がその神事が行われる日である。氏子中から選ばれた力自慢の男性たちが力士と行司に扮し、ミタラセ（境内の御手洗）の水で身を浄め、境内に設けられた土俵に上がってお払いを受ける。その後、行司が、東西に分かれた白鉢巻の乳幼児（生後6か月から3歳くらいまで）二人を呼び出す。力自慢の力士が行司の軍配を合図に乳幼児を抱き上げて、「ヨイショ、ヨイショ」とかけ声もろとも頭上高く揺すり上げ、先に泣いた方を勝ちにする。現在は、勝敗を決せず両方に勝ち名乗りを挙げる形をとっている。

　この神事の発祥時期は不明であるが、神社に奉納された絵馬等から江戸時代末期にはすでに子供相撲が行われ、「泣き相撲」はそこから発生したものとされる。

　「泣く子は育つ」という言い伝えに基づき、子供の無事な成長を願う地域の伝統的な神事であったものが、時代の変遷とともに参加する乳幼児が増え、今では広く県内外からの参加者で賑わう。相撲講が組織され、この行事を主催している。

　1990年（平成2）に鹿沼市の無形民俗文化財に指定され、1996年（平成8）に国の選択無形民俗文化財に指定された。

days on the 19th or on a Sunday immediately after the 19th). The brawny men who have been selected from among the shrine parishioners are dressed as Sumo wrestlers and referees get exorcised on the Sumo ring after being purified with the water of "Mitarase" (holy water trough). After that the Sumo referee calls the two babies (from 6 months to 3 years old), both wearing a white head band, being divided as East or West. The Sumo wrestlers who boast their great physical strength lift the babies in their arms at a sign from the referee and shake and put them high up above their head, shouting "Yoisho, Yoisho." The baby who cries first wins the competition. Nowadays there is no outcome of the competition but both of the babies win the match.

Although when this Shinto ritual originally began is unknown, it is believed that children's Sumo matches were held at the end of Edo Period according to the image drawn on some votive wooden tablets that were dedicated to the shrine and "Nakizumo" was started from there.

Based on the tradition, "the child who cries grows up in good health," it used to be a traditional Shinto ritual of the area to pray for children's growth in good health. As times change, more babies participate recently and it is crowded with the participants from not only inside but outside of the prefecture. A Sumo association is organized to spon-

なお、生子神社の名前の由来については、もともと籾山明神といわれる古い社であったものが、戦国時代のある時、氏子である村人の子が天然痘に罹り死去してしまった 。そこで、その両親が我が子の蘇生を祈願したあと境内に湧くミタラセの池で水行を行ったところ、三日後に願いが叶い、子供が生き返ったという。以来「生子神社」と呼ばれるようになったといわれる。このような由来もあわせて「泣き相撲」の起源に関係していると思われる。

sor the event.

It was designated as Intangible Folk Cultural Properties by Kanuma City in 1990 and as Selected Intangible Folk Cultural Properties by the country in 1996.

Regarding the origin of the name, "Ikiko Shrine," it used to be "Momi-yama Myojin," the name of an old shrine. During the Age of Civil Wars, a child of one of the shrine parishioners in the village died of smallpox. The parents prayed for the child's resuscitation and practiced asceticism (pouring water over themselves) at the pond of "Mi-tarase." 3 days after that, their prayers were answered and the child revived. Since then, the shrine was called "Ikiko Shrine" (Child Resuscitation Shrine). The history of this kind also seems to be related to the origin of "Nakizumo."

鹿沼今宮神社の屋台行事
Imamiya Shrine and its Yataigyoji

鹿沼市今宮町　今宮神社

今宮神社

　鹿沼市の今宮神社は、日光二荒山神社の分社的性格を持ち、日光山鹿沼今宮権現と称した。1608年（慶長13）、徳川幕府から50石の朱印地を与えられ、今宮権現が、現在みられるような優美な権現造りの社殿（県文化財指定）に整備された。明治維新とともに今宮神社と称号が改められ、1931年（昭和6）には栃木県社に昇格した。

付け祭り・ぶっつけ

　18世紀後半頃から今宮神社の氏子が主体となって鹿沼宿の通りを囃子と歌舞で練り歩く「通り祭り」が盛んになった。各町が競い合って江戸から役者や振付師を呼び寄せ、山車・屋台の上で芝居を披露するなど、祭礼を盛り上げた。これが「付け祭り」と呼ばれ、神社が主体となって行なう本祭に附属する祭りという

Imamiya Shrine

The Imamiya Shrine in Kanuma City is a branch shrine of the Nikko-san Futarasan Shrine and it was once called Nikko-san Kanuma Imamiya Gongen. In 1608, it was awarded a vermillion-seal certificate of land rights of 50-koku* by the Tokugawa shogunate and was rebuilt into an elegant-looking shrine of 'gongen-zukuri' (a style of Shinto architecture) that we see today. Its name was changed to the Imamiya Shrine at the beginning of the Meiji Era, and in 1931 it was promoted to the rank of the prefectural shrine.

＊ koku: a measure of volume used for rice. A koku of rice equaled about 180 liters, enough rice to feed one person for a year.

Tsuke-matsuri and Buttsuke

In the latter half of the 18th century, Tori-matsuri Festival came to be held by local residents, mostly parishioners of the Imamiya Shrine. They paraded down the streets of Kanuma dancing to the music of flutes and drums. Each area of Kanuma competed with each other and invited actors and choreographers from Edo (now, Tokyo) to add excitement and pleasure to the festival. They staged shows on dashi (floats) and yatai

意味を持っている。

「ぶっつけ」は、主要交差点において、2台以上の彫刻屋台が向き合い、大銅・締太鼓・鉦・笛の構成による囃子の競演のことである。ちなみに、鹿沼には34の氏子町があり、現在、27台の彫刻屋台がある。

(stages). This is called Tsuke-matsuri. Tsuke-matsuri, as its name suggests, is a festival subordinate to the main festival.

In Buttsuke, more than two yatai decorated with elaborate carvings confront with each other at intersections on streets. People on them play big drums, shime-drums, gongs and flutes, and dis-

鹿沼彫刻屋台　yatai decorated with elaborate carvings

山・鉾・屋台行事

　山・鉾・屋台行事とは、山や鉾などの山車を担いだり、引いたりして練り歩く神社の祭礼の一般呼称である。本来、ダシは「出し物」の意味で、祭りに招き寄せる神の依代になるものである。山車は地方によって呼称や形式が異なり、「曳山」「祭り屋台」（または単に屋台）などとも呼ばれる。

　2016 年、ユネスコは日本の重要無形民俗文化財 33 件を「山・鉾・屋台行事」として世界無形文化遺産に登録した。33 件の中には、既に登録されている茨城県日立市の「日立風流物」と京都府京都市の「京都祇園祭の山鉾行事」も含まれている。栃木県からは「烏山の山あげ行事」と「鹿沼今宮神社の屋台行事」がこの 33 件に含まれている。

屋台

　屋台の始まりは氏神へ奉納する踊りなどの舞台で、移動できる簡単な「屋根付きの台」である。全国的な分類から見ると、鹿沼の屋台は単層舘型の四輪形式で「囃子屋台」の部類に入る。装飾から見ると、「彫

play their skills. Incidentally, 27 out of 34 residential areas of Kanuma City own their yatai.

Yama・Hoko・Yataigyoji

'Yama・Hoko・Yataigyoji' is another name for shrine festivals that feature a parade of 'dashi'. 'Dashi,' a shortened form of 'dashimono,' is a vehicle for the deity of a festival. In some places, 'dashi' is called 'hikiyama' or 'matsuri yatai' (sometimes, shortened to 'yatai')

In 2016, UNESCO registered 33 Important Intangible Folk-Cultural Properties of Japan under the name of 'Yama, Hoko and Yataigyoji' as Would's Intangible Cultural Heritages. Two properties ('Hitachi Furyumono' of Hitachi City and 'Yamahoko of the Gion Festival' of Kyoto) which are already registered are included in the list of the 33. The two properties in Tochigi Prefecture, Yataigyoji of Imamiya Shrine in Kanuma and Yamaagegyoji in Karasuyama are among the 33.

Yatai

Yatai was originally a stage where people offered dances to local deities. It has a roof and can be moved easily. According to the nation-wide classification, yatai in Kanuma is a one-storied type with four wheels, and it can be included as 'Hayashi yatai.' It is a type of Chokoku

刻屋台」に分類される。

　大正時代には「踊り屋台」が数多く制作されていた。「踊り屋台」はすべての部分が折りたたみ構造で、車輪が取り付けられており、機動性を活かし彫刻屋台の前に据え、彫刻屋台が舞台背景となり、本体は囃子などの鳴り物場の役割をしていたことが屋台記録に記されている。

地域伝統芸能

　鹿沼の彫刻屋台の制作・修復に携わる職人、車師、屋台大工、彫工、彩色師の４人が鹿沼の名匠として、一般財団法人地域伝統芸能活用センターの2016年度地域伝統芸能大賞支援賞に決定した。栃木県内では2000年度に受賞した烏山山あげ保存会以来である。

　木工、金工、漆塗、染織などの伝統的な工芸技術が何世紀にもわたり彫刻屋台の維持・修復を支えてきた証である。「動く東照宮」の異名を持つ屋台群は、まさに祭りの主役なのである。

yatai.

During the Taisho period, many odori yatai were built. Odori yatai is so made that it can be folded easily. It has wheels and can be moved easily. It is placed in front of Chokoku yatai and works as a fore-stage of Chokoku yatai. Old records tell us that the odori yatai was used as a stage for musicians.

Traditional Folk Performances

Four people (kuruma-shi, yatai-dai-ku, choko and saishiki-shi) who are engaged in the making and maintaining of chokoku yatai of Kanuma were chosen as excellent craftsmen and were awarded the grand prize in the Traditional Folk Performances of 2016 by the Center for Promotion of Folk-performing Arts. This is the second case that a traditional folk performance in Tochigi Prefecture was awarded a prize. In 2000, Yamaage Festival of Karasuyama was awarded a prize.

This shows that traditional craftsmanship like woodwork, metalwork, lacquerwork, and dyeing have greatly contributed to maintaining or repainting chokoku yatai for centuries. Yatai, which is sometimes called 'Toshogu Shrine that Moves,' is playing a central role in the festival.

野木神社の提灯もみ
Chochin-momi Festival at Nogi Shrine

野木町　野木神社

野木神社

　野木神社は野木町の南西部にある。源頼朝 (1147-1199) とのかかわりが深く、鎌倉幕府の記録である「吾妻鏡」には「野木宮」と記されている。この神社は旧郷社である。

　「野木宮由来」によると、仁徳天皇の御代、下毛野国の国造として赴任した奈良別王は、応神天皇の御子の神霊を山城国の聖廟より笠懸野台手箱（現、野木町野渡台手箱）の地に祠を建てて祀ったのが始

Nogi Shrine

The Nogi Shrine is in the south-western part of Nogi Town. It is closely related with Minamoto no Yoritomo (1147-1199). In *Azuma Kagami* (a historical account of the Kamakura Shogunate), this shrine is listed as Nogi-no-Miya. This shrine was formerly ranked as 'Go-sha.'

According to *the Origin of Nogi-no-Miya*, the origin of this shrine goes back to Narawake no Kimi, who came to the province of Shimotsuke as regional administrator. He built a small shrine in a

野木神社　Nogi Shrine

めという。この祠は、現在の野木神社の南西約800mのところにあり、小さな鳥居と祠が現在も宮地として残されている。

延暦年間 (782-806)、坂上田村麻呂は蝦夷征討の際、当神社に戦勝を祈願し、目的を達成できたので、帰途、祈願成就のお礼として、神霊を現在の地に遷し、社殿を建立したという。

提灯もみ

野木神社では、毎年12月3日に「提灯もみ」と呼ばれる奇祭が行なわれる。この祭りは、戦前まで行なわれていた「七郷巡り」の風習が始めといわれている。「七郷巡り」とは、神官が馬に乗り、神輿が氏子の地域を巡って神社に帰ってくる神事で、古く鎌倉時代の建仁年間 (1201-1204) に始まったと伝えられる。七郷とは、旧寒川郡内の迫間田、寒川、中里などの七つの郷で、かつて源頼朝から寄進された神領であったところである。

「七郷巡り」の際、各郷では裸男が手に手に提灯を持って、郷境で互

place named Kasagake-no-dai Tebako, and asked for a ceremonial transfer of a divided deity of Emperor Ojin's Prince from the holy tomb in the province of Yamashiro (now, part of Kyoto). Its torii and building still remain in a place about 800m south-west of the Nogi Shrine.

During the Enryaku Period (782-806), Sakanoue no Tamura-maro visited this shrine on his way to northern Japan to subdue Ezo tribes. He prayed for the victory in the coming battle. After he successfully subdued Ezo tribes, he visited this shrine again to thank the deity. And he built a new shrine building for the deity in a place where the Nogi Shrine is now.

Chochin-momi Festival

A strange festival named 'Chochin-momi' is held at the Nogi Shrine on December 3rd every year. It is said that the origin of this festival can be traced back to the pre-war custom of 'Shichigo Meguri (lit. going round 7 districts).' In the festival, the Shinto priest goes round his 7 parishes on a horse with a portable shrine. It is believed that this ritual began during the Kennin Period (1201-1204). The 7 parishes are Hazamada, Samukawa, Nakazato, etc., within the former county of Samukawa, land given by Minamoto no Yoritomo.

When the portable shrine came to a border between parishes to be handed over to the next parish, men on the sending side and men on the receiving

提灯もみ（柏村祐司氏撮影）　Chochin-momi Festival (Photo by Yuji Kashiwamura)

いにぶつかりもみ合いながら神霊を熱狂的に迎え、送り出した。神霊を少しでも長く留め置こうとする郷と少しでも早く自分たちのところに招こうとする郷との間で激しいもみ合いがあったという。

　この神事は次第に姿を変え、現在では、長い竿竹の先に提灯を付け、神社の参道で男たちがぶつけ合ってもみ合い、相手の提灯の火を消し合うものとなった。これが「提灯もみ」である。祭りの日には境内の神楽殿では「太々神楽」が演じられる。

side bumped and jostled against each other because the sending side wanted to keep the shrine in their parish as long as possible and the receiving side wanted to receive the shrine as soon as possible. Men on both sides wear only a loincloth.

　The form of this ritual has gradually changed. Today people get together on the approach of the Nogi Shrine with a long bamboo which is tied with a chochin on its top. They bump and jostle against each other trying to put out the fire in the chochin. This is the present form of Chochin-momi. On the day of the festival Daidaikagura Dance is performed in the Kagura-den Hall of the shrine.

ニッコウキスゲ(日光黄菅)

ススキノキ科ワスレグサ属

禅庭花とも言われる。
日本の中部以北の高地に生じ、しばしば大群落をなす。
花は黄色で、葉が笠菅に似ているのでキスゲと呼ばれる。

第6章
受け継がれる名産品
Local Products

東昌寺梵鐘　Bell at Tosho-ji Temple

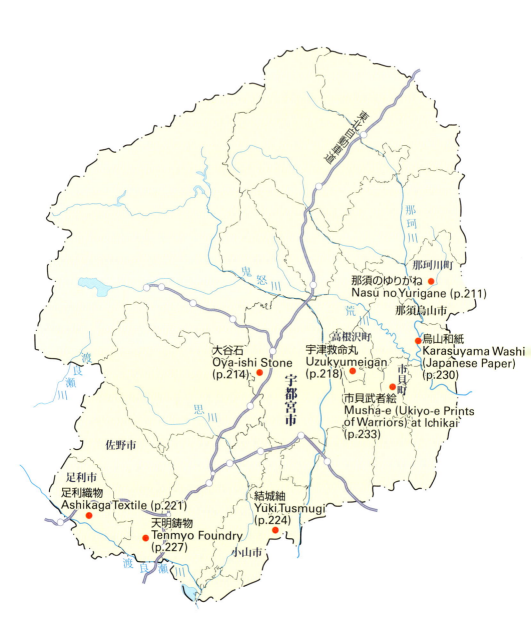

那須のゆりがね
Nasu-no-Yurigane

那珂川町健武

　那珂川町健武(旧馬頭町健武)にある健武山神社は、日本武尊と金山彦命の２柱をご祭神とする神社で、延喜式内社＊の一つである。

＊延喜式内社：平安時代の延喜式神名帳に記載されている格式の高い神社

　この神社のある一帯はわが国で最初に金を産出したとされるところで、平安末期に編集された「東大寺要録」によると、東大寺の大仏の

The Takebu-yama Shrine at Takebu, Nakagawa Town, enshrines Yamato Takeru-no-mikoto and Kaneyamahiko-no-mikoto. This shrine is one of the prestigious shrines listed in *Engi Shiki*＊.

＊ Engi Shiki is a collection of books compiled by order of Emperor Daigo during the Engi Era (901-922).

It is believed that the first gold in Japan was discovered in the area around this shrine. According to *Todaiji Yoroku*, which was compiled during

健武山神社　Takebu-yama Shrine

鍍金に必要な「金」が747年（天平19）に下野国で産出された、とある。「那須のゆりがね」として知られる砂金である。

「続日本紀」によると、陸奥国小田（現、宮城県遠田郡涌谷町黄金山神社付近）から大量の「金」がもたらされたのは749年（天平21）のことであるので、「那須のゆりがね」より2年後にあたる。

12世紀前半頃に書かれた「今昔物語」（巻十一）には、次のように書かれている。「陸奥ノ国・下野ノ国ヨリ色黄ナル砂ヲ奉レリ。鍛冶共ヲ召テ吹下サルニ、実ニ色目出タク、滉イ黄ナル金ニテ有リ。…（中略）…此ノ国ノ金ノ出来レル始也。」（聖武天皇、始造東大寺語）

「延喜式」によると、「那須国が毎年納める税は、砂金百五十両、練金八十四両（1両=37.5g）」であった。東大寺の大仏の鋳造が開始されたのは749年（天平勝宝1）であり、その開眼供養が行われたのは752年であった。「続日本紀」は、また、「承和2年（835年）「下野国武茂神に従五位下を授け奉る。この神は砂金を採る山上に座す」と書いているが、これはこの神社が大仏造立に功績があったことを称えたものと想像される。

「古代産金の里」の碑
Monument that tells 'Gold was once found here'

the late years of the Heian period, gold necessary to plate Great Buddha of the Todaiji Temple was first discovered in the province of Shimotsuke in 747. The gold is popularly known by the name of 'Nasu-no-Yurigane'.

Shoku Nihongi tells us that, 2 years later, a large amount of gold was found in Oda in the province of Mutsu (now, Miyagi Prefecture) in 749.

The 11th Book of *Konjaku Monogatari* ('Tales of Times Now and Past') written during the first half of the 12th century says: "Yellow-colored sand was presented from the provinces of Michinoku and Shimotsuke. Smiths were gathered and told to refine it, and gold

ちなみに、東大寺の大仏に鍍金をするのに必要とされた金の量は、約58.5kgであったという。

マルコ・ポーロ (1254-1324) は「東方見聞録」(the Travels of Marco Polo) の中で、日本を「黄金の国ジパング (Zipangu)」と紹介している。「東方見聞録」によるとジパングの人々は、偶像崇拝者で、外見がよく、礼儀正しいが、人喰いの習慣がある、と書かれている。マルコ・ポーロは日本には来ていないので、恐らく、モンゴルに滞在中にでも耳にした話に基づいてこのように書いたものであろう。

of high-quality was obtained. ...This is the first time that gold was obtained in our country."

Engi Shiki says, "The province of Nasu paid taxes of 150-ryo in gold dust and 84-ryo(1-ryo=37.5g) in refined gold." The making of the Great Statue of Buddha began in 749 and the ceremony to consecrate the Statue was held in 752, and *Shoku Nihongi* writes: In 835, 'Jugoi-no-ge' (Junior Fifth Rank, Lower Grade) was given to the god of Mumo located on a gold-producing mountain in the province of Shimotsuke." It is believed that the shrine was ranked 'jugoi-no-ge' because it greatly contributed to the building of the Great Buddha.

Incidentally, the total amount of gold needed to make the Buddha was 58.5kg.

In *Travels of Marco Polo*, Marco Polo (1254-1324) described Japan as "Zipangu of Gold Country." It also tells us, "People in Japan are idol worshippers, good-looking, and polite, but they have habits of man-eating." He did not come to Japan and he may have been told stories like this while he was in Mongolia and recorded them in his journal.

大谷石
Oya Stone

宇都宮市大谷

　宇都宮市の中心部から北西に約7kmの地に石の里大谷がある。大谷は「陸の松島」「関東の耶馬渓」などと称され、里のあちこちには「天狗の投げ石」「亀岩」などの奇岩や怪岩を見ることが出来る。
　大谷地区で産出される緑色の凝灰岩は大谷石と呼ばれ、建築用資材をはじめ様々な用途に使われ

Oya lies about 7 km north-west from the center of Utsunomiya City. Oya is often called "Matsushima on Land" or "Yabakei in Kanto." Here and there in Oya, we can see strange and interesting rock formations like 'Tengu-no-Nageishi" (Rock thrown by a tengu) or "Kame-iwa" (Tortoise Rock).

The green tuff stone produced in Oya is called Oya stone. It is well-known nation-wide as building materials. It

大谷寺　Oya-ji Temple

ている。この地域の地下には東西8km、南北 37km にわたって大谷石があると推定されている。

下野国分寺礎石

大谷石が建築材料として利用されるようになった歴史は古く、壬生の車塚古墳や奈良時代 741 年（天平 13）に下野国分寺が建立された際、礎石として大谷石が使われたことが分かっている。

日本最古の磨崖仏

大谷寺の壁面には、本尊の石造千手観音立像（高さ約 4m90cm）をはじめ、平安時代（794-1185）から鎌倉時代（1185-1333）にかけて彫られた計 10 体の磨崖仏があり、国の特別史跡・重要文化財の二重指定を受けている。日本最古の磨崖仏である。

帝国ホテル

大谷石を全国的に有名にしたのはなんと言っても帝国ホテルの建築である。

1917 年（大正 6）頃、財界人大倉喜八郎を中心に、外国人客を対象にした高級ホテルを建築しようと

is estimated that Oya stone lies underground 8 km east and west and 37 kilometers north and south.

Cornerstones of Shimotsuke Kokubunji Temple

Oya stone has been used as building materials since old days. It is known that the stone was used for the building of Kurumazuka Tumulus in Mibu. It is also known that it was used as cornerstones of the Shimotsuke Kokubunji Temple which was built in 741.

the Oldest Rock Carvings in Japan

On the rock face of the Oya-ji Temple, there is a carving of Thousand Armed Kannon (about 4.90 meters in height) together with 9 other carvings. They were carved during the Heian (794-1185) and Kamakura (1185-1333) periods and are designated as National Historic Site and as National Important Cultural Property. They are the oldest carvings on rock face in Japan.

Imperial Hotel

Oya stone was used for building the Imperial Hotel, which made Oya stone famous all over Japan.

Around 1917, Okura Kihachiro and some financiers began to feel the need for a high-class hotel for visitors from foreign counties and asked an American

明治村に移築された旧帝国ホテル　Former Imperial Hotel (Museum Meiji-mura)

する動きが起り、その設計をアメリカの建築家フランク・ロイド・ライト(1869-1959)に依頼した。

　ライトはその建築材料として大谷石に着目した。当時、倉庫などにしか使われていなかった大谷石を高級ホテルに使うことに、はじめ、大倉達の反対があったが、最終的にはライトの考え通り大谷石が使用されることになった。

　ホテルは1922年(大正11)に営業を開始したが、翌1923年9月1日に起きた関東大震災でもほとんど被害を受けず、当時は大谷石が

architect, Frank Lloyd Wright (1869-1959), to make a plan.

　Wright's attention was attracted to Oya stone as building materials of the hotel. At first, Okura and others objected to Wright's idea, because, in those days, Oya stone was used only for building warehouses and, to use it as materials for high-class hotels was considered undesirable. However, Wright's idea of using Oya stone was finally accepted.

　The Imperial Hotel was opened in 1922. On September 1st, following year, Kanto area was severely hit by a devastating earthquake, but the hotel was damaged only slightly. People thought that Oya stone was an excellent build-

耐震性、耐火性にすぐれた建築材料であるとして話題となった。

当初の帝国ホテルの建物はその後の再建に伴い、愛知県犬山市の明治村に移された。

日本民藝館

大谷石は、東京の駒場にある日本民藝館の一階の外壁および一階ホールの床部分にも用いられている。日本民藝館は柳宗悦（むねよし）(1889-1961)、濱田庄司 (1894-1978) ら が中心となって 1936 年に開設された日本の伝統的工芸品を収蔵展示している建物で、初代館長に柳宗悦、二代館長に濱田庄司がなっている。

松が峰教会

宇都宮市に、1932年（昭和7）に完成したカトリック松が峰教会も大谷石を使用した双塔を持つ美しい建物で、その建設はカジャック神父 (R. P. Hippolyte Cadilhac 1859-1930) によって構想されたものである。

この他、大谷石を用いた建造物として、栃木市入舟町の横山郷土館の蔵や宇都宮市の旧大谷公会堂など多数ある。

また、大谷石は花瓶、置物、灯籠などの大谷石細工にも利用されている。

ing materials for withstanding fires and earthquakes at the time.

The hotel was renovated and the original hotel buildings were moved to the Museum Meiji-mura in Inuyama City, Aichi Prefecture.

Japan Folk Crafts Museum

Oya stone is also used for the outer walls and the hall of the 1st floor of the Japan Folk Crafts Museum in Koma-ba, Tokyo, which was opened in 1936 by Yanagi Muneyoshi (1889-1961) Hamada Shoji (1894-1978) and others. The museum displays a collection of traditional works of folk crafts. The first director of the museum was Yanagi Muneyoshi and the second was Hamada Shoji.

Matsugamine Catholic Church

The two-steepled Matsugamine Catholic Church in Utsunomiya, which was completed in 1932, is also built of Oya stone. The church was designed by R.P.Hippolyte Cadilhac (1859-1930).

Many other buildings such as the Store-house of Yokoyama Kyodo-kan at Irifune, Tochigi City, and Oya Civic Hall in Utsunomiya are also made of Oya stone.

Oya stone is also used for making vases, ornament articles and lanterns.

宇津救命丸
Uzu Kyumeigan
高根沢町　上高根沢

宇津救命丸薬師堂　Uzukyumeigan Yakushido

　高根沢町にある御料牧場の東約500mのところに宇津救命丸高根沢工場がある。この工場は、1597年（慶長2）に宇津権右衛門によってはじめられたものである。権右衛門は宇都宮家第22代城主 国綱の御殿医であったが、国綱が豊臣秀吉から突然改易を言い渡されたのを期に、高根沢の地に帰農して半農

　The Takanezawa plant of Uzu Kyumeigan is located about 500m east of Imperial Stock Farm. It was founded by Utsu Gon'emon in 1597. Gon'emon was once a family doctor of Kunitsuna, the 22nd lord of Utsunomiya Castle. But when Kunitsuna was suddenly deprived of his fief by Toyotomi Hideyoshi, Gon'emon became a farmer, and continued to practice medicine in the village of Takanezawa.

半医の生活をはじめた。

　宇津家の秘薬、金匱救命丸（宇津救命丸はかつてこう呼ばれた）は子供の薬として一粒が米俵一俵に値するといわれたが、近郷近在の人々に無償で分け与えられていたという。

　金匱救命丸の製法は、代々、宇津家の長男だけに口伝されたという。この薬の優れた効能の評判は次第に関東一円から全国に広がり、多くの家庭では金匱救命丸を置薬とした。

　1781年（天明元）になって、宇津家は新領主の一橋家（徳川御三卿のひとつ）にこの薬の献上を始めた。

　宇津家は、また、1876年（明治9）、明治初期には全国的に極めて珍しい私立小学校、宇津学校（最初は「博愛館」と呼ばれた）を設立した。そこでは、修身、漢文、算数、習字を教え、教師は宇津家一門の兄弟たちが務めたという。教師の病・死などで、1935年（昭和10）頃、廃校を余儀なくされたが、宇津資料館には当時の立派な卒業証書が展示されている。

　宇津救命丸高根沢工場に隣接する宇津薬師堂（高根沢町指定文化財）の敷地内には、その業績・社会貢献を称える石碑が立っている。当時の貴族院議長で学習院院長でも

Kinki Kyumeigan (later called Uzu Kyumeigan) was a secret family medicine of the Utsu Family for young children. It was said that a pill of Kinki Kyumeigan was worth a bag of 60 kg of rice. The Utsu Family gave the medicine free to people living nearby.

It is said that the secret recipe for this medicine was handed down by word of mouth from the eldest son of one generation to the eldest son of the next generation. The efficacy of this medicine gradually came to be known not only in the district of Kanto, but in the whole nation. And many families kept Kinki Kyumeigan as household medicine.

In 1781 the Utsu Family began to present this medicine to the new lord, Hitotsubashi Tokugawa family (one of the 3 privileged branches of the Tokugawa family).

In 1876, the Utsu family established a private elementary school called Private Utsu School (named Hakuai Kan at the beginning). In the early days of the Meiji period, it was quite rare to establish a private elementary school. Subjects taught were: morals, Chinese, arithmetic, and calligraphy. They were taught by the sons of the Utsu Family. Around 1935, the school was forced to close down due to the teachers' illness and death. We can see the beautiful diploma of those days displayed in the Utsu Museum.

Within the precincts of Utsu Yakushido (one of the cultural properties of

あった近衛篤麿（1863-1904）が建てたものと伝えられている。

現在、第18代当主の宇津善博氏が宇津救命丸株式会社の社長をしている。本社は東京にある。

高根沢工場の敷地内、木立の中には、江戸時代に薬の調合をしたという「誠意軒」や宇津資料館が建っている。工場入口の松、屋敷前の堀、中央の長屋門などは、江戸時代の名残を今に伝えている。代々、教育家、篤志家として存続してきた宇津家の歴史を感じさせる高根沢の一隅である。

Takanezawa Town) near the Takanezawa plant, there is a stone monument which praises Utsu family and the school for their achievement and contribution to the society. It was built by Konoe Atsumaro (1863-1904), Chairman of the House of Peers and President of Gakushuin School at that time.

The president of Uzu Kyumeigan Corporation today is Utsu Yoshihiro, the 18th family head of Utsu Family. Its head office is in Tokyo.

In the grounds of Takanezawa plant among pine trees, there is a building called Sei'i Ken where medicines were mixed during the Edo period. There is also Utsu Museum. The pine trees at the entrance to the plant, moats in front of the house, Nagayamon gate in the center and so on are remainders of the Edo period. It is a nook in Takanezawa where you can feel the history of the Utsu family as a family of education and benevolence that has continued to exist for generations.

宇津救命丸長屋門　Nagaya-mon Gate, Uzukyumeigan

足利織物
Ashikaga Textile
足利市

絹の生産は紀元前3000年頃に中国で始まったとされ、日本には弥生時代に伝わった。

709年（和銅2）、皇大神宮＊の遷宮に際し、足利地方から絹織物が献上されたとの記録がある。

＊皇大神宮：三重県伊勢市五十鈴川上にある神道で一番重要な神宮。ご祭神は天照大神。

また、正倉院の文書に明記されているように、752年（天平勝宝4）東大寺の大仏開眼の際にも足利地方から織物が献上され、平安時代に入ってもなお献上が続いたとされる。

さらに、鎌倉時代末期に書かれた「徒然草」第216段には足利義

ノコギリ屋根工場 Factory with saw-tooth shell roof

It is generally believed that silk production began in China around 3000 BC. It was introduced to Japan during the Yayoi period (about 300 BC-about AD 300).

It is recorded in an old document that silk fabrics were presented from Ashikaga to the Kotaijingu Shrine* when its deity was transferred to a new shrine building in 709.

* the Kotaijinngu Shrine: one of the most important Shinto shrines in the upper reaches of Ise City, Mie Prefecture. Enshrines Amaterasu Omikami.

The documents kept in the Shoso-in tell us that some textiles were presented from Ashikaga to the Todai-ji Temple when the ceremony to consecrate the Great Buddha was held at the temple in 752. Textiles continued to be presented into the Heian period.

Furthermore, it is written in the 216th Chapter of *Tsurezuregusa (Essays in Idleness)* that every year Ashikaga Yoshiuji presented Ashikaga dyed fabrics to Hojo Tokiyori (1227-1263), shogunal regent to the Kamakura Shogunate at the time.

At the end of the 18th century, tall looms were brought in from Nishijin, Kyoto, via Kiryu to Ashikaga, and full-

氏が鎌倉幕府執権北条時頼 (1227-1263) に毎年足利染物（織物）を贈った、とある。

足利では 18 世紀末、京都西陣より桐生経由で高機（たかばた）を移入、本格的な商品生産を開始した。

1820 年前後からは、木綿織物や絹綿交織物も人気を博し、足利市場が隆盛した。こうして足利織物業は、上州（現、群馬県）西部の養蚕地帯、中部の製糸地帯、東部の織物地帯、館林・真岡付近の綿糸地帯と共に大きな地域的分業の一環を形成するようになった。

1880 年（明治 13）には、米大統領であったグラント将軍 (1822-1885) が足利来遊の折、白縮緬（ちりめん）を贈られたという。

1890 年代には、手工業形式の工場が出現した。現在、ノコギリ屋根工場は日本の近代化産業遺産として登録されている。足利市内に現存するものは、旧足利模範撚糸工場（現アンタレススポーツクラブ）と旧足利織物㈱（現トチセン）の二棟である。

1920 年（大正 9）には足利模様銘仙が起こる。銘仙の源流は屑繭や玉繭からとった太い糸を緯糸（よこいと）に用いた先染平織（さきぞめひらおり）の絹織物で、柄合（がらあい）は縞・絣（かすり）が中心で、丈夫で安価、

scale silk commodity production started.

Around 1820, cotton fabrics and mixed fabrics of cotton and silk became popular and the Ashikaga market became livened up. Silkworm raising in the western Joshu district, silk reeling in the middle Joshu district, weaving in the eastern Joshu district, and cotton fabrics in Tatebayashi/Moka area came together to form the link of regional specialization as Ashikaga Textile Industry.

In 1880, when General Ulysses S. Grant (1822-1885), the former president of the USA, visited Ashikaga, a fabric of white crepe was presented to him.

During the 1890s, fabrics came to be manufactured in small-scale mills. Today, the silk mills with saw-tooth shell roof are registered as the heritages of industrial modernization. Two buildings of those days still exists in Ashikaga: Former Ahsikaga Model Silk Mill (now, Antares Sports Club) and Former Ashikaga Textile Co. (now, Tochisen Co.).

In 1920, they started weaving Ashikaga Design Meisen (coarse silk cloth). The origin of Meisen can be traced back to the silk fabrics which are made of waste cocoon and of thick yarn taken from cocoon. The patterns were mainly either stripes or Kasuri (splashed pattern). Since it was durable and inexpensive. Kasuri was widely used for women's everyday clothes and bedclothes.

In the Taisho period, it came to be

女性の普段着や夜具に用いられた。

　大正期には伊勢崎、桐生、秩父、足利、八王子等、北西関東を中心に生産されるようになった。工場で大量生産される安価な銘仙の出現によって、それまで木綿しか着られなかった庶民の女性までが絹の着物に袖を通すようになり、東京を中心に中産階級の普段着、庶民のおしゃれ着、カフェ女給の仕事着として定着した。

　特に足利の「解し織*」で作った柄が友禅染や抜染や捺染の如く際立たず上品で、嗜好に適し、喜ばれた。

＊解し織：栃木県指定伝統工芸品

　今、足利市は「解し織」や踊り用の着物に使う織物づくりによって、また、編メリヤス、横メリヤス、ニット製品の染色総合生産として、その伝統と技術を引き継ぎ、新たな機業地として活躍している。

produced mainly in the north-west part of Kanto region, such as Isesaki, Kiryu, Chichibu, Ashikaga and Hachioji. As meisen became inexpensive because of mass production, common women who used to wear only cotton kimono started wearing silk kimono. In Tokyo and in some other places, meisen came to be used for everyday wear of the middle class people, for stylish garments of common people, or for working clothes of the café maids.

The design made from Ashikaga "Hogushiori*" was more gradated and elegant than that of the Yuzen dyeing, the Discharge dyeing, or the Textile printing. So it was considered more "refined" and was welcomed by people because it matched their taste.

＊ Hogushiori: a splashed pattern called 'fraying weave'. Traditional Crafts Products designated by Tochigi Prefecture

Today, the city of Ashikaga is thriving as a city of Total Dyeing Industry by taking over the traditional technologies of producing not only "Hogushiori" and fabrics for dancing wear, but also knitted fabrics, weft-knitted fabrics, and other fabrics.

結城紬
Yuki-tsumugi
小山市、下野市

結城紬の起源は、古代に遡り、「常陸国風土記」（721年成立）に記されている「長幡部絁」に結びつくものと考えられている。絁とは粗製の絹布のことである。

「庭訓往来」（1322年発行）には、諸国の名産品の一つとして「常陸紬」の名前が見える。室町時代にこの地方を治めていた結城氏から幕府や鎌倉管領にこの織物が献上されたことから「結城紬」と呼ばれるようになった。

近世になり、この地方の代官となった者が染色と織り方の技術の改良を行い、「結城紬」の知名度を高めた。その結果、生産が増大し、「和漢三才図絵」に国内最上級の紬ということで紹介された。幕末から明治にかけて、より高度な絣織りや縮織りの技術が取り入れられて生産が増大した。

一方、織機の出現により伝統的な「結城紬」本来の機織りの消滅が危惧されるようになり、伝統的な技術を残すよう技術保存運動が展開された。

The origin of Yuki-tsumugi goes back to ancient times. It is believed that Yuki-tsumugi is related with Nagahatabe-no-Ashiginu recorded in *Hitachi-no-kuni Fudoki* (written in 721). Ashiginu is a kind of rough cloth of silk.

In *Teikin Orai* (publ. in 1322), Yuki-tsumugi is listed by the name of Hitachi-Tsumugi as one of the noted products in Japan. Yuki-tsumugi came to be called by the present name after the Yukis presented textiles to the Kamakura Shogunate and the Shogunal deputy for the Kanto region.

Yuki-tsumugi came to be widely known after a local 'daikan' (local administrator) improved the techniques of dyeing and weaving textiles. As a result, the production of Yuki-tsumugi greatly increased. *Wakan-Sansai-Zue* writes that Yuki-tsumugi is one of the best tsumugi in Japan. From the end of the Edo period till the beginning of the Meiji period, higher techniques of 'kasuriori' (splashed pattern) weaving and 'chijimiori' (cotton crepe) weaving were adopted and the production greatly increased.

When weaving machines were introduced, people began to fear that the traditional method of weaving Yuki tsumugi by hand would die out, and the

亀甲柄　Tortoise-shell pattern

　1956年（昭和31）には国の重要無形文化財に指定され、同時に従事者6名が技術保持者に認定された。

　その後、1977年（昭和52）には国の「伝統工芸品」にも指定され、同年、結城紬伝統工芸士（染2名、絣くくり6名、織り6名）が認定された。

movement to preserve the traditional method began.

Yuki-tsumugi was designated as a national intangible important cultural asset in 1956 and, at the same time, 6 persons were certified as holders of techniques of traditional tsumugi-weaving.

In 1977, Yuki-tsumugi was designated as a national traditional handicraft, and several persons (2 for dyeing, 6 for kasuri-kukuri, and 6 for weaving) were certified as craftsmen of traditional Yuki Tsumugi.

結城紬とは？

　結城紬の重要無形文化財としての指定要件は次の3点である。
1. 手つむぎ：使用する糸はすべて真綿から手で紡いだものとする。
2. 手くびり：絣模様を付ける場合は手くびりによること。
3. 地機（居座機）で織ること。

　これら3つの要件を満たさない場合は重要無形文化財とは見なされない。

　制作工程には非常に手間がかかり、そのことから女性の着物一着分（普通の亀甲のもの）が100万円くらいで取引される。

　結城紬の主な生産地は、栃木県では小山市から下野市付近まで、茨城県では結城市である。小山ものを「結城」と呼ぶことに違和感を覚える人もいるが、この地域は歴史的には小山氏とその一族の結城氏が支

What is Yuki-tsumugi?

　In order to be called Yuki-tsumugi, a fabric must meet the following 3 requirements:
1. All yarns for Yuki-tsumugi must be spun manually from floss silk.
2. Patterns of 'kasuri' (ikat) must be made by hand-tying.
3. All yarns must be woven with a back-strap loom

　Fabrics that do not meet these 3 requirements can not be recognized as important intangible cultural assets.

　It takes very long time to weave Yuki-tsumugi and the cloth (with tortoise-shell patterns) needed for a kimono costs about 1,000,000 yen.

　Yuki-tsumugi is mainly produced in Oyama City and Shimotsuke City in Tochigi Prefecture and in Yuki City in Ibaraki Prefecture. Some people may find it strange to call products of Oyama by the name of Yuki, but people in the area do not feel it incongruous to use the name of Yuki tsumugi because the

地機織　Back-strap Loom

配した地域であり、産地の人々には違和感はない。

もともとこの地方では養蚕が盛んであって、紬織りは農閑期の副業として、農家の女性の大切な収入源となっていたが、現在は生産が激減している。

ユネスコ無形文化遺産

2010年（平成22）11月、結城紬がユネスコの無形文化遺産保護条約に基づき、「人類の無形文化遺産の代表的な一覧表」に記載（登録）され、結城紬がこれまで守り続けてきた高い技術が世界的に評価された。日本では、これまでに能楽、歌舞伎など21件（2016年現在）がユネスコ無形文化遺産に登録されている。

結城紬は、もともと丈夫で日常衣料や野良着として、親から子へ数代にわたって着続けられていた。それを江戸時代の通人が見い出し、色合いが渋いうえに絹なのに絹らしい光沢を発しない、独特の風合いを出す粋な反物として人気を博していった。

現在、小山市福良にある栃木県産業技術センター紬織物技術支援センターでは、紬織物についての試験研究、技術支援及び後継者育成を行っている。

area was once governed by the Oyama family and and its branch family, Yuki.

Sericulture has been prospering in this area, and was an important source of income for women of farming families as a side business during the agricultural off-season.

UNESCO Intangible Cultural Heritage

In November, 2010, Yuki-tsumugi (handwoven silk fabric) was inscribed on the 'Representative List of the Intangible Cultural Heritage of Humanity' based on 'UNESCO Convention for the Safeguarding of the Intangible Cultural Heritage.' This means that its sophisticated techniques of weaving Yuki -tsumugi were universally recognized. So far, 21 items in Japan including 'noh plays' and 'kabuki plays' have been inscribed on the list of Intangible Cultural Heritage.

Yuki-tsumugi has been used for everyday or farmers' working clothes, and has been worn from generation to generation. It was found by a man-about-town during the Edo period and gradually gained popularity as stylish fabrics because it was quiet in color even thought it was silk and had unique feeling.

Today, Tsumugi-orimono Technology Support Center (a branch center of Industrial Technology Center of Tochigi Prefecture) in Fukura, Oyama City, is doing experimental studies of Yuki-tsumugi, offering technical supports, and taking charge of upbringing successors.

天明鋳物
Tenmyo-foundry

佐野市

天明鋳物の最盛期は室町時代 (1392-1573) から江戸時代 (1603-1867) 初期といわれている。特に、茶道が隆盛を迎えた安土桃山時代 (1573-1600) には、天明鋳物の茶釜は、九州・福岡県の芦屋町産の茶釜と併せて、「西の芦屋、東の天明」と並び称され、もてはやされた。

芦屋釜は地肌が滑らかで地紋が鮮麗なのに対し、天明釜は寂びた肌合いに素朴で力強い造形という特徴を有している。

江戸時代の釜の鑑定控えには、「上作の天明釜は、大判金で50枚程」との記述もあるとのことである。（現代の通貨に換算する場合、一両を6.6万円、大判金を十両とすると、およそ3,300万円となる）

天明鋳物を有名にしたのは、京都・方広寺の「国家安康」の梵鐘の鋳造である。数千人ともいわれている全国の鋳物師とともに、佐野からも39名の天明鋳物師が参加し、脇棟梁を務めたとのことである。その梵鐘が、のちに、大坂の陣による豊臣家滅亡を招いたとされる方広寺鐘

It is believed that Tenmyo Foundry was at its peak from the Muromachi period (1392-1573) to the early Edo period (1603-1867). Especially, during the Azuchi Momoyama period (1573-1600) when tea-ceremony was most popular, the tea-kettles of Tenmyo Foundry as well as those made in Ashiya, Fukuoka Prefecture, was highly valued. It was often said said, "Ashiya in the west Japan and Tenmyo in the east Japan."

While Ashiya tea-kettles have smooth surface and vivid pattern in design, Tenmyo tea-kettles have quiet and subdued refinement in temperament and simple and sturdy shaping.

One memorandum of the tea-kettle evaluation in the Edo period says, "a well-made Tenmyo kettle is worth 50 large oval gold coins." (If converted into modern currency with a large oval gold coin being worth 66,000 yen, it will be about 33,000,000 yen.)

What made Tenmyo Foundry famous was that together with thousands of founders over the country, 39 Tenmyo founders from Sano participated as the side leaders in the project of "Kokka Anko" temple bell foundry for Hoko-ji Temple in Kyoto. Later, this temple bell caused "Hoko-ji Temple Bell Inscrip-

銘事件を引き起こした。

　現存する最古の天明鋳物は1321年銘の梵鐘で、鋳物師名は大工甲斐権守　卜部助光、茨城県五霞町にある東昌寺に寄進されている。

　千年の歴史を持つ天明鋳物は多種多様で、武器の製造で始まったが、その後、梵鐘、鰐口、銅祠、釣り灯篭、擬宝珠、茶釜、仏像に及び、現代では機械の部品なども作られている。かつて、佐野には100軒の鋳物屋と300人を超す鋳物師がいたと言われているが、明治以降、佐野の鋳物業は衰退し、どちらかとい

tion Incident," which is said to have led Toyotomi Family to fall after the Siege of Osaka.

Among all the foundry works presently existing that are recognized as Tenmyo Foundry, the oldest one is the temple bell inscribed as Founder, Carpenter Kai Gonnokami Urabe Sukemitsu, 1321, which has been donated to Tosho-ji Temple, Goka Town, Ibaraki Prefecture.

Tenmyo Foundry, which has a history of 1,000 years, started with the manufacture of weapons and then a great variety of kinds of works such as temple bells, prayer gongs, small copper shrines, hanging lanterns, ornamental

佐野市の鋳造所　a foundry factory in Sano City

うと伝統工芸として存続、2014年時点で佐野旧市街地に残る主な現役の天明鋳物の鋳物師・鋳造所は、栗崎、正田、若林の3軒にまで減少している。

　新しい取り組みとして花器、文鎮、ベーゴマなどを商品化し、最近の話題として、佐野市ゆかりの有名人、ダイヤモンド・ユカイ、石井琢朗らの手型などがある。

caps of a railing post, tea-kettles, Buddhist images, and so forth. Machinery parts are also made today. It is said that there used to be 100 foundry factories and over 300 founders in Sano in the past. After the Meiji Period, the foundry in Sano declined and continued to exist as traditional craft. As of 2014, only 3 Tenmyo foundry factories are on active service in the old Sano City area. They are Kurisaki, Shoda, and Wakabayashi.

　Recently new attempts have been made to produce vases and bowls, paper weights, spinning tops, and so on. One of the attempts that have attracted the attention of people was casting handprints of famous people like Diamond Yukai, Ishii Takuro, etc., who were born or grew up in Sano City.

東昌寺梵鐘　Bell at Tosho-ji Temple

烏山和紙

Karasuyama Washi (Japanese Paper)

那須烏山市

　烏山和紙を代表するものに程村紙（程村は那須烏山市下境地区にあった地名）を挙げることができる。元来、原料に那須楮を使った手すき和紙である。

　手漉き和紙の作業工程は、原材料の楮をカセイソーダ液で煮て繊維を柔らかくすることから始まり、流水の中でのアク抜き、同じく流水の中で楮の皮についた塵を手で取り除く塵取り、楮の繊維を細かく砕く叩解、繊維を漉きフネに入れ、水とトロロアオイの根を加えて攪拌、漉き桁での漉き、水分を搾り出し、最後に一枚ずつ乾燥機にかけて干す、というものであり、手作業が基本である。

　1213〜1219年に那須十郎が越前五箇荘から紙漉き職人を招き、那須奉書を漉き始めたのが起源とされる。この技法は国の無形重要文化財に選ばれており、今では主に地元の山あげ祭りのハリカ（野外歌舞伎の、山と呼ばれる舞台背景）や県内の小・中・高の卒業証書に使われている。2007年、烏山和紙を使っ

Hodomura-shi (Hodomura is the name for the area that used to exist in Shimozakai, Nasukarasuyama City) represents Karasuyama Washi (thick Japanese paper). It is originally the handmade Japanese paper using Nasu Paper Mulberry.

Its making work process is as follows. First, the fibers of the raw material, Kozo (Paper Mulberry) need to be softened by boiling them in caustic soda. Then the lye must be washed away in the flowing water (Akunuki). At the same time, the dust should be removed by hand from the Kozo skins (Chiritori). After that the Kozo fibers need to be smashed and broken into pieces (Kokai). Then the fibers are stirred in a boat with water and roots of Sunset Hibiscus added in it (Kakuhan). From the boat, the fibers are scooped and spread thin using the reeds (Suki). At the end, the sheets are hung one by one in the drying machine after the water is squeezed out. This whole process is basically done all by hand.

It is believed to be its origin that Nasu Juro invited some paper makers from Echizen Gokanosho between 1213 and 1219 and started making Nasu thick Japanese paper for ceremonial use. This

た照明器具や工芸家具商品が、国の「中小企業地域資源活用プログラム」に認定された。厚み、光沢があり、熱に強い烏山和紙の特性を活かし、細切れの紙を利用した押し絵やつなぎ目のない3m四方の大きな和紙を用いた「ついたて」などの商品化にも取り組んでいる。

paper making technique has been designated as one of the National Important Intangible Cultural Properties and used mainly to make the Graduation Certificates for the elementary, junior high and high schools in the prefecture as well as to make the stage set called Yama for the local outdoor Kabuki, "Yamaage Festival" in Karasuyama. The lighting apparatus and craft furniture products using Karasuyama Washi were recognized by the government's Small and Medium-sized Enterprise Regional Utilization Program in 2007. Taking advantage of the characteristics of Karasuyama Washi, that are thick, glossy, and heat-resistant, some attempts are made to commercialize the rag pictures using small pieces of Karasuyama Washi and the portable partitioning screens using large seamless Karasuyama Washi, as large as 3 m square.

漉き桁での漉き　Washi making

武者絵
Musha-e : Ukiyo-e Prints of Warriors
市貝町田野辺

　市貝町には、全国で唯一の武者
絵の資料館「大畑武者絵資料館」
がひっそりと存在する。築300年
の古民家を改装、江戸時代から現
代までの武者絵のぼり、大畑家制
作ののぼり、武者絵皿、壺、屏風、
型紙、大畑家にある古文書、大畑
家以外で制作されたのぼり等、100
点を展示する。

　大畑家では江戸時代から代々、
紺屋を営んでいたが、1889年（明
治22）からは、本格的に武者のぼ
り絵の製作を開始した。赤穂浪士
の討ち入り装束や名力士雷電の浴
衣を染めた、などの口碑伝承がある。
1954年、日本民芸協会褒賞を受
賞、1965年、日本ナンバーワン展
表彰、1975年、栃木県文化財功労
賞受賞（二代目、耕雲）、1976年、
天皇皇后両陛下の御前にて実演、
1978年、栃木県無形文化財に認定
（二代目、耕雲）された。

　絵柄は鍾馗のほか、八幡太郎義
家、源義経、武田信玄、上杉謙信、
新田義貞、織田信長、徳川家康な
ど、主に戦国武将15種類に及ぶ。

Ohata Musha-e Museum, an only Musha-e (Ukiyo-e prints of warriors) museum in the country, quietly and even forsakenly stands in Ichikai Town. The 300-year-old traditional Japanese house was remodeled into a museum to display 100 items, such as Musha-e flags from Edo to modern times, flag Musha-e platters made by Ohata family, pots, folding screens, dyeing stencils, historical documents Ohata family owns, flags made by others, etc.

Since the Edo period, Ohata family had operated a dyer's shop generation after generation until they started their full-scale production of Musha-e flags in 1889. According to the oral tradition, they made the costumes for Ako Roshi (lordless samurai of Ako domain) Raid, and dyed Yukata for Raiden, a popular sumo wrestler. They were awarded the Japan Folk Crafts Association prize in 1954, and Japan Number One Exhibition Commendation in 1965. The second, Koun received the award for Cultural Distinguished Service by Tochigi Prefecture in 1975, and provided Their Imperial Majesties Emperor and Empress with his painting demonstration in 1976 before he got certified as Intangible Cultural Assets by Tochigi Prefec-

かつては全て手書きであったが、現在は一つの絵柄について約30枚の型紙による型染めと手書きの併用となっている。

のぼり絵は5月の節句の際物(きわもの)にふさわしく、面相が勇壮で気品にあふれ、刷毛(はけ)つかいが見事で、伝統工芸として価値の高いものとなっている。

ture in 1978.

The designs are mainly of 15 different kinds of Bushos (military commanders) of the Sengoku (warring states) period, such as Hachiman Taro Yoshiie, Minamoto no Yoshitsune, Takeda Shingen, Uesugi Kenshin, Nitta Yishisada, Oda Nobunaga, Tokugawa Ieyasu, and so on as well as Shoki (Image of Plaque Queller). Although they used to be all hand-painted, nowadays printing using about 30 dyeing stencils per design is adopted together with hand-painting.

As it is suitable for the May seasonal festival goods, the flag design has a brave and graceful look with excellent brushwork, which also makes it valuable traditional art and craft.

武者絵（鍾馗）　Musha-e (Shoki)

しもつかれ
Shimotsukare

　「しもつかれ」は栃木県（および茨城県・群馬県の一部）を中心に伝わる伝統の郷土料理で、2月最初の午の日である「初午」の朝に、赤飯とともに稲荷神社に供え、五穀豊穣・商売繁盛を祈るという行事食でもある。

　「しもつかれ」の材料は、塩鮭の頭、大豆（節分の福豆の残り）、大根、人参、酒粕などである。

　作り方は、鮭の頭を骨が柔らかくなるまで、時々、アクを取りながら煮込み、炒り豆（大豆）と「鬼下ろし*」で粗く下ろした大根と人参を加え、酒粕を入れて煮込む。地域によっては、少量の酢、刻んだ油揚げを入れることがある。調味料を一切用いず、調理するのが一般的である。

*鬼下ろし：木の枠の中に突起のある竹を組みこんだ大きなおろし器具。大根、人参などをすりおろす

　栄養豊富な食べ物として、各家庭それぞれで工夫が凝らされ、味や製法、材料などが伝承されてきたもので家庭ごとに特徴的な味がある。

　正月の塩鮭の頭は悪霊を追い払う呪力を持ち、節分の福豆にも「破魔招福」の力があるとされ、「しもつ

"Shimotsukare" is a traditional local food eaten mainly in Tochigi Prefecture (and in some parts of Ibaraki and Gunma Prefecture). It is offered to the Inari-jinja Shrine together with red rice on Hatsu-uma day in February to pray for a good harvest of the five grains and for good business.

Ingredients for making shimotsukare are: head of salted salmon, parched beans (leftovers of beans used for bean-scattering ceremony), radishes, carrots, 'sake' lees, etc.

To make shimotsukare, you first cook the head of salted salmon, sometimes skimming off the scum, until its bones become soft. You then add roasted beans, radishes and carrots which are roughly grated with oni-oroshi,* and sake lees. A little vinegar and deep-fried chopped tofu are sometimes added. Usually it is cooked without any seasoning.

* oni-oroshi: a large grater made of a forked piece of wood with some saw-toothed bamboo sticks bridged in between

Shimotsukare is a very nutritious food. Each household uses different ingredients and has its own way of cooking. Naturally shimotsukare has taste and flavor slightly different from household to household.

かれ」は厄除けを願う縁起物の信仰食という面があった。

「しもつかれを7軒食べ歩くと中風(ちゅうぶう)にならない」「多くの家のしもつかれを食べると無病息災だ」などという俗言が伝えられ、昔は隣近所で重箱に入れた「しもつかれ」をやりとりする風習があったという。

「しもつかれ」は、地域によって、しみつかり、しみつかれ、すみつかれ、すみつかり、とも呼ぶ。

起源由来については、「下野ばかり」あるいは「下野家例」がなまったものという説がある。さらに、「宇治

There once was a popular belief that a head of a salted salmon has a magical power of driving away evil spirits. Parched beans were also believed to have not only the power of driving away evil spirits but also the power of inviting good fortunes. People believed that shimotsukare was a food that brings in good luck.

People used to say, "If you eat shimotsukare made at 7 different homes, you will not be stricken with paralysis." or "You will enjoy good health if you eat shimotsukare made at many different homes." This explains why people used to exchange shimotsukare with their neighbors in a lacquer ware box.

しもつかれ　Shimotsukare

著者略歴

大關 篤英 (おおぜきあつひで)

栃木県立宇都宮高等学校卒業
東北大学文学部英語科卒業
ハワイ大学大学院修士課程修了（英語教授法学専攻）
（元）文部省教科書調査官
（元）宇都宮大学教授（教育学部）
（現）宇都宮大学名誉教授、宇都宮共和大学名誉教授

外山 智子 (とやまともこ)

栃木県立宇都宮女子高等学校卒業
宇都宮大学教育学部英語科卒業
（元）文部省学習指導要領（外国語科）調査協力研究委員
（元）宇都宮大学教育学部英語教育法実施指導講師
（元）栃木県立公立学校校長
（現）宇都宮短期大学付属高等学校講師
（現）栃木県立衛生福祉大学校講師

古口 紀夫 (こぐちのりお)

栃木県立栃木高等学校卒業
東京教育大学文学部社会科学科卒業
（元）栃木県立宇都宮高等学校長
（元）栃木県教育委員会教育長
（元）栃木県立博物館長
（元）下野市教育委員会教育長

福田 繁人 (ふくだしげと)

栃木県立宇都宮高等学校
早稲田大学政治経済学部経済学専攻
滝の原塾(有)　主宰
（現）宇都宮短期大学附属高等学校講師
（現）栃木県立宇都商業高等学校講師
（現）国際情報ビジネス専門学校講師

村松 英男 (むらまつひでお)

栃木県立宇都宮高校卒業
東京理科大学理工学部建築学科卒業
一級建築士
（元）㈱宇都宮イングリッシュセンター代表

なぜ、人は栃木に魅せられるのか
The Appeal of Tochigi
栃木の自然と文化再発見

2018年2月15日　第1刷発行

編著者　**Delphiの会**（代表 大關篤英）

発　行　**随想舎**
　　　　〒320-0033　栃木県宇都宮市本町10-3　TSビル
　　　　TEL 028‐616‐6605　FAX 028‐616‐6607
　　　　振替 00360‐0‐36984
　　　　URL：http://www.zuisousha.co.jp/

印　刷　**モリモト印刷株式会社**

装丁●栄舞工房
定価はカバーに表示してあります／乱丁・落丁はお取りかえいたします
©Ohzeki Atsuhide 2018　Printed in Japan　ISBN978-4-88748-352-1